The Spread of Islam

Other Books in the Turning Points Series:

Turning|Points

IN WORLD HISTORY

The Spread of Islam

David L. Bender, *Publisher*
Bruno Leone, *Executive Editor*
Bonnie Szumski, *Series Editor*
Clarice Swisher, *Book Editor*

Greenhaven Press, Inc., San Diego, California

Every effort has been made to trace the owners of copyrighted material. The articles in this volume may have been edited for content, length, and/or reading level. The titles have been changed to enhance the editorial purpose.

Library of Congress Cataloging-in-Publication Data

The spread of Islam / Clarice Swisher, book editor.
    p.   cm. — (Turning points in world history)
  Includes bibliographical references (p.   ) and index.
  ISBN 1-56510-967-8 (lib. bdg. : alk. paper). —
ISBN 1-56510-966-X (pbk. : alk. paper)
  1. Islam—History. 2. Islam—20th century. I. Swisher, Clarice, 1933– . II. Series: Turning points in world history (Greenhaven Press)
BP55.S68 1999
297'.09—dc21
                                             98-16517
                                               CIP

Cover photo: Peter Newark's Pictures

©1999 by Greenhaven Press, Inc.
P.O. Box 289009, San Diego, CA 92198-9009

Printed in the U.S.A.

Contents

Chapter 4: The Spread of Factions Within Islam

Chapter 5: The Modern-Day Resurgence of Islam

Foreword

Certain past events stand out as pivotal, as having effects and outcomes that change the course of history. These events are often referred to as turning points. Historian Louis L. Snyder provides this useful definition:

> A turning point in history is an event, happening, or stage which thrusts the course of historical development into a different direction. By definition a turning point is a great event, but it is even more—a great event with the explosive impact of altering the trend of man's life on the planet.

History's turning points have taken many forms. Some were single, brief, and shattering events with immediate and obvious impact. The invasion of Britain by William the Conqueror in 1066, for example, swiftly transformed that land's political and social institutions and paved the way for the rise of the modern English nation. By contrast, other single events were deemed of minor significance when they occurred, only later recognized as turning points. The assassination of a little-known European nobleman, Archduke Franz Ferdinand, on June 28, 1914, in the Bosnian town of Sarajevo was such an event; only after it touched off a chain reaction of political-military crises that escalated into the global conflict known as World War I did the murder's true significance become evident.

Other crucial turning points occurred not in terms of a few hours, days, months, or even years, but instead as evolutionary developments spanning decades or even centuries. One of the most pivotal turning points in human history, for instance—the development of agriculture, which replaced nomadic hunter-gatherer societies with more permanent settlements—occurred over the course of many generations. Still other great turning points were neither events nor developments, but rather revolutionary new inventions and innovations that significantly altered social customs and ideas, military tactics, home life, the spread of knowledge, and the human condition in general. The developments of writing, gunpowder, the printing press, antibiotics, the electric light, atomic energy, television, and the computer, the last two of which have recently ushered in the world-altering information age, represent only some of these innovative turning points.

Each anthology in the Greenhaven Turning Points in World History series presents a group of essays chosen for their accessibility. The anthology's structure also enhances this accessibility. First, an introductory essay provides a general overview of the principal events and figures involved, placing the topic in its historical context. The essays that follow explore various aspects in more detail, some targeting political trends and consequences, others social, literary, cultural, and/or technological ramifications, and still others pivotal leaders and other influential figures. To aid the reader in choosing the material of immediate interest or need, each essay is introduced by a concise summary of the contributing writer's main themes and insights.

In addition, each volume contains extensive research tools, including a collection of excerpts from primary source documents pertaining to the historical events and figures under discussion. In the anthology on the French Revolution, for example, readers can examine the works of Rousseau, Voltaire, and other writers and thinkers whose championing of human rights helped fuel the French people's growing desire for liberty; the French *Declaration of the Rights of Man and Citizen*, presented to King Louis XVI by the French National Assembly on October 2, 1789; and eyewitness accounts of the attack on the royal palace and the horrors of the Reign of Terror. To guide students interested in pursuing further research on the subject, each volume features an extensive bibliography, which for easy access has been divided into separate sections by topic. Finally, a comprehensive index allows readers to scan and locate content efficiently. Each of the anthologies in the Greenhaven Turning Points in World History series provides students with a complete, detailed, and enlightening examination of a crucial historical watershed.

Introduction

The emergence of a major religion in the Middle East changed the tide of history, but not in a single day or month or year. Islam has evolved from its origins in seventh-century Arabia to spread across many continents; today nearly a billion people claim to be Muslims. Within this phenomenon are several turning points that determined the course of Islamic, and world, history.

The beliefs and practices of Islam were revealed to Muhammad in messages from Allah over a period of twenty-three years; since Muhammad's death, Muslims have spread and interpreted his messages and struggled to observe them as faithfully as possible in a changing world. Islamic history can be described in three phases: classic, decline, and resurgence. Several significant turning points occurred during the early classical period as Muhammad acted on Allah's messages and the religion gained its first adherents. A few centuries later, the emergence of strong Islamic leaders and the influence of external events were pivotal to Islam's rise. After a period of decline in the Islamic empire, the third phase is marked by a resurgence of Islamic power and popularity.

The essays in this companion focus primarily on the major turning points in Islamic expansion. The contributors, drawn from both Western and Islamic traditions, are researchers and scholars of Arab history and the religion of Islam. The introductory overview provides a context for understanding Islamic beliefs and practices and how and why the religion has spread.

This companion also includes many special features that make research efficient and understandable. An annotated table of contents lets readers quickly preview the contents of individual essays. An appendix of primary documents supports historical events discussed in the essays. A glossary of Arabic words offers quick access to unfamiliar and specialized terms. A chronology of significant events in the history of Islam places the turning points in a broader context. The bibliography includes useful titles for additional research on the turning points and related topics.

Each essay has aids for clear understanding. Individual introductions serve to explain the main points, which are then identified by subheads within the essays. Footnotes explain uncommon references and define unfamiliar words. Taken together, these aids make the Greenhaven Press *Turning Points in World History* an indispensable research tool.

Islam: An Overview

Muhammad's Arab Culture

Muhammad, a member of the Quraish tribe, lived in Mecca, a trading city in central Arabia near the Red Sea. The whole population of the Arabian peninsula lagged behind other areas of the ancient Near East in their religion and culture. Though Muhammad's tribe of Quraish people were settled and prosperous, most of the Arabian peninsula was inhabited by small tent-dwelling, nomadic tribes called Bedouins. Their sparse, dangerous existence forced them to build strong blood and kinship loyalties for protection. Few could read or write and human rights were unknown. Jews and Christians had tried to teach the ways of their religions to the Arabian tribes, but with little success; consequently, Muhammad knew little about important Hebrew figures or Jesus.

The Arab tribes nonetheless had strong religious beliefs and regularly worshiped at the Meccan shrine Kaaba. Many believed there was one god, al-Llah, "the God," the same God that Jews and Christians worshiped, but felt themselves to be outsiders because God had never sent them a prophet nor given them a book as he had the Jews and Christians. Many Arabs were still devoted to pagan gods, especially to the three daughters of al-Llah: the Goddess in the city of Taif, the Mighty One in the city of Nakhlah, and the Goddess of Fate in the city of Qudayd. Each had a shrine in which the goddess was represented by a stone.

Few documents record Muhammad's life before he became a prophet, but the Koran reveals much about him after. Muhammad's father died before Muhammad's birth, his mother when he was six, and his grandfather when he was eight; from then on he was raised by Abu Talib, an uncle who saw that Muhammad had military training and learned the skills of a merchant. He married Khadija bent Khuwaylid, an older woman. Together they had two sons who died, four daughters—Zaynab, Ruqayyah, Umm Kulthum, and Fatimah—and two foster sons—the slave boy Zayd ibn Harith and Ali, orphaned son of Muhammad's uncle Abu Talib.

Muhammad Becomes the Prophet

Islam originated in 610, when Muhammad was forty years old, during the seventeenth night of Ramadan (the month of religious tributes and pilgrimages to holy shrines) in a cave on Mount Hira outside the city of Mecca. Muhammad ibn Abdallah, on a spiritual retreat with his wife and family, awoke from his sleep, felt a divine presence, and heard an angel command, "*iqra!*"—"recite." Over a period of twenty-three years, Muhammad recited messages direct from God—line by line, verse by verse, chapter by chapter—to others who memorized them and to those who could write them down. The messages have been recorded in the Koran—the "Recitation." On his own, Muhammad spread the word of Allah throughout Arabia and attracted followers who carried his message across Africa and the Middle East and into India and China. In her biography, *Muhammad*, Karen Armstrong considers Muhammad "one of the greatest geniuses the world has known. To create a literary masterpiece, to found a major religion and a new world power are not ordinary achievements. . . . When he began his mission, a dispassionate observer would not have given him a chance."

Muhammad's first visitation by an angel terrified and revulsed him. Thinking he had been possessed by the *jinn*, spirits despised for their power to possess poets and affect others, he rushed from the cave to climb to the summit and jump to his death, but the angel Gabriel appeared again, identified himself, and assured Muhammad that he, Gabriel, was the means by which God reveals himself to humans. Shaking, Muhammad crawled on his hands and knees until he reached Khadija, asking her to cover him and shield him from the presence. She held him in her arms, soothed him, and tried to take his fears away, the comfort she offered each time Muhammad saw visions and heard voices. All sources report Muhammad's profound dependence on his wife as his spiritual adviser, a reassuring person who helped him accept the authenticity of his strange and unusual revelations.

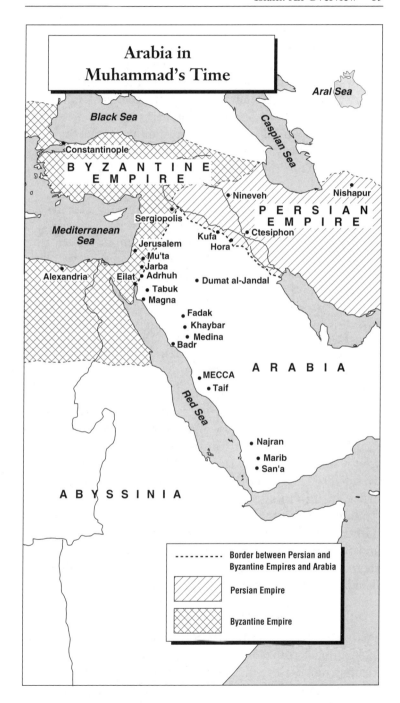

Arabia in Muhammad's Time

Aral Sea

Black Sea

Caspian Sea

Constantinople

B Y Z A N T I N E
E M P I R E

Nineveh

Nishapur

Sergiopolis

P E R S I A N
E M P I R E

Mediterranean Sea

Kufa • Ctesiphon

Jerusalem

Hora

Mu'ta

Alexandria   Eilat • Jarba

Adrhuh

• Dumat al-Jandal

• Tabuk

• Magna

• Fadak

• Khaybar

• Medina

• Badr

A R A B I A

• MECCA

• Taif

Red Sea

• Najran

• Marib

• San'a

A B Y S S I N I A

- - - - - - - -   Border between Persian and
Byzantine Empires and Arabia

Persian Empire

Byzantine Empire

Muhammad always insisted he was human, not a divine figure like Jesus. Muhammad resembles prophets and leaders in Jewish scriptures—Moses, David, Solomon, Elijah, Isaiah—men with a religious passion, but not saintly or necessarily virtuous. Muhammad never dreamed he had the gift of prophecy and had no vision of a world religion. In the beginning he spent all his energy struggling to put the messages into words. Armstrong paraphrases early historians who quote Muhammad:

> Muhammad once said: "Never once did I receive a revelation without thinking that my soul had been torn away from me." It was a process of creation that was agonizing. Sometimes, he said, the verbal content was clear enough: he seemed to see the angel in the form of a man and heard his words. But at other times it was more painful and incoherent: "Sometimes it comes to me like the reverberations of a bell, and that is hardest upon me; the reverberations abate when I am aware of the message." We shall see him turning inward and searching his own soul for a solution to a problem, rather as a poet listens to the poem that he is gradually hauling to light. The Qu'ran warns him to listen to the inarticulate meaning carefully.

A two-year period of silence followed the first messages, during which Muhammad wondered if he had been deluded or if God had abandoned him as incapable of articulating divine revelation. Some writers have described him in a state of suicidal despair during this period. Finally the silence broke in brightness and reassurance, as described in Sura (Chapter) 93: "By the white forenoon / and the brooding night! / Thy Lord has neither forsaken thee nor hates thee / and the Last shall be better for thee than the First." Until this time the revelations were the secret of Muhammad, Khadija, and her cousin Waraqa ibn Naufal.

The First Followers

With new faith that the messages were indeed authentic, Muhammad realized he must take them to others, but Waraqa warned him that he would meet resistance and scorn. No savior, messiah, or political leader, Muhammad thought at most he had been designated a *nadhir*, a "warner" to his own Quraish people to return to the practice of caring for the disadvantaged people of the tribe. His decision to share the messages with others was the first turning point in the spread of Islam. During the next three years Muhammad recruited followers among his own family and among others attracted by word of mouth. His first recruit outside the family, Abu Bakr, in turn recruited young men from the community. A small group, mostly those with little wealth and power in Meccan society, held prayers each morning and evening.

Gradually Muhammad widened his audience to include the rich and successful Quraish. He presented not a list of requirements but praise for the virtues of being generous with wealth, giving to the poor, living simply and frugally, and creating a new spirit of unity in the tribe. He urged them to accept their obligations to God as their creator and the essential force and energy in the universe. Animals, he said, automatically surrender to the forces and order of the universe; only humans can make a choice not to surrender and, thus, must make a choice to surrender. Gradually, Muhammad raised the issue of the Last Judgment, when all people would be accountable for their deeds; he described an eternity of hell for the wicked and a garden paradise for the good. The uneasiness felt by many wealthy Quraish at this message turned to protest after Muhammad's next message: He told them that because there was only one God, Allah, they would have to put aside other gods. Though many Arabs only halfheartedly believed in the three daughters, they clung to their worship out of the security of a long tradition. A crisis soon developed.

Opposition to Muhammad's Messages Grows

When Muhammad asked people to abandon worship of other gods and embrace a new religious attitude, essentially he was asking too much. When the Quraish, viewing him as a dangerous heretic, accused him of betraying the religion of their fathers, Muhammad reiterated his message of divine unity, of one God. The Quraish then campaigned to get rid of Muhammad, although many families within the tribe were divided. He was verbally harassed; enemies pulled him by his robes when he performed his rituals around the Kaaba; others tried to bribe him to be quiet. Opponents threatened Muhammad's uncle Abu Talib, persecuted slaves of Muhammad's followers, and boycotted all Muslims, or adherents of Islam. Fifty-three Muslims and their families fled to Abyssinia for safety.

Late in 616, one of Muhammad's most ardent enemies, Umar ibn al-Khattab, set out to kill Muhammad in the house where he was spending the afternoon. Thinking Umar was safely gone for the day, his sister and her husband, who had secretly become Muslims, invited the Muslim blacksmith Khabbab ibn al-Aratt to recite the most recent sura to them. In the street, another secret Muslim of the clan stopped Umar and told him to go back to his house to see what was happening. As he neared, he heard the words of the Koran from his own window. He burst in and beat his sister, but when he saw that he had drawn blood, a change came over his face, and he picked up the Koran that Khabbab had dropped and read the opening lines of Sura 20. "How fine and noble is this speech!" he said. He picked up his sword, ran into the street, and, as Armstrong describes,

> burst into the house where Muhammad was. Obviously thinking that attack was the best means of defence, Muhammad seized him by the cloak: "What has brought you, son of Khattab?" he cried. Umar replied: "O apostle of God, I have come to you to believe in God and his apostle and what he has brought from God." Muhammad gave thanks so loudly that everybody in the large house (who had hidden in terror at Umar's approach) realised what had happened.

This story illustrates the power of the Koran's words in Arabic, especially when heard aloud. Many converts, moved by the beauty and power of the language, accepted Islam upon hearing the suras read.

Though many Quraish converted to Islam, attacks by Muhammad's enemies intensified, and events in his personal life worsened. The year 619 was a year of sadness: first Khadija, his wife and devoted supporter, died, followed by his uncle Abu Talib, one of the tribal chiefs. The new chief promised Muhammad protection, but did so grudgingly. Muhammad was devastated by the deaths and fearful for his life. Tricks became more insulting: Someone threw animal parts at him and another threw a a sheep's uterus in his cooking pot. Enemies pelted him and his daughter with dirt in the streets. He decided to seek protection in the merchant city of Taif, home of the shrine of the Goddess, one of the three daughters of al-Llah. He approached three guardians of the shrine and asked them to accept his religion and give him protection. Incensed by his request, they ordered their slaves to chase Muhammad through the streets. He escaped by diving into the orchard of a Quraish resident, who, feeling sorry for anyone so badly treated, sent a slave to Muhammad with a plate of grapes. Muhammad, touched by the kindness but feeling desperately alone, realized at that moment that his only refuge was with God. Historian Ibn Ishaq reports his words:

> O al-Llah, to Thee I complain of my weakness, little resource, and lowliness before men. O Most Merciful, Thou art the Lord of the weak and Thou art my Lord. To whom wilt Thou confide me? To one afar who will misuse me? Or to an enemy to whom Thou hast given power over me? If Thou art not angry with me, I care not. Thy favour is more wide for me. I take refuge in the light of Thy countenance by which the darkness is illumined, and the things of this world and the next are rightly ordered, lest Thy anger descend upon me or Thy wrath light upon me. It is for Thee to be satisfied until Thou art well pleased. There is no power and no might save in Thee.

From this point on, Muhammad had faith that Allah would guide him in events as they occurred, even when God's plan was not clear to him.

Amid his continuing trouble, in 620 Muhammad had a dream; though the story was never recorded in the Koran, historians call it the Night Journey to Jerusalem. One night while Muhammad was reciting the Koran at the Kaaba, he fell asleep. In his dream Gabriel awakened him, lifted him onto a heavenly steed named Buruq, and the two miraculously flew to Jerusalem and landed on the Temple Mount. Greeted by Abraham, Moses, Jesus, and a crowd of other prophets, all prayed together, after which Muhammad was offered his choice of water, milk, or wine. He chose milk because it symbolized the "middle way," or moderation, advocated by Islam. Then a ladder appeared, and Muhammad and Gabriel climbed to the seven heavens, each leading closer to the throne of God. Adam presided over the first heaven, Jesus and John the Baptist the second, Joseph the third, Enoch the fourth, Aaron and Moses the fifth and sixth, and Abraham the seventh, at the threshold of the sphere of God. There Muhammad was told that Muslims must make *salat*, or pray, fifty times a day. On his way down Muhammad was stopped by Moses, who told him to go back and get the number reduced; again and again Moses sent Muhammad back until the number fell to five, which Moses still thought was too high, but Muhammad was too embarrassed to ask for less. After the dream, Muhammad instructed Muslims to turn toward Jerusalem while praying. After Muhammad's death, the Muslim tradition of praying five times a day remained a fundamental practice.

The *Hijra*: Muhammad's Move to Medina

At the time of Muhammad's search for a safe place, tribes in Yathrib, an oasis settlement several miles north of Mecca, were struggling to make the transition from nomadic to settled life. Three Jewish tribes and a number of Arab tribes living around the oasis were caught in a web of competition and violence. Muhammad met six tribal leaders from Yathrib, read the Koran to them, and the six became Muslims and asked Muhammad to try to unite them. In 622, after a year of preparation, seventy Muslims and their families emigrated from Mecca to Yathrib, followed by Muhammad. A treaty, which survives, was drawn up stating the rules of the new community, the *umma*. Armstrong explains:

> It stated that Muhammad was entering into a covenant with the Arab and Jewish tribes of Medina. [The Jews gave this Aramaic name to Yathrib.] All the different tribes of the oasis

were to bury their old enmity and form as it were, a new super-tribe. The Muslims and the Jews were to live peaceably with the pagans of Medina, as long as they did not make a separate treaty with Mecca in an attempt to get rid of the Prophet. . . . God was the head of the community and the only source of security. . . . Hitherto the tribe had been the basic unit of society; the *umma*, however, was a community which was based on religion rather than kinship. This was unprecedented in Arabia.

The move to Medina is known as the *hijra*, the "emigration." It is a major turning point in Islam, so important that Muslims date their era from this event. That Muhammad succeeded in unifying the community and that he established economic and political power sufficient to dominate all of Arabia makes this turning point important; failure in either task might have meant the end of Islam and Islamic expansion.

Muhammad succeeded by means of his messages from God, the force of his leadership, and the wisdom of his strategy. He created a unified community, the *umma*, by tolerating the tribes' differences. For example, he accommodated the Arab tribes in 624 when he changed the *qibla*, the direction to face while praying, from Jerusalem to Mecca; this gave Arab Muslims the feeling that they had their own religion. Muhammad accommodated the Jews by identifying their day of fasting as the official day for everyone and by respecting their stories of past Hebrew prophets. He accommodated the pagan tribes by letting them live peaceably under the protection of the city. Allah's guidance and Muhammad's governing strategies established practices that became part of the Islamic tradition. By the example of his behavior and by settling disputes equitably, he established principles of equality and justice in Islam.

Once settled in Medina, Muhammad took new wives. Polygamy was common practice at the time, often arranged for political or economic reasons. Muhammad married thirty-year-old Sawdah and six-year-old Aisha, who lived with her parents until she came of age. He also married the widow of a Muslim who had died on return from Abyssinia,

Umar's daughter Hafsah, and Zaynab, whose husband offered to divorce her if Muhammad would marry her. When sixty-five men from the community were killed in battle, Muhammad urged surviving men to marry the widows. His concern was for the welfare of the women who, without husbands, had no protection or support.

In early Medina days, Muhammad built a mosque which provided living and worshiping quarters. He built an apartment for each of his wives but none for himself since he stayed with each wife in turn. Though he came to prefer Aisha in later days, he provided for and treated each wife equally. The mosque, finished in 623, was a central place of prayer. Bilal, Abu Bakr's freed slave, was the first muezzin, the one who calls the faithful to prayer. Before dawn he climbed onto the roof of the tallest house, and at dawn, he stretched out his arms and called, "O God, I praise Thee and ask Thy help for Quraish that they may accept Thy religion."

Gaining Economic and Political Power in Medina

The oasis of Yathrib gradually evolved into the *umma* of Medina, but in 623 it was still surrounded by enemies, and its safety depended on Muhammad's establishing economic and political power. Muhammad turned to the common Arab practice for gaining wealth, the *ghazu*, raids on caravans traveling the trade routes. One raid was particularly significant; it brought Muhammad prestige, reconfirmed his belief in God's intervention, and provided guidelines for the treatment of defeated enemies and the handling of war booty. In 624, Muhammad led an army of 350 volunteers to the Well of Badr near the Red Sea and waited to raid the largest Meccan caravan of the year. Hearing of Muhammad's plan, its leader rerouted the caravan and sent a call to arms to Mecca. About a thousand soldiers responded. The caravan got safely past Muhammad's army, but one of the leaders persuaded the Quraish to fight the Muslims in revenge for a past Muslim murder of a Quraish man (the custom of the blood feud). Muhammad exercised sound strategy and discipline by positioning his men to take advantage of wells for water, the direction of the sun, and the most solid terrain, and he trained his soldiers to move in disciplined formation. His effort resulted in the defeat of an army twice the size of his. The victors followed the usual Arabian custom of killing the defeated and fighting over the spoils, but a revelation came to Muhammad from Allah that prisoners must be fed, housed, and treated decently, and the booty divided equally, a plan he implemented swiftly and strictly. To honor the day of victory at Badr, Muhammad changed the day of fasting from the Jewish Ashura to the ninth day of Ramadan, beginning the Islamic tradition of fasting during Ramadan.

Knowing that he had been born into a world of warring and disorder, Muhammad believed he could bring peace and order in some instances with tolerance, kind acts, and cooperation, but accepted that in other circumstances he had to fight the way to a God-centered orderly world. The Koran began to urge Muslims to participate in jihad, a word usually translated into English as "holy war" but signifying a larger connotation of physical, moral, spiritual, and intellectual effort. When unavoidable, Muhammad did not flinch from physical violence and bloodshed, but balanced the physical aspect of jihad with elements of spirituality and discipline. After the victory at Badr, the Quraish continued to follow the laws of the blood feud and attack. To survive, Muhammad needed to preserve the *umma*'s unity and defeat the Meccan army.

He first tried the least bloody ways to accomplish his goals. Muhammad acted twice against disloyal tribes within the *umma*. The first time one of the weak Jewish tribes threatened the *umma*, Muhammad expelled the tribe, but some members returned to help the Quraish against the Muslims. When a second tribe planned to help the Quraish from within Medina, Muhammad had the men tied, beheaded, and buried in a trench, and sold the women and children into slavery. Muhammad had hoped to win the Quraish without violence, but their army launched new attacks. Since his army was much smaller, Muhammad relied on superior strategy and tricks. In March 627, the Quraish started a march toward Medina with three thousand men, three thousand camels, and two hundred horses. Because cliffs and rock surrounded three sides of Medina, he had only the north to secure. With time to prepare, Muhammad brought all crops and animals within the city, leaving nothing for the attacking army to eat. He then involved the whole *umma* in digging a deep trench on the north and building a dirt mound to shield them. Armstrong describes the bewilderment of the Quraish soldiers' arrival:

> Indeed, as the Meccan army stared at the trench in bewilderment a shower of arrows warned them that they were sitting targets and they hastily withdrew until they were out of range. . . . Salman's [the Persian convert who thought of the idea] trench effectively stymied the whole massive offensive and the Qurayshi leaders simply did not know how to deal with it. . . . But the cavalry, of which they had such hopes, was now completely useless, because the horses could not get over the trench.

Unable to get into Medina, the Quraish mounted a siege, but when food ran out, their horses and camels were dying, the temperature dropped, and the wind and rain came, they lost their resolve. As the defeated army turned and left, one of the leaders said, "Every man of sense now knows that Muhammad has not lied." He had defeated one of the largest Arab armies and quashed the opposition within the *umma*, proving that he was the most powerful man in Arabia. The spread of Islam had reached another turning point.

In 627 and 628 Muhammad began building a confederacy to extend the influence and range of the *umma*. He invited Bedouin tribes to convert to Islam, established trade with Syria to weaken the Meccan monopoly, and used small acts of generosity and kindness to foster brotherhood. He made a treaty with the Quraish that arranged for Muhammad to lead a three-day pilgrimage to the Kaaba. When the time came, the astonished Quraish watched Muhammad, on his favorite camel, and twenty six hundred pilgrims clad in white garments file into the city and circumambulate the shrine. They watched a former Meccan slave, Bilal, climb on top of the Kaaba and call the Muslims to prayer. When a Quraish leader told Muhammad his three days were up, Muhammad moved in disciplined fashion, and the whole pilgrimage filed out of the city before nightfall. The pilgrimage was a moral triumph for Muhammad; many Quraish subsequently converted to Islam, and outlying Bedouin tribes, seeing the shift in power, joined Muhammad. Since entering Yathrib in 622, Muhammad had gained political power that dominated nearly all of Arabia and had laid the foundations for a new policy that would enable Muslims to govern a large empire for more than a thousand years.

Muhammad's Death and the Passage of Power

In 632, Muhammad sensed that the end of his time was near. He made a last pilgrimage to Mecca and preached his farewell sermon at the mosque of Nimera near Mount Arafat. He told his audience to deal justly with one another, to treat women kindly, to abandon blood feuds, to treat the *umma* as one and all Muslims as brothers, and to take only what a Muslim brother willingly gives. Before he died on June 8, 632, he warned those close to him not to give him too much honor and to remember that he was mortal.

At Muhammad's death, Islam was a faith of clear beliefs and practices, but Muhammad left little guidance about the passage of power after he was gone. The use and abuse of power determined the expansion and control of the Islamic empire for a thousand years. Within a century after Muhammad's death, Arab armies had mastered the territory from the south of France to the Indus River in India, an empire that existed until the 1200s.

After Muhammad's death the four men closest to him established a form of government called a caliphate. A caliph, a designated successor of the Prophet, headed the Muslim state, but did not serve as the spiritual successor. Abu Bakr, Umar, Uthman, and Ali, Muhammad's son-in-law, were the *rashidun*, the rightly guided caliphs who governed by Muhammad's principles; they comprised the first caliphate (632–661). From the first, the caliphs differed about the passage of power from one caliph to the next: Should power be passed to the Muslim who best can lead and best represents the Prophet? or should it pass according to family and blood

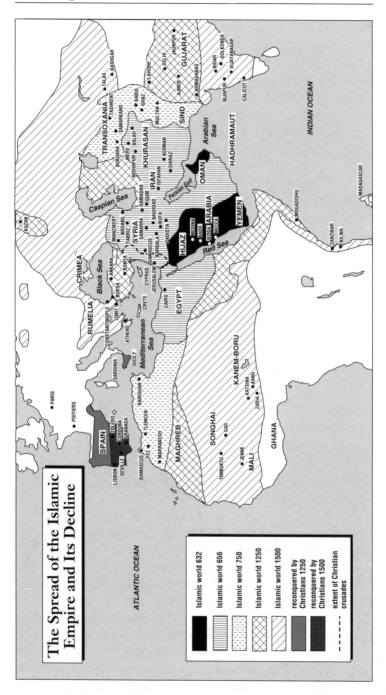

The Spread of the Islamic Empire and Its Decline

Islamic world 632
Islamic world 656
Islamic world 750
Islamic world 1250
Islamic world 1500
reconquered by Christians 1250
reconquered by Christians 1500
extent of Christian crusades

ATLANTIC OCEAN
INDIAN OCEAN

PARIS
POITIERS
SPAIN
LISBON
TOLEDO
CORDOBA
GRANADA
SEVILLE
DAMASCUS
FEZ
MARRAKESH
TLEMCEN
KAIROUAN
SARDINIA
SICILY
MAGHREB
Mediterranean Sea
CRETE
CYPRUS
ATHENS
CONSTANTINOPLE
IZMIT
BURSA
RUMELIA
Black Sea
CRIMEA
KAZAN
Caspian Sea
ANKARA
KONYA
JERUSALEM
DAMASCUS
MANZIKERT
ARDABIL
TABRIZ
SYRIA
SAMARRA
KARBALA
KUFA
QADISYA
BAGHDAD
QUM
HAMADAN
ISFAHAN
IRAN
NISHAPUR
MERV
KERMAN
SHIRAZ
KHURASAN
BALKH
BUKHARA
SAMARKAND
TASHKENT
TRANSOXANIA
TALAS
KASHGAR
GHAZ.
KABUL
MULTAN
SIND
LAHORE
DELHI
JAUNPUR
GUJARAT
AMER
AHMADABAD
BIDAR
GOLKONDA
VIJAYANAGAR
BIJAPUR
CALICUT
HIJAZ
MEDINA
JIDDA
MECCA
ARABIA
Red Sea
YEMEN
HADHRAMAUT
OMAN
Arabian Sea
Persian Gulf
EGYPT
CAIRO
KANEM-BORU
SONGHAI
GHANA
MALI
TIMBUKTU
JENNE
GAO
KATSINA
KANO
ZARIA
MOGADISHU
ZANZIBAR
KILWA
MADAGASCAR

lines as power passes in monarchies? The difference of opinion was peaceable in the first years, but eventually led to violence, assassinations, civil war, and the division into the sects, the Shi'a and the Sunni. Muhammad had laid the groundwork for a confederation, and the first caliphs followed his personal and political practices to create an empire. As Islam fanned outward from Arabia, the Persian and Byzantine empires were weakening, and the peoples under their control, who hated their conquerors, saw Arab invaders with a degree of approval, making Muslim expansion easier. Arab tribes migrated into new territories and established military garrisons of disciplined administrators and well-trained soldiers. Non-Muslims were taxed, but converts could avoid the tax by attaching themselves to Arab tribes. Many converted, but those who did not were granted protected status, and Muslims continued to be pluralistic, coexisting with Jews, Christians, and Zoroastrians. Muslims left existing infrastructure and administrative systems in place and refrained from imposing their faith and habits on their subjects. With tolerance, like Muhammad's in Medina, Arab armies took Iraq and Syria by 634 and Egypt by 640.

Civil War Leads to Decline

The Rashidan caliphate ended when members of the Umayya family from Mecca opposed Uthman, and Ali was killed in 661 after a battle with Mu'awiya from the house of Umayya. Mu'awiya became the caliph and moved the center of Islam from Medina to Damascus in Syria, establishing the Umayyad dynasty. The Umayyads extended the Islamic empire east to Byzantium and west to Spain by 711 and dominated the Mediterranean Sea by 750, after which civil war broke out. In 750 Abu Hashim and his son defeated the Umayyads with the help of an army recruited in Persia. The last Umayyads fled in 756 to Spain, where they established a kingdom that produced a fine culture of Arabian art and poetry. Also in 756 Abu Hashim moved the capital to Baghdad and established the Abbasid caliphate (750–1258), the last Sunni. Under the Abbasids, the empire spread east and thrived, producing its highest achievements in art, science, and medicine during the period from 786 to 809. This was the age of *The Arabian Nights*, major works in theology and literature, and translations of Greek scientific and philosophical works into Arabic, many of which were subsequently translated into Latin for European scholars. With the decline of the Umayyads in the west, those who believed power descended from Ali, the husband of Muhammad's daughter Fatimah, gained power and established the Fatimid caliphate. The Fatimid caliphate took control of Egypt and North Africa in the 900s.

By the mid–tenth century, the Islamic political empire had begun to decline, but Islam continued to grow in the east. There was no jihad to resist three forces attacking the empire: Europeans, Mongols, and Ottoman Turks. During the Dark Ages, Europe had been culturally far behind the Muslim world, but in the tenth and eleventh centuries Europeans mobilized to reclaim territory lost to the Muslim empire. In 1061 the Normans, determined to drive Muslims out, attacked them in southern Italy and Sicily. In 1085 Christian forces and knights from throughout Europe defeated the Muslims in Cordova, the center of Islamic power in Spain. Knights on the Christian Crusades conquered Jerusalem in 1099, recaptured the lost shrines, and established the first European colony in the Middle East. In the eastern part of the Islamic empire, Mongols from central Asia, under the leadership of Genghis Khan, attacked Baghdad, ending the Abbasid caliphate in 1258. Then Ottoman Turks, also from central Asia, crossed the Middle East to Egypt and created a vast empire, which they controlled until the 1500s.

Though Christians drove Muslims out of Spain, Islam continued to gain large numbers of converts in North Africa and in the east. Both the Mongols and the Turks liked Islam, converted, and spread the religion to India, Indonesia, and into China. Military leaders practiced Muhammad's principles of tolerance, allowing, for example, the Hindus, Christians, and Parsis to retain their beliefs and administrative institutions in India. In the Middle East at the end of the eighteenth century, colonialism and the advent of Western culture, technology, and capitalism perplexed Muslims. Western values conflicted with Muhammad's stress on egalitarianism, his concern for the poor and unfortunate, limitations on vast accumulations of wealth, and simple and frugal living, dividing Muslims into those who wanted to isolate themselves from the west and those who thought the advance of the West was inevitable and wanted to modify Islam to find a suitable compromise; Muhammad, after all, was a pragmatist. This problem of responding to the dominant West is still unresolved in the Muslim world.

Islamic Duties, Beliefs, and Practices

The major sources for the beliefs and practices of the millions of modern Muslims are the Koran, in Arabic Qu'ran, and the Hadith, a collection of Muhammad's words and practices. In 653 the caliph Uthman commissioned scholars to produce a definitive text of the Koran. In the ninth century two scholars reviewed and codified each tradition in the Hadith. All Islamic law, called the Shari'a—the religious and secular duties, beliefs, and practices of the faithful—derive from these two sources.

The so-called five Pillars of Islam identify the chief duties and beliefs of the Shari'a expected of Muslims. First is the *shahada*, or the profession of faith as recorded in the Koran: "There is no deity but God, Muhammad is the messenger of God." Second is the *salat*, or formal worship performed with words and actions five times a day—before sunrise, noon, afternoon, sunset, and evening. When called to prayers, Muslims enter the mosque, stand in rows facing Mecca and perform cycles of standing, raising hands, bowing, kneeling with forehead on the ground, and sitting. Formerly, only men attended prayers; today women also attend, but usually in an area separate from the men. The third pillar is the *zakat*, or legal alms, a poor tax. Muslims are asked to pay a tenth of their wealth to help poor people and to carry out political purposes. Giving, it is thought, benefits and purifies the giver. The fourth pillar is the fast of Ramadan, which lasts thirty days. During this month Muslims abstain from eating, drinking, smoking, and sexual intercourse from before sunrise until after sunset. In the holiday atmosphere of the fast, families and friends gather for meals and celebrations after sunset. The fifth pillar is the hajj, the once-in-a-lifetime trip to Mecca. Usually hajj activities—circumambulating the Kaaba, *salat*, and ceremonies in other locations—take several days. Those without the means or time for the hajj can fulfill this duty in alternate ways. Sometimes jihad is considered a sixth pillar in the sense of striving in the way of God and fighting evil in oneself.

Besides pillars, there are basic doctrines of Islam, called faiths. The absolute unity of God is a faith to be accepted intellectually and spiritually, since all theological issues are founded on this oneness. Second is the belief in angels who work as God's messengers and helpers, such as the good angels Gabriel and Michael, and the belief in fallen angels, Satan and Harut. Third, Muslims believe that Muhammad was the last in a long line of prophets who brought scriptures to their peoples by means of revelations from God in the form of suggestions or inspirations. The Koran lists twenty-five prophets, including Jesus, starting with Adam and ending with Muhammad. The fourth belief concerns final judgment when the world will be turned to chaos, and Muhammad will be able to help only with God's permission. In *An Introduction to Islam*, Frederick Mathewson Denny explains:

> Each human being has a record book that will be examined at the Judgment, with each individual being handed his or her book in either the right or the left hand. This is symbolic of the association of the right with goodness and purity and the left with evil and pollution. As in Muslim social relations, so also at the Judgment, the giving of something into the left hand symbolizes contempt. . . . The final outcome is either eternal paradise or eternal hell, the former a blissful retreat and the latter a horrible punishment of fire.

The fifth belief, called the "Divine Decree and Predestination," creates tension between God's intervention and humans' free will. The Koran says in Sura 7, "whomsoever God guides, he is rightly guided; and whom He leads astray, they are the losers." The word *Islam* means "surrender";

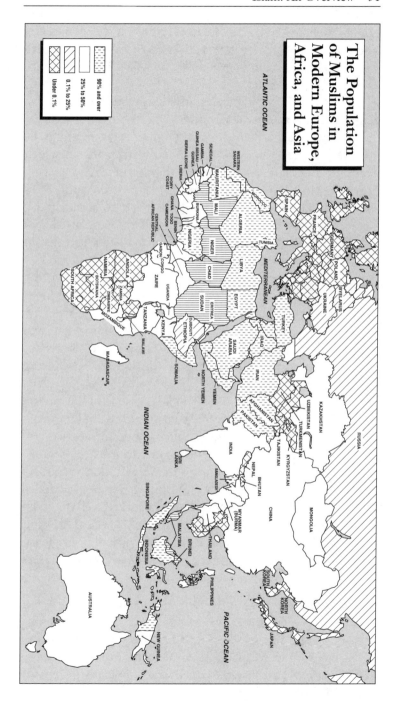

The Population of Muslims in Modern Europe, Africa, and Asia

Muslim means "one who surrenders." The tension arises when individuals search for the balance between surrendering to God and taking responsibility, as Muhammad practiced and encouraged.

Islamic law also identifies practices guiding Muslims' daily lives, not to overwhelm them, but to assure them that they are living according to their religion. A few examples illustrate laws as they came to Muhammad, many of which were more humane and equitable than those they replaced. According to the Koran, Muslim men may have four wives and a woman one husband. At a time when no authoritative government or police force existed, Muslims were instructed to seek justice by taking a life for a life, an eye for an eye, but to avoid excesses and blood feuds. Both men and women could inherit property, but a woman received one-half the amount of a man's share. Today this law seems discriminatory, but in Muhammad's time, it greatly advanced women's rights. Prior to Muhammad, tribal women had no rights and were regularly treated physically and sexually with no regard for their dignity or pain. Muhammad instituted laws giving women rights to be protected behind a veil, to be treated kindly, and to own property. Food laws restrict the eating of pork, blood, any meat dedicated to pagan gods, and meat not properly killed according to Islamic precepts. Wine was also prohibited; one historian speculates that this restriction may be the result of early Muslim leaders' reputation for drinking wine to excess. The law prohibiting usury, the practice of charging interest for the use of money, worked well in the Islamic empire, but caused many problems when Muslims began working with Western capitalism. A final example instructs Muslims on purification, in particular to wash before prayers. Denny explains:

> Purification, then, both logically and temporally precedes worship. It is, in fact, a sort of entry into sacred time and space. As one washes, one is symbolically as well as physically separated from the mundane marks of normal living and working and made new for the conscious entry into the presence of God.

Interpreting the Koran and the Hadith for twentieth-century societies causes different problems in different parts of the world, but evokes similar reactions everywhere. Some extremists want to ignore Islamic traditions and adopt Western dress, enjoy Western entertainment, and participate in the material luxuries that can be acquired under Western capitalism. Other extremists want to adopt a strict interpretation of the Koran and Islamic traditions. The large majority fall in the middle and search for ways to practice their religion and also live realistically in the modern world.

The most dramatic turning point marking the resurgence of Islam in the modern world was the Shi'a revolution in Iran in 1978–1979, but reform and change had been occurring for many decades before that. Colonialism had brought Western schools to Islamic countries, separating those who wanted their children to learn Western science and ideas and those who denounced these schools as heretical and kept their children in traditional Islamic schools. Rapid globalization of transportation and communication systems in the twentieth century resulted in masses of country people flocking to the cities where they lived in poor, crowded conditions, separated from middle- and upper-class Muslims. Social reform in North Africa attracted many converts to Islam, and missionary efforts have increased the numbers of Muslims in Africa, Asia, Europe, and America.

The Iranian Shi'a revolution, led by the exiled Ayatollah Khomeini, brought into sharp focus many of the divisions and changes that had been stirring in the Muslim world. Its immediate cause was a revolt against Shah Reza Pahlavi and his program to modernize the Iranian economy, society, educational system, and military. According to Denny:

> The shah was an autocrat who dealt very harshly with his opponents. . . . On the surface and in public, the shah tried to present an image of a benevolent monarch bringing his people into prosperous and progressive modern times. And many people in the middle and upper classes did indeed prosper, especially from the country's oil wealth. Western-style recreations, fashion, social life, music, entertainment, and consumer goods were abundantly available in all the

cities and large towns, accompanied by garish posters, billboards, and shop fronts. Women in the cities went about in short dresses and without the traditional Islamic covering of the hair and arms, something shocking and unacceptable to more conservative Muslim sensibilities, which were all the time still very strong, although beneath the surface and waiting to reemerge.

Khomeini, returned to Iran and installed as the country's absolute authority when the shah was deposed, gained a following by insisting that in Islamic tradition priests, not kings, rule, and enjoyed popularity as an activist priest who aimed to change the world and not retreat from the challenges of modernism. Today Iran symbolizes Islamic revival and reform and promotes its brand of political Islam to other Islamic nations, both Shi'a and Sunni. Denny says, "There is a conviction that the old sectarian (Shi'a-Sunni) split no longer makes any sense but serves only to divide and confuse Muslims."

Americans and Europeans take interest in three elements of the Islamic resurgence: fundamentalism, treatment of women, and Muslim immigration. Frederick Denny thinks the label "fundamentalism," originating in America to describe ultraconservative Protestants, is inappropriate to describe the renewed voice in the Islamic community; better, he believes, to call the movement "traditionalism." Islamic specialist John O. Voll, however, finds the term "fundamentalist" appropriate because it suggests "a great urgency," a characteristic he sees in growing numbers of Muslims. In *Islam: An Introduction*, Annemarie Schimmel offers her insight into this movement:

> The emergence of an attitude deemed "fundamentalist" . . .
> is understandable and, for the historian of religion, appears
> almost logical. The entire inherited value system seemed to
> have lost its importance and been replaced with radically different values under the influence of the West (the influence
> of Western movies and videos cannot be overrated in this
> process). Now the hope is to find a certain protection from
> Western civilization, or rather its caricatures as marketed in
> the mass media, by returning to the good old days of the

Prophet when things were as they ought to be.

In the process of returning to the traditions of the Prophet, some extremists misinterpret the intent of Muhammad and fail to heed his warnings against violence and excess; consequently, Westerners fear these extremists as terrorists. An important issue in the resurgence of fundamentalism is the status of women. In its most extreme form, fundamentalism keeps women isolated and their bodies covered. In many Islamic countries, however, large numbers of well-educated, professional women—professors, politicians, and lawyers—counter fundamentalist dictates as advocates of equal rights for ordinary Muslim women. Women converts to Islam tend to follow traditional patterns of dress called *hijab*—the head scarf and long coat—to conform to Islamic piety or to avoid criticism. Muslim feminists, both men and women, seek to emphasize Islamic principles and also modernize, but in their minds modernizing is not synonymous with Westernizing.

Today large numbers of immigrants flow into European and North American countries, presenting tremendous challenges of enculturation. In America the Muslim population is growing even faster than in European countries as African Americans convert to Islam. African American converts are increasing in response to recent awareness of an Islamic heritage in Africa before slavery and the influence of strong American Muslim leaders from Elijah Muhammad and Malcolm X to Louis Farrakhan, who emphasizes economic and social justice for blacks. Many African Americans are converting to Islam in U.S. prisons, where Muslim religious leaders provide counseling and instruction. Inmates find the strict observation of Islamic practices appealing because it gives order to prison life and the dignity of receiving rights to regular prayer and special foods.

Because this turning point—the resurgence of Islam—is a present-day phenomenon, it is unclear what its historical impact will be. Islamic modernists quote over and over these lines from the Koran, Sura 12–13: "Verily God does not change the fate of a people unless the people change what is in themselves."

Chapter 1

The Origin and Growth of Islam in Arabia

Turning | Points

IN WORLD HISTORY

The Birth of Islam in the Arabian Desert

Muhammad Munir

Muhammad Munir describes the wilderness, the environment surrounding Mecca and the wild Bedouin tribes that inhabited it. Munir explains how Muhammad, an honest and reputable orphan, became the Prophet who heard Allah's words and suffered persecution when he tried to spread the message of the new religion. Islamic historian Muhammad Munir, former chief justice of Pakistan, a Muslim society, researched both remote Islamic history and present-day attitudes toward and economic influences of Islam.

There was no law and order or organised government as we understand it before Arabia came under the control of the holy Prophet of Islam. Though Arabia had been a Roman Province and Yemen had been successively subdued by the Abyssinians[1] and Persians, the Arabs in fact remained always independent. The towns of Mecca and Madina [Medina] had also bowed under the Scythians[2] but it did not in the least affect their independence. Much later the Sultans of Egypt and Turks claimed Arabia as their conquered territory and attempted to bring it under their effective administrative control but in vain; the Arabs remained independent in point of fact and law, the imposed suzerainty over them being merely nominal and theoretical. Even the armies of such powerful monarchs and emperors as Sesotris, Cyrus, Pompey, Trajan and August could not conquer this wild re-

1. Ethiopians 2. nomadic people from ancient Eurasia

Excerpted from *Islam in History*, by Muhammad Munir. Copyright ©1974 by The Law Publishing Company, Lahore, Pakistan. Reprinted by permission of the publisher. All rights reserved.

gion. The secret of the independence of Arabs lay in their martial spirit, the terrain of the country and the effective use by them of their horses and camels. Each tribe was independent under its own leader and had nothing to do with other tribes except when one tribe engaged in a feud with another resulting from a fancied or real injury, which once begun continued for centuries. And when Arabia was invaded by a foreign power, the tribes forgot their old jealousies, rivalries and blood feuds and presenting a united front against the enemy charged on them with bows, spears, swords and javelins, sure of a victory; but if defeated they would, with their camels who could easily travel 50 miles a day and horses who could gallop like no horse can, retreat to the wilderness of burning sand dunes, leaving the enemy to die of thirst and hunger or being lost in the pursuit. Some two years before the birth of the holy Prophet, Abraha, the Ethiopian general, invaded Arabia, bent upon destroying the Kaba,[3] but his elephants and African soldiers and he himself had to retreat disgracefully, having been struck by small-pox and enveloped in a hail storm. There is an allegorical reference to this incident in the Quran [Koran], as Allah speaks to mankind in allegories, 24:35.

Tribal Life Untouched by Civilization

The Arabs living in tents in the wilderness never came into close contact with civilisation which surrounded them on three sides. They had no political system and their economic life was simplicity itself. With no proper roads or navigation and their chiefs having only a casual trade connection, the nomads led a life of wandering, moving from place to place where their horses and camels could graze and they themselves could get some food. Once in a year only, on the occasion of the Hajj,[4] the nomads would meet other tribesmen and hear what people returning from their trade expeditions would say or what a poet had to tell of a feud heroically

3. today the most sacred shrine of Islam, believed to have been erected originally by Abraham. A boxlike structure standing in the courtyard of the Great Mosque at Mecca, it has no devotional significance other than its history.   4. pilgrimage to Mecca

fought or of the beauty of a real or imaginary woman. Of course they would perform the Hajj, worship the gods that were installed in the Kaba and pray for the aversion of an apprehended calamity or the fulfillment of a cherished wish. Though each tribe had its own dialect, it never concealed its preference for the pure Arabic of Mecca which was also used by the famous poets who came there to sing their love or epic poems.

Before the birth of Islam, women were treated as mere chattels. On the death of a father his widow and concubines, which could be as many as he could afford, devolved on the son who could take all or any one of them except his own real mother for his sexual satisfaction. In the same manner a woman could have connections outside the wedlock with as many men as she liked though there was always a possibility of a feud being started by the aggrieved husband or his relations. Though the definition of incest, a horrid crime in modern society, has varied from age to age, in ancient Arabia the offence, except in a few cases, was hardly defined or the conventional prohibition against it observed. Slaves, of course, had no rights and their treatment was worse than that of animals. The use of alcohol was general and profuse and gambling in various forms was a cherished game with them. Giving a daughter in marriage to another family was a humiliation and female infanticide was practised without reproach or shame. Daylight robberies and murders were the order of the day. Even human sacrifices were not unknown. This gloomy picture of ancient Arab society is not however all that one can paint; the Arabs had their own redeeming features. They were scrupulously honest in keeping their word and promise. Their valour, love of independence, eloquence and hospitality were proverbial.

Bedouin Hospitality and Religion

One had merely to enter the tent of a Bedouin for refuge or food and both were immediately available to him with a parting gift according to the resources of the host, and any desert dweller would defend with his life any helpless man who asked for his protection. One outstanding characteristic of ancient Arabia was the Arab's tolerance for the religious beliefs of others. He would on no account interfere with others' belief or worship. Thus before the birth of the Prophet of Islam, Jews, Christians, Zoroastrians, Sabaeans and Magis were living in Arabia unhindered and without

---

The Desert Camel

The odes of seven ancient Arab poets capture the life of pagan tribal dwellers near Mecca, the environment out of which Muhammad came. In the following excerpt, Tarafa, one of the seven poets, creates a picture of his camel racing.

Ah, but when grief assails me, straightway I ride it off
mounted on my swift, lean-flanked camel, night and day racing,
sure-footed, like the planks of a litter; I urge her on
down the bright highway, that back of a striped mantle;
she vies with the noble, hot-paced she-camels, shank on shank
nimbly plying, over a path many feet have beaten. . . .
Reddish the bristles under her chin, very firm her back,
broad the span of her swift legs, smooth her swinging gait;
her legs are twined like rope uptwisted; her forearms
thrust slantwise up to the propped roof of her breast.
Swiftly she rolls, her cranium huge, her shoulder-blades
high-hoisted to frame her lofty, raised superstructure. . . .
Her long neck is very erect when she lifts it up
calling to mind the rudder of a Tigris-bound vessel.
Her skull is most like an anvil, the junction of its two halves
meeting together as it might be on the edge of a file.
Her cheek is smooth as Syrian parchment, her split lip
a tanned hide of Yemen, its slit not bent crooked;
her eyes are a pair of mirrors, sheltering
in the caves of her brow-bones, the rock of a pool's hollow. . . .
Her ears are true, clearly detecting on the night journey
the fearful rustle of a whisper, the high-pitched cry,
sharp-tipped, her nobel pedigree plain in them,
pricked like the ears of a wild-cow of Haumal lone-pasturing.

A.J. Arberry, *Aspects of Islamic Civilization: As Depicted in the Original Texts.* London: George Allen and Unwin, 1964.

molestation. The Arab's hostility to Islam was based on an entirely different ground. The ancient Arab loved his personal and political freedom as much as his freedom of worship and thought; but Islam required him to give up the worship of his gods and to adopt the worship of only one God and this the ancient Arab felt as an irksome restriction on his freedom of thought and worship which was eventually to affect his personal and political freedom. He did not realise, until it actually happened, that worship of only one God would mean unity and one nation, and could give him strength and power which at the moment he could not dream of.

To the general idolatry mentioned earlier, Arabs were no exception. According to Muslim traditions Kaba was built by Abraham and Ismail[5] on old foundations which had since long lain buried. But by floods, fire and wear and tear, the new structure was damaged more than once and the Quraish[6] had to rebuild it and at the time of its construction there stood outside it 360 idols, more important idols having been installed inside it. The great idol Hubal had also been an inmate of the Kaba. After the holy prophet proclaimed the new religion and started his denunciation of idols, the idols or material representation in or outside the Kaba were all destroyed. It will thus be apparent that before the birth of Islam Arabia was steeped deep in idol worship, and almost every tribe had its own idol. But though this was so, Jews, Christians, Sabeans and Magis had long been settled in some parts of Arabia and they were professing their faiths and practicing their religious rites without opposition by the idol worshipping Arabs. The idea of one God had been the fundamental trait of the preachings of Moses, and Jesus of Nazareth had been converted into Christ, the son of God. The Sabeans also were Judeo-Christians who were considered among the people of the Book with Jews and Christians. . . . And then there was a body of thinkers (called Hanifs) who had come vaguely to conceive of a being above the

5. Ishmael, the son of Abraham cast out to wander; the forebear of the Arabs   6. a tribe in Mecca

gods. And as far back as 539 B.C. when the Jews returned to Jerusalem, there arose among them a number of prophets who began to talk of one universal God and of a promise by Him that the world would one day be a place of unity, peace and happiness. This God lived in a temple, not made with hands, eternal in the heavens. Thus an inchoate idea of a Supreme Being had existed in Arabia before the birth of Islam but the attributes of this Supreme Being had either not been fully comprehended or existed only for the children of Israel led by Moses. . . .

Muhammad's Background

Conditions in the world and Arabia were as just described when from the west of Arabian desert land there appeared the faint precursor of a storm, not of the usual poisonous simoom,[7] but entirely different in its potentiality from all other storms, that was to envelop the world, free an enslaved humanity and pull down from their high pedestals gods which had ruled over human destinies for centuries and bring down the thrones of the proudest and most powerful kings, Caesers and emperors, and humble civilizations which from Knossus to Byzantine the world had accepted for more than two thousand years. Muhammad was born in a Quraish family of Mecca in 570–571 A.D. . . .

Muhammad was the posthumous son of Abdulla, a custodian of Ka'aba and one of the most handsome and influential noblemen of the Quraish tribe. So the future Prophet was born an orphan and the initial responsibility of nursing him fell on his mother, the lady Amina. The tribe of Quraish were also known as Bani Kin'ana, and were the most distinguished of the descendants of Ismail who after his father, patriarch Abraham, had left him and his mother Hagar in Arabia and himself returned to Palestine, had settled in Arabia among the local tribes and taken part in the erection of Ka'aba with his father when he paid his third or fourth visit to Arabia. The present rites of Hajj are not very dissimilar to those performed by Abraham.

---

7. a strong, hot, sand-laden wind of the desert

It is unnecessary to give a full genealogical table of the Prophet. It will be sufficient to look at the short pedigree-table below which admits of no dispute:

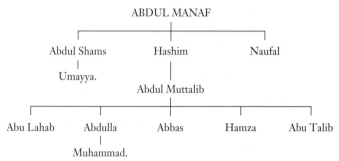

ABDUL MANAF

| Abdul Shams | Hashim | Naufal |

Umayya.

Abdul Muttalib

Abu Lahab   Abdulla   Abbas   Hamza   Abu Talib

Muhammad.

Mecca by reason of the Ka'aba and of its being situate on a trade route was the most important town in Arabia and Abdul Muttalib, the grandfather of the Prophet, was Ka'aba's custodian, the highest office that an Arab could claim. On Abdul Muttalib's death the office devolved on Abdulla, the father of the Holy Prophet. . . .

Muhammad's Life as an Orphan

As Muhammad's father Abdulla had in the course of a trade journey died at Madina, the care and custody of the orphan was taken by his grandfather Abdul Muttalib. As a child, according to the Arab custom, he was given to a lady of the desert, Halima, to be nursed by her for some years. The infant remained for a few years in the tents of Banu Sa'd, noted for the beauty and sweetness of their tongue. But Halima returned the child to his mother Amina while he was still 5 years old. The mother took the child to Madina to show him the grave of his father but while she was returning to Mecca, she died on the way and the child was brought back to Mecca. The infant was only 8 years of age, when his grandfather also died and his custody was taken by his uncle Abu Talib. He was twelve years old when his uncle took him with himself on a trade journey to Syria in the course of which he was introduced to Bahira, a Christian ascetic. Apart from the legends which differ in details relating to some supernatural phenomena there is nothing of importance to mention in the life of the boy, except that he developed into a young man of exemplary character. . . . His occupation was to graze his uncle's cattle and though he was coming to adolescence in the traditional atmosphere of Arabia, he never liked idol worship, and never committed any evil. On the contrary he was so scrupulously honest that he came to be called "Amin" (honest or trustworthy). . . .

It was at this time that Abu Talib thought of arranging his nephew's marriage with Khadija [a widow of high rank in Mecca]. The lady welcomed the proposal and the young man of 25 was linked in wedlock to the lady who was then 35 or 40 and thus his senior by 10 or 15 years. . . .

Muhammad's Sojourn to the Cave

After this marriage, life for the young man became somewhat comfortable and his mind was at peace. Though *Ummi*, illiterate, he had always been thoughtful since his adolescence and now that his mind had been maturing he looked at the skies, the sun, the stars, and planets and their regular annual movements, and at the species of animal and vegetable life, and began to ask himself how all these forms of life were born, developed and decayed without notable increase or decrease in their number, how regular were the changes in seasons, and he was seized with a powerful mood of reflection and contemplation; but finding no answer to his questions, he chose a lonely cave named Hira near Mecca where he often went and stayed for long hours, contemplating in solitude. While he was in one of these contemplative moods, he thought he saw an apparition in the form of an angel who asked him to recite a verse. The prophet said that he could not read but on the insistence of the angel and on his body being squeezed by the visitor three-four times, he recited after the angel a sentence, which broadly meant that Rabb (Allah) was the Creator and that he had made man from a clot of flesh. This happened some 15 years after he had been married to Khadija. Feeling an acute sense of fear he returned home and told his wife what had happened and asked her to wrap him in a blanket. The lady felt puzzled for some time and then consoled her husband by saying that what he had seen was true and that he should be happy, as no harm could be caused or intended to him whose life was spotless and dedicated to the service of those who deserved. After this he continued visiting the cave and some time later the angel again appeared and addressing him as the wearer of the sheet of prophethood asked him to apprise his near relations to fear the wrath of Allah. Returning home he mentioned this incident also to his wife who unhesitatingly proclaimed her belief in him and thus she was the first person to believe in Islam. Abubakr, one of his friends, soon joined and he was followed by the prophet's cousin Ali who was then just a youth, and by the manumitted[8] slave Zaid. All these were persons who were thoroughly acquainted with the character and conduct of the Holy Prophet. He then openly began to proclaim the new creed but could convert during three years only forty persons. One day he was required by a revelation to proclaim his new creed more openly and not to mind those who opposed him. Accordingly the prophet called the people of Mecca and climbing on the mount of Safa he first asked them to judge him by the life he had been leading among them and after they agreed that his life was spotless, that he had never lied and had the reputation of being an *amin*, he forbade them to worship anything but Allah and to lead clean moral lives. This was resented, particularly by his uncle Abu Lahab, who said that his nephew was in an eccentric mood which would soon pass away.

Preaching and Persecution

The Prophet continued preaching in Mecca for ten years whenever and wherever he found the time and the place to be suitable. There used to be an annual fair in Mecca to which people came from all over Arabia to display their arts, games and wares, read their poems and perform the Hajj. The Prophet would go and address them about his mission on their way to and from the fair but everywhere he was ridiculed, insulted and called bad names. In these demonstrations the leading part was taken by Abu Lahab, his uncle,

8. freed from bondage

who would say that his nephew had gone out of his mind. It is not necessary to describe at length the indignities and humiliations to which he was subjected and the physical threats that were held out to him and his followers, particularly for the three months after Abu Talib's and Khadija's deaths which occurred within a few weeks of each other. His social and commercial boycott was proclaimed by a placard that was hung in front of the Ka'aba. The Prophet and his followers then felt more helpless but he continued his mission and for three months he was subjected to the most cruel and barbarous treatment. After three trying months following the two deaths, he decided to go to Taif, an important town 60 miles from Mecca, alone or with Zaid, hoping that he would there have a more favourable audience but he had hardly been there for about a month when he found further stay there impossible. The elderly preacher was ridiculed and literally stoned out of the town by the street urchins, with bleeding legs and feet. Praying Allah for help he returned to Mecca, only to meet fiercer opposition. He then attempted to convince of his mission some of the interior Arab tribes but without any success. His assertion that he was an apostle of God went unheeded, but despite this the new movement continued gaining ground. He was offered the most alluring temptation if he withdrew from his mission—money, chieftainship, women but the offer was emphatically spurned. In every book on the life of the Prophet a full description of the brutalities practiced on him and his followers have been described in detail and at one time they became so intolerable that a batch of 11 men and 4 women including Usman and his wife and the Prophet's daughter Ruquiya, decided to emigrate to neighbouring Habsha of which the Christian Negus was the king. This incident describes an interesting dialogue between the leaders of the emigrants and the king and shows the firm conviction of those who after embracing Islam had left their homes where they had not been feeling safe. Next year some more Muslims went to Habsha with a view to settling there. But persecution has never stemmed the tide of a liberal movement firmly believed in, and the small body of Muslims received fresh strength when Umar embraced Islam.

In the 11th year of prophethood six persons of a leading tribe of Yathrib [Medina] came to Mecca for Hajj, they all, after a short audience with the Prophet in the solitude of a valley, accepted Islam. Next year 12 more men came from Yathrib and accepted the new faith having given an undertaking to be true to the new faith. On their return to Yathrib a companion of the Prophet accompanied them who proved so effective a preacher that Yathrib became practically a Muslim town. In the following year, 72 Muslims from Madina came to Mecca for Hajj, met the Prophet and their leader entered into a pact promising to receive the Prophet in Madina and protecting him with his life and property. In return the Prophet promised an alliance with them in peace and war.

In the 13th year of revelation, the Prophet informed his companions that he had been directed in a revelation to migrate to Madina with his followers. Thus began the Hijrat to Madina, the companions leaving Mecca in batches, with all their property and assets left behind. Within two months all the companions had migrated to Madina, and it took each batch two months to reach its destination. Only three persons were left behind, namely, the Prophet himself, Abu Bakr and Ali. The leaders of the tribes now found a convenient opportunity to murder the Prophet. A conspiracy was hatched according to which when the Prophet lay on bed, the leaders of all the tribes were simultaneously to attack and murder him so that the responsibility for the murder may not be fixed on any single tribe or person. The Prophet came to know of the design and defeated the plan by himself and Abu Bakr leaving before the time of the intended attack and making Ali sleep on the bed. In the morning when the intending assassins found Ali on the bed and the Prophet and Abu Bakr gone, they were sorely disappointed. After leaving Mecca the Prophet and Abu Bakr had taken shelter in a cave called Thaur, a few miles from Mecca, where they hid themselves for three day. The conspirators spread in all directions to overtake the fugitives and when some of them came near the cave, Abu Bakr felt fear for their lives, because they were only two against many but the Prophet said to him that they were not only two but three, as Allah was with them. Some scouts of the conspirators had come to the mouth of the cave but finding a spider's web spun across the entrance they thought that the place was deserted and went away. Commenting on this incident a Roman historian remarks that one tiny insect "had changed the history of the world" (cited by Wollaston in "Half an hour with Muhammad"). From the day on which they left the cave, June 20, 622 A.D., a day from which henceforth the chronology of Islamic world was to be computed, the first Hijri year had commenced. After three days the Prophet and his companion set out on the journey to Madina where after a short sojourn in a suburb of Madina they took the road to that city where they were enthusiastically welcomed. With the Hijrat to Yathrib begins a new chapter, in fact the most important chapter, in the history of Islam.

The Spread of Islam in Arabia

Thomas W. Lippman

Thomas W. Lippman traces the turns in Muhammad's fortunes as he moved from Mecca to Medina and back to Mecca seeking converts to the religion of Allah. According to Lippman, in Medina Muhammad established a power base from which he conquered Mecca and influenced outlying Bedouin tribes. While in Medina, Muhammad's messages from Allah expanded the Koran beyond its basic theology to include guidelines for earthly conduct. In Cairo, Egypt, as the *Washington Post*'s Middle East bureau chief, Lippman gained insight into the complexities of the Arab countries and the Islamic world. He is the author of *Egypt After Nasser*.

In 620 Muhammad made what Muslims call his night journey, in which he was transported to Jerusalem and ascended from there into the heavens. This was probably a mystical experience or vision but many Muslims believe Muhammad was actually transported physically, by a miracle, to Jerusalem, the sacred city of monotheism. . . .

The Egyptian scholar Ahmad Galwash, in *The Religion of Islam*, which was published with the approval of the religious authorities at Cairo's al-Azhar University, says of the night journey (as it is called), "All that Muslims *must* believe respecting this journey is that the prophet saw himself, in a vision, transported from Mecca to Jerusalem and that in such vision he really beheld some of the greatest signs of his Lord. However, some trustworthy tradition insists that this journey was a real bodily one and not only a vision."

In either case, it was an exalting spiritual experience,

which consoled Muhammad in his darkest hour and marked the beginning of a change in his fortunes. Shortly after the night journey, the Prophet was at a pilgrim fair outside Mecca where he met a group of men from Yathrib [Medina], an important town to the north, some of whom were probably Jews. It was an encounter that changed the history of Islam and of the world.

It was evidently not a chance meeting; the men from Yathrib sought him out. . . . Unlike Mecca, which was ruled by the Quraish and prosperous in its stability, Yathrib was exhausted by a power struggle among two Arab and three Jewish tribes, and its citizens were looking for a unifier and mediator. Fazlur Rahman suggests that they sought out Muhammad because even though he had failed to convert the Meccans word of his "moral prestige and statesmanlike ability" had already spread beyond his native city.

The men went back to Yathrib, about 280 miles north of Mecca, and told of their meeting. At the fair the following year, 621, a delegation of twelve returned to Mecca and entered into an agreement with Muhammad. They pledged to refrain from idolatry, promiscuity, and infanticide, and they offered a welcome to the Prophet and his followers. Muhammad dispatched one of his disciples to Yathrib to instruct the people in his teachings. In 622, a delegation of seventy-five citizens of Yathrib formally invited the community of Muslims to move to their town.

The Hegira: The Migration to Medina

Muhammad was not primarily interested in Yathrib. His objective was the conversion of Mecca, which was in effect the religious capital of Arabia. But he was making little headway there, and practicality dictated that he accept the invitation, which would enable him to establish a useful power base at last. This decision prepared the way for the seminal event in Islamic history, the *hijra* (or *hegira*, as it is usually spelled in English), the migration of Muhammad and his followers from Mecca to their adopted city. The Muslims left Mecca in small groups, so as not to arouse suspicion. The migration was completed on September 24, 622. . . .

Yathrib, the new home of Islam, was renamed al-Medinat al-Munawara, "the illuminated city," or al-Medinat al-Rasul, "the City of the Messenger" (accounts vary), and has been known ever since as Medina, the Arabic word for city.

There Muhammad was in wholly different and more promising circumstances than he had been in at Mecca. He was free to preach openly and was heard with respect. The scorned outcast of Mecca was welcomed by the Medinese, who had no tribal hostility to him and no vested interest in the commerce of the pilgrimage to the Kaaba.[1] Muhammad was no longer a solitary troublemaking mystic; he was the leader of a growing community, its judge and lawgiver, and soon would be its military commander as well.

In the absence of a strong ruling power at Medina, Muhammad's temporal authority grew rapidly. It was reinforced by Koranic revelations that put the seal of divine authority on his position as "Commander of the Faithful" and equated Muhammad's instructions to the community with the divine will: "He that obeys the Apostle obeys Allah himself" (4:80). In the *hadith*,[2] Muhammad is quoted as telling the Muslims, "What I have forbidden to you, avoid; what I have ordered, do as much of it as you can. It was only their excessive questioning and their disagreeing with the prophets that destroyed those who were before you."

The basic doctrines of the faith had been established at Mecca. Now, at Medina the Koranic revelations and Muhammad's teachings dealt less with eschatology[3] and more with the social and legal issues confronting the community. The mundane supplanted the mystical in the revelations. The exalted prophetic visions gave way to long lessons on social behavior, family life, justice, law, prohibited conduct, and the obligation of the faithful to fight for their beliefs. Muslims, having learned what to believe about God and the Last Day, were now taught how to act on earth in accordance with that belief.

---

1. the sacred shrine of the gods in Mecca   2. a supplement to the Koran recording the actions and sayings of the prophet Muhammad   3. theology dealing with death and human destiny

Muhammad's Rule in Medina

Muhammad's first act of governance is said to have been the issuance of a charter establishing the relationship of the three groups that made up the population of Medina: his followers from Mecca, the indigenous Medinese *ansar* (helpers), and the Jews. The charter guaranteed religious freedom for the Jews, urged cooperation and unity among the Muslims, and declared that Muhammad should be the arbiter of disputes. With that the Prophet established two principles that were revolutionary in their time and place and had been rejected at Mecca. One was that Islam was the source of temporal as well as spiritual authority, and the other was that faith, rather than tribe, should be the bond that regulates the affairs of men.

Both principles are still basic to Islam. The brotherhood of Islam, the *umma*, or community of believers, has existed ever since in a bond of faith that transcends race and politics. "The believers," says the Koran, "are a band of brothers" (49:10).

The working agreement with the Jews, however, did not survive long. Muhammad naively expected them to accept his religious message as well as his temporal authority and he was angry when they did not. The Jews mocked his revelations and scorned him for his imperfect understanding of the Jewish scriptures, to which he frequently alluded. Muhammad suspected that the Jews were giving secret support to the Quraish of Mecca, whose hostility to him did not abate after the *hijra*.

This tension with the Jews is said by some authorities to account for decisions the Prophet made early in his sojourn at Medina, which effectively Arabized the new faith. Islam became less an extension of Judaism and more a specifically Arabian creed.

In accordance with new instructions from Allah, Muhammad changed the *qibla*, the direction of prayer, from Jerusalem to Mecca, and he incorporated into Islam the pilgrimage to the Kaaba. Friday replaced Saturday as the day of congregational prayer. "We will make you turn toward a qibla that will please you," says the Koran. "Turn toward the Holy Mosque [of Mecca]; wherever you be, face towards it" (2:144). . . .

Muhammad still viewed Mecca as his objective and still hoped to convert the Quraish. In dropping the Jewish Sabbath and in making Islam a faith focused on Mecca instead of Jerusalem, he may have been making overtures to the hostile Meccan rulers. The Koran emphasizes the Arabness of Muhammad's mission, his role as prophet to a people who had no scripture of their own; and to the Arabs, Mecca was the traditional center of worship. Even at Medina, Muhammad referred to Mecca as "the sacred city." Medina was only a temporary sanctuary, from which he sought to implant Islam in the city that had denied it. The change in the *qibla* and the inclusion of a pilgrimage to the sites of Abraham (not to the pagan gods of Mecca) could only make Muhammad's faith less alien to the Meccans.

Before resuming his mission to Mecca, however, Muhammad had first to consolidate his power at Medina.

Aside from the Jews, his chief source of difficulty was a group of Medinese Arabs who resented his influence and sought to sabotage him. Their tactic was to pretend to embrace Islam while secretly working in concert with the Jews against Muhammad. They were known as the Hypocrites. Muhammad and his sincere followers are said to have known perfectly well what the Hypocrites were up to, but Muhammad accepted their false professions of faith and even allowed them to fight with his troops, saying that it was up to God to determine what is in men's hearts. . . .

When the leader of the Hypocrites died, Muhammad is said to have attended the funeral and led prayers for him, thus winning over into genuine faith many of those who had been secretly opposed to him.

The last ten years of Muhammad's life is a story of government and diplomacy more than a story of religion. The fundamentals of the faith were well established; but if Islam was to survive its founder, it had to become irreversibly ascendant in Arabia within his lifetime, and it was to that objective that the Prophet devoted his energies in conflicts with the Jews and Hypocrites of Medina that alternated with recurring military skirmishes against the Quraish of Mecca.

The skirmishes evidently originated in the need of the

Muslim community in Medina for food and money, which impelled them to resort to the traditional kind of caravan-raiding that was indistinguishable from banditry except perhaps in motive. Even if the Muslims had not been obliged to raid, however, armed conflict with the Quraish was probably inevitable, given the Prophet's determination to implant Islam in Mecca.

Battles with the Quraish

Two years after the *hijra*, a small band of believers attacked a caravan and carried off the spoils. Muhammad himself did not participate, but he was criticized for allowing the attack to take place during a month regarded as holy by the Arabians when, by tradition, a truce was in effect. Thus, this first Muslim skirmish was a tactical success but a political liability for Muhammad.

His justification for the breach of taboo is recorded in the Koran: "They ask you about the sacred month. Say, 'To fight in this month is a grave offense; but to debar others from the path of Allah, to deny Him, and to expel His worshippers from the Holy Mosque is far more grave in His sight. Idolatry is worse than carnage'" (2:217).

The Prophet and his followers were city-dwellers, not bedouin, and any analysis attributing the behavior of Muslims to bedouin tradition is specious. But the Muslims evidently adapted themselves quickly to the techniques of desert warfare. Their next recorded encounter, a real battle with lasting significance, was a spectacular success. It was the Battle of Badr, which took place in March 624. It is analyzed in Sura 8 of the Koran, which says that Allah caused Muhammad to underestimate the enemy's numbers so he would not shrink from the encounter. Muslims still give thanks for that today.

Ten accounts of Badr by Muslim and Western chroniclers may give ten different versions of the details, but there is no dispute about the scope of the incident or its outcome. The Muslims prepared to raid a caravan that was passing southward on its way to Mecca. The Meccans, alerted, reinforced. Muhammad and about 300 followers encountered a Meccan force of nearly a thousand at Badr, eleven miles southwest of Medina, and routed them.

To the Muslims and to other Arabs of the peninsula, this demonstrated that Allah was indeed on the side of Muhammad. The victory, against such great odds, reinforced Muhammad's claim to be the true prophet built the confidence of the community, and prepared the way for decisive encounters with both the Quraish of Mecca and the Jews of Medina. A Koranic revelation told the Muslims that Allah had sent a thousand angels to help them and would always ensure the triumph of the believers. Other revelations instructed the believers in their obligation to join the fight when the call to do so was issued. It was not their arms but the power of God that achieved the victory, the Koran told the Muslims, and God will always be with those who fight for the faith. . . .

The year after Badr, the Quraish sought revenge. They counterattacked with 3,000 men. Muhammad organized a defense on a slope at Uhud, north of Medina, but his troops were defeated when archers on the flank left their posts, apparently fearful that they would be cut out of the booty. Muhammad himself was wounded in the rout.

Then in one of those unaccountable blunders that fill the pages of military history, the Meccans withdrew after the battle instead of entering Medina, failing to press their advantage. Perhaps they believed that the defeat they had administered to the Muslims would suffice, but the result was to leave the community of the faithful intact and to leave Muhammad's authority over the Muslims unchallenged. Far from losing control because of the defeat, Muhammad chastised his followers for their weakness and laid down regulations for the division of the spoils in future engagements, which were not long in coming.

The Quraish sent another expedition northward in 627. Muhammad foiled it by ordering a trench dug around Medina. When the Meccans withdrew their siege after this Battle of the Trench, the nature of the military struggle between the two communities changed. The Quraish were never again able to challenge the Muslims at Medina, and the initiative passed to Muhammad, who resumed his efforts to implant Islam in the sacred city.

Conflicts with the Jews

Between skirmishes with the Quraish, Muhammad pressed his campaign against the Jews of Medina. The olive branch that he had held out to the Jews in the early days of Islam, when he still believed the Jews would accept his message as a continuation of their own beliefs, he withdrew in disillusionment. He saw them as treacherous, supporting the Quraish and violating their charter with the Muslims. The Jews not only rebuffed his message, they also ridiculed him. Muhammad retorted that they had corrupted and rejected their own scriptures. Koranic revelations spoke of the Jews in harsh terms.

In the Koran, God says, "Because of their iniquity, we forbade the Jews good things which were formerly allowed them; because time after time they have debarred others from the path of Allah; because they practice usury—though they were forbidden it—and cheat others of their possessions" (4:160). Respect for Jews as "people of the book" gave way to excoriation and contempt; the Koran denounces the Jews as blasphemers and corrupters, and even associates them with pagans as the strongest enemies of Islam (5:85). "Those to whom the burden of the Torah was entrusted and yet refused to bear it" says the Koran, "are like a donkey laden with books" (62:5).

Two of the three Jewish tribes of Medina were expelled from the city. The third, the Qurayza, supported the Quraish during the Battle of the Trench, and when that engagement ended, the Muslims extracted a terrible vengeance. All the men, six hundred to eight hundred in number, were beheaded; the women and children were sold into slavery. That is one of the few recorded incidents of its kind in the early history of Islam; the Prophet preached tolerance and compassion, not blood lust, and generally conquered groups were treated with mercy. The mass execution of the Jews of Medina is justified by Muslim commentators on the ground that they had not only rejected Islam but actually conspired against the Muslims in violation of a solemn agreement. . . .

After the Battle of the Trench and the elimination of Jewish opposition, events moved swiftly, as Muhammad felt himself strong enough to challenge the Meccans. Rather than undertake direct military confrontation, he devised a political stratagem.

Muhammad Gains Mecca and Arabia

He and a large band of the faithful, said to number more than a thousand, set out for Mecca not as an army but as pilgrims desirous of visiting the sacred shrine. As the Muslims approached the city, the Meccans sent out a delegation to negotiate with Muhammad. The outcome was a pact known as the Treaty of Hudaibiya. Muhammad and his followers agreed to put off their pilgrimage until the following year, and the Meccans acknowledged their right to make it. The Quraish accepted Muhammad's right to preach and in effect acknowledged his legitimacy.

This diplomatic compromise upset some of Muhammad's more zealous followers, but it demonstrated once again that Muhammad was a flexible pragmatic leader, not a fanatic. He was willing to see blood shed when necessary, as at Badr, but he was also willing to negotiate and compromise to minimize violence, as he did when he agreed to the Treaty of Hudaibiya, which served his objectives to establish himself and Islam in Mecca. The pact with the Meccans was evidently seen by members of other Arabian tribes as authorization for them to embrace Islam, and it is said that more people then did so than had accepted the faith in all the preceding years of Muhammad's mission.

The treaty was signed in 628. The following year, as agreed, Muhammad and some of the Muslims did make the pilgrimage. They spent three days in Mecca, and by all accounts the citadel of idolatry began quickly to crumble when confronted with the power of Islam. The Muslims won some illustrious converts who had formerly opposed Islam. Among them was Amr ibn al-As, who a few years later was to conquer Egypt in the name of Islam.

Muhammad's was not a mission of half measures or partial successes. He wanted Mecca. . . . In January 630, Muhammad assembled an army of 10,000 men and marched on Mecca, where he met little resistance, either because the Meccans finally accepted the message of Islam or because they bowed to superior numbers. The Quraish were undone when their leader, Abu Sufyan, embraced Islam and threw in his lot with Muhammad. The Muslims marched into the city, and Muhammad personally directed the destruction of the pagan idols in the Kaaba. He himself is said to have wrecked the wooden image of a pigeon that was hanging from the shrine's roof.

The ascendancy of Islam in Arabia was assured, if not yet complete. It was manifest that Islam was the true religion of Allah. How else could the scorned upstart Muhammad and his few persecuted followers have overcome not only the Quraish but also the power of all the tribal gods and all the idols of the Kaaba? It was just as Muhammad had been saying all along; the power of the true God would reveal itself, and when it did, all the false gods would crumble. With the acceptance of Allah and of Islam by the Meccans and the neighboring tribes, Muhammad's mission was nearly complete.

Muhammad's Message of Tolerance, Equity, and Piety

The occupation of Mecca appears to have been a model of mercy and charity. Muhammad pardoned most of his foes, and if they embraced Islam, he shared with them the tribute that began to flow in from tribes of the peninsula who submitted to Muhammad's temporal authority, if not entirely to his creed. The Prophet preached tolerance, equity, and piety, and he evidently practiced what he preached. The brief time remaining in Muhammad's life was devoted mostly to consolidating details, such as the exclusion of non-Muslims from the holy places—a rule that is still enforced by the government of Saudi Arabia—and a ban on visiting the shrines except in proper raiment. Those who accepted Islam were welcomed into the faith; those who did not were excluded from power and booty, but not killed or exiled. . . .

In February 632, [Muhammad] undertook a last pilgrimage to Mecca. On the Plain of Arafat he preached a farewell sermon still admired by Muslims for its virtuous tone and effective delivery.

He reminded the faithful, "Ye shall have to appear before your Lord Who shall demand from you an account for all your actions." And he told them again, "Know that all Muslims are brothers. Ye are one brotherhood, no man shall take aught from his brother unless by his free consent. Keep yourselves from injustice. Let him who is present tell this to him who is absent. It may be, that he who is told this afterward may remember it better than he who has now heard it."

With that final restatement of his message—remember Allah and the Last Judgment, shun injustice, spread the word, and embrace all Muslims as brothers—Muhammad's mission was completed. He returned to Medina and died there in the arms of his favorite wife, Aisha, on June 8, 632.

Idealizing Muhammad and Early Islam

William Montgomery Watt

William Montgomery Watt argues that many modern Muslims idealize Muhammad and romanticize early Islam. After depicting the primitive social environment from which Muhammad came, Watt warns of the dangers in reinstating ancient laws prescribing stoning and cutting off of limbs to control wayward behavior. Watt suggests that modern Muslims study the past to gain insight for solving present problems rather than try to re-create the past. William Montgomery Watt has been professor of Arabic and Islamic studies at the University of Edinburgh in Scotland. He is the author of *The Formative Period of Islamic Thought*, *Muhammad at Mecca*, *Muhammad at Medina*, and many other books and articles.

Prior to the coming of Islam the nomadic Arabs had only a very limited historical awareness, and even the urban Arabs were probably not much better informed. They were not greatly interested in anything beyond their own immediate circles. They were aware of how in desert life there could be a rise and decline of tribes. They saw tribes becoming weaker and fading away, while others grew in numbers and importance; and then the latter might also fade away and be replaced by yet others. Slight memories had been preserved, as we learn from the Qur'ān, of the no longer extant tribes of 'Ād and Thamūd. The historical material known to the pre-Islamic Arabs was mostly in the form of stories about 'the days of the Arabs' (*ayyām al-Arab*), which were primarily the days on which there had been important battles. A rough chronological framework for this material was provided by genealogy, so that the Arabs thought in terms of generations rather than of years and decades. Centuries were beyond their ken. They had no long perspectives, since most tribes had existed for only a few generations. There was no conception of a continuing historical process such as is described in the Bible. This lack of historical awareness may have contributed to the absence of a concept of development.

A little was known in Mecca about Biblical history, and this was made use of in the Qur'ān and perhaps added to. The various Biblical personages and events mentioned there were not presented in historical order; the stories came separately and in haphazard fashion, so that there was no idea of the linear history of the Israelites. This may explain, for example, why in the Qur'ān (19.28) there is apparent confusion between Miriam, the sister of Aaron, and Mary, the mother of Jesus, both of whom are Maryam in Arabic.

Into this formless world Muḥammad was sent by God as a prophet, 'out of the blue', as it were; or, if there was a reason for his being sent when he was sent, it was that the Arabs had never had a prophet—at least not since the time of Abraham and Ishmael who had founded a community at Mecca which had since disappeared. In later passages of the Qur'ān it was claimed that Muḥammad was a prophet for all humanity. Such a view was strengthened by the remarkable successes of the Arab armies in the century after Muḥammad's death. Westwards they had conquered all North Africa, had occupied much of Spain and raided as far as the centre of France. Eastwards they had overrun the Persian empire and penetrated into Central Asia and the Punjab. This expansion of Muḥammad's city-state into an empire was taken to show that the Muslims were continuing to be supported by God, as they had been at the battle of Badr in 624;[1] and it came to be expected that the Islamic empire would expand to include the whole human race.

1. a major victory for Muslims, whose small force defeated the wealthy, powerful Quraish tribe outside Medina

This expectation or assumption came to be expressed by contrasting 'the sphere of Islam' (*dār al-islām*) with 'the sphere of war' (*dār al-ḥarb*). The sphere of Islam embraces those regions under Islamic rulers in which the provisions of the Islamic Sharīʿa[2] are observed and Muslims can practice their religion, even if there are also non-Muslims with the status of protected minorities, following their own laws in personal matters. The sphere of war consists of the regions and peoples not under Muslim rulers. . . .

In the present there are difficulties in Islamic states having permanent treaties with non-Muslims. The medieval jurists held that a treaty with a state or ruler in the sphere of war should not be for longer than ten years. Modern Muslim statesmen have, of course, entered into binding agreements with non-Muslims—in the United Nations, for example—but this practice has never been sanctioned by the traditional exponents of the Sharīʿa. Thus the division of the world into the sphere of Islam and the sphere of war is by no means a thing of the past. In so far as traditionalist Islam grows in strength it could come into the forefront of world politics. . . .

The colonialism from which Muslim countries have suffered in recent times was in part parallel to the occupation of Palestine and some surrounding regions by the Crusaders in the eleventh and twelfth centuries. The significance of the Crusades for Muslims and for Christians was in fact very different. The actual Crusaders were supported by a great tide of religious fervour in Western Europe, and religious aims were uppermost in the minds of most of them. For the Muslims in general, however, the Crusades were of little concern. . . .

Some Muslims today, however, see various forms of Western aggression against the Islamic world as a recrudescence of the crusading movement. Colonel Qadhafi of Libya goes so far as to speak of Napoleon's invasion of Egypt in 1798 as the Ninth Crusade and the establishment of the state of Israel with American support as the Tenth Crusade. This last is somewhat inappropriate, since the aim of most of the orig-

2. the code of laws and rules governing the life and behavior of Muslims

inal Crusaders was to bring the Christian holy places under Christian control.

The Idealization of Muḥammad and Early Islam

Associated with this perception of the place of Islam in world history was an idealizing and romanticizing of Muḥammad and the early Muslims. Muḥammad was held to be perfect in every way, and never to have been a pagan, despite the fact that the Qur'ān (93.7) speaks of him as 'erring' (ḍāll), and other sources report that he had sacrificed to the local deities. This idealization of Muḥammad leads modern Muslims to reject the story of the 'satanic verses' although it is accepted by the eminent historian and exegete[3] aṭ-Ṭabarī and has some support from a verse in the Qur'ān (22.52). The story is that on one occasion, while Muḥammad was hoping that he might receive a revelation which would bring over to his side the leaders of Quraysh hostile to him, Satan inserted verses into the revelation permitting intercession to three local goddesses. Muḥammad thought these verses were part of the genuine revelation, proclaimed them publicly, and was joined by the Meccan leaders in an act of Islamic worship. Later he realized that he had been mistaken about these verses and proclaimed a revised form, not allowing intercession, and thus caused the Meccans to turn away from him. It seems impossible that any Muslim could have invented this story, or that aṭ-Ṭabarī would have accepted it from a non-Muslim. Yet most traditionalist Muslims today reject it.

This process of idealization was not restricted to Muḥammad himself and his Companions, but extended to the whole period of the first four 'rightly guided' caliphs, the Rāshidūn, and further. Thus it is supposed that the men in the early Muslim armies were motivated chiefly by zeal for Islam and for its spread, though this is not borne out by an objective look at the historical sources. The expeditions did not at first lead to conversions on any great scale (except in Iran), since the status of 'protected minorities' was given to most of the inhabitants of the occupied territories. The primary aim of

3. one who is skilled in the analysis of a text, here the Koran

most of the expeditions—like that into France in 732 which was defeated at Tours—was the acquiring of booty, and this is doubtless what was uppermost in the minds of the troops. Muslims today sometimes claim that the early Islamic conquests were not a 'colonial phenomenon' but 'conquests in the field of creed and the construction of the human personality', though the writer [in *Risalat al-Jihad*] from whom these phrases are quoted somewhat contradictorily asserts that Islam did not spread by the sword.

Another aspect of the idealization of the early Muslims is the view that their religious devotion was such that they remembered the verses of the Qur'ān perfectly and that, when they copied it as scribes, they never made mistakes. Ordinary Muslims today will argue that there are no textual variants for the Qur'ān as there are for the Bible. The scholars, how-

---

Punishments Recorded in the Koran

The fifth surah, or chapter, of the Koran, entitled The Table, *designates punishments for specific wrongdoings in verses 35, 37, and 40, but also offers forgiveness for the repentant.*

Those that make war against God and His apostle and spread disorder in the land shall be put to death or crucified or have their hands and feet cut off on alternate sides, or be banished from the country. They shall be held up to shame in this world and sternly punished in the hereafter: except those that repent before you reduce them. For you must know that God is forgiving and merciful. . . .

As for the man or woman who is guilty of theft, cut off their hands to punish them for their crimes. That is the punishment enjoined by God. God is mighty and wise. But whoever repents after committing evil, and mends his ways, shall be pardoned by God. God is forgiving and merciful.

Did you not know that God has sovereignty over the heavens and the earth? He punishes whom He will and forgives whom He pleases. God has power over all things.

N.J. Dawood, translator, *The Koran: With a Parallel Arabic Text*. New York: Viking, 1990.

ever, are well aware that there are seven (or some other number) sets of readings, all of which are accepted as canonical, in accordance with a Ḥadīth[4] to the effect that God revealed the Qur'ān according to seven *ḥurūf* (literally 'letters'). They thus maintain that what the Western scholar sees as textual variants are not variants but alternative forms of genuine revelation. Modern Western scholars have in addition drawn attention to works by medieval Muslim scholars which contained lists of non-canonical textual variants which were in circulation prior to the standardizing of the text of the Qur'ān in the caliphate of 'Uthmān about 650. ...

Dangers in the Idealization of Early Islam

The modern Western observer cannot fail to be aware of great dangers inherent in the idealization of early Islam. There is a sense in which it is similar to the Christian slogan of 'Back to the Bible' which has been used as a rallying cry for reform; but there is an important difference. The forms of life depicted in the Bible cover many centuries, and Christian reformers were selective in what they imitated. It was chiefly some aspects of the New Testament that were followed, and there was no question of copying the crudities of the Old Testament. In Islam, however, the idea of going back to the Qur'ān and the example of Muḥammad means the idealization of a period of little more than twenty years in a region of the world where life was still somewhat primitive and barbaric. Nearly all Westerners, whether God-fearing or not, are horrified that Muslims of today can contemplate the amputation of a hand as a punishment for theft or stoning as a punishment for adultery, even if only in a few precisely defined cases.

The amputation of the thief's hand is certainly prescribed in the Qur'ān (5.38), and was presumably sometimes carried out. In a modern society this would make a man or woman incapable of earning a living honestly and instead become a burden on the community; and one can only think that in Muḥammad's time the person thus punished would have had

4. the sayings of Muḥammad, collected in medieval times, a supplement to the Koran

some sort of family support, and that it may have been felt appropriate that the whole family should suffer for the fault of one member.

Stoning for adultery is not a punishment prescribed in the Qur'ān according to the standard text. One verse (4.15) speaks of a guilty woman not being allowed to leave the house; and a later verse (24.2) says that a guilty man and woman are both to be flogged. . . .

In Mecca and even more in Medina in pre-Islamic times many strange forms of 'marital' relationship were found, such as polyandry (one woman having several 'husbands'), and these forms were regarded as socially acceptable. One of the aims of the Qur'ānic rules was to ensure that a woman had sexual relations with only one man at a time; but it seems to have been realised that this ideal could not be achieved all at once, since it was contrary to many hitherto normal practices. The Qur'ān thus seems to distinguish between women who accept and observe the restriction to one man (whom it calls *muḥsināt* or *muḥsanāt*) and those who do not observe the restriction. All this makes it difficult to know what the *zinā'* (translated 'adultery') could have been for which stoning was prescribed. . . . The conclusion to which this points is that there was no stoning for adultery in Islam until a least a generation after Muḥammad, by which time the earlier polyandric practices had faded out and been forgotten. . . .

The introduction into the Sharī'a of stoning as a punishment for adultery must have been the work of Muslim religious scholars in the latter half of the first Islamic century, but it is difficult to know the precise social circumstances with which they were concerned. What can be said here is that in accepting stoning as a possible punishment for adultery Muslims of today are idealizing not the earliest Islam as it really was, but as it was alleged to have been by later scholars.

It also seems incredible that in the later twentieth century some people should claim that an ideal for human life is to be found in a society in which the *lex talionis*[5] was in opera-

---

5. the law dictating that the punishment shall be identical to the offense; for example, the death penalty for murder

tion at least to some extent. This point deserves to be explained at length. Many Christians think that the principle of 'an eye for an eye' is something inferior, since it has been—to use an Islamic term—'abrogated' by the teaching of Jesus in the Sermon on the Mount. [John 8:4f] To think it inferior, however, is in part a misapprehension. In a society where there is no strong ruler with an effective police force the *lex talionis* or retaliation (life for life, eye for eye, etc.) is probably the best way of maintaining a degree of public security. For this reason it is prescribed in both the Old Testament and the Qur'ān. Since there was no central authority capable of punishing a murderer it became the sacred duty of the next of kin to avenge a person's death. The Bible distinguishes between deliberate killing and unintentional killing, and insists that in the former case retaliation *must* be carried out. Even before the revelation of the Qur'ān some Arabs seem to have been substituting a blood-wit (camels or money) for an actual life; but conservative moralists taunted those who accepted camels with being content with milk instead of blood. The Qur'ān encourages the remission of the full penalty and the acceptance of a blood-wit. . . .

The basic reason why 'private' retaliation, despite its being prescribed in the Qur'ān, cannot be accepted as an ideal for human society today is not that it is immoral in itself, but that it belongs to, and presupposes, a more primitive structuring of society. In our more civilized and more organized modern societies we have effective police forces and judiciaries, which in most cases are capable of arresting murderers, bringing them to trial and punishing them. Our societies therefore rightly forbid 'private' retaliation, or individuals 'taking the law into their own hands', since there is always the danger that the avenger will exact more than like for like. The Qur'ān, too, insists that the retaliation should be no more than the injury suffered. In pre-Islamic Arabia on one occasion, when a great chief was killed and a young man of the murderer's tribe killed in retaliation, the chief's tribe maintained that this victim counted for no more than a chief's shoe-latchet; and this led to a bloody war. These observations leave open the possibility that there may be a valid principle implicit in the Qur'ānic prescription of retaliation but such a principle can only be applied in modern circumstances if it is admitted that there has been a development in the structuring of human society and that this excludes any right or duty of 'private' retaliation.

Idealization of the Past Blinds the Community to Problems of the Present

Apart from the particular dangers inherent in the idealization of early Islam there is a general danger, namely, that the community becomes so obsessed with recreating something past that it fails to see and deal with the real challenges and problems of the present. Arnold Toynbee in his *Study of History* spoke of the idolization (not idealization) of an ephemeral self or institution, and gave several illustrations at some length. Though he does not mention contemporary Islam, his conception might be applied to it. As has already been suggested, what has been idolized is not early Islam as it actually was, but the self-image of Islam created by the religious scholars in the subsequent three or four centuries. With this image was bound up a structuring of Islamic society based on the elaboration of the Sharī'a and the formation of a religious institution, which partly worked with the political leadership but was partly independent of it. The creation of the Islamic world community, as it existed from 1000 or earlier until about 1600, is a remarkable achievement, to be reckoned among the finest achievements of humanity as a whole. The inhabitants of a vast area of the world's surface were given a high degree of social stability, which was not seriously disturbed by great political upheavals. Despite this success, however, any attempt to recreate a community based on the same image of early Islam is unlikely to have satisfactory results. What is required is a deeper appreciation of the essential principles implicit in Qur'ān and Ḥadīth, so that solutions to contemporary problems may be found which grow naturally out of the fundamental experiences of the earliest Islam.

This critique of the idealization of early Islam is intended to leave open the possibility that Muslims of today may by meditating on the Qur'ān and the Sīra find inspiration to deal with contemporary problems. To emphasize this point and to suggest more profitable ways of 'going back' to the past, it may be helpful to give a statement about Christianity by [M. Ramsey and L.J. Suenens,] two prominent Christian leaders:

> Everywhere throughout the Christian world, as if led by the Spirit, Christians are going back to their roots again. It is not 'Primitivism', the conviction that to find the authentic church we must go back to the first century . . . and then childishly try to recreate some romantic illusion of what seems an ideal age. Rather it is as if the thought of these first ages and their priorities helps Christians to sort out, in the light of many new insights from other disciplines, the elements of their denominational stances that are of lasting relevance and those which are ephemeral and stultifying.

Chapter 2

The East-West Spread of Islam

Turning Points

IN WORLD HISTORY

The Geographic Expansion of Islam

Richard M. Eaton

Richard M. Eaton traces Arab Muslims' conquest in the 130 years after Muhammad's death, a period of rapid expansion extending from Europe to China. He discounts traditional theories explaining this growth and identifies recent, more complex reasons why Arabian forces succeeded. Eaton has taught history at the University of Arizona, specializing in research of Indian and Islamic history. He is the author of *Sufis of Bijapur, 1300–1700: Social Roles of Sufis in Medieval India* and *Islam and the Bengal Frontier, 1200–1760.*

During the ten years immediately following the Prophet's death, from 632 to 642, Arab Muslims erupted out of the Arabian peninsula and conquered Iraq, Syria, Palestine, Egypt, and western Iran. The movement did not stop there, however. To the west, Arab ships sailed into the Mediterranean Sea, previously a "Roman lake," taking Cyprus (649), Carthage (698), Tunis (700), and Gibraltar (711), before conquering Spain (711–16) and raiding southern France (720). Sicily, Corsica, and Sardinia suffered repeated pillaging during those years. Meanwhile, Arab armies during the 650s marched eastward across the Iranian plateau and completed the destruction of the Sasanian Empire,[1] forcing the son of the Persian "King of Kings" to flee to the Tang court in China. By 712 Arab armies had seized strategic oases

1. In the sixth century the Sasanian emperors of Persia controlled the Middle East from Iran to the eastern part of the Fertile Crescent, while the Byzantine Roman emperors controlled Asia Minor. The two powers were foes.

Excerpted from *Islamic History as Global History*, by Richard M. Eaton. Copyright ©1990 by the American Historical Association. Reprinted with permission of the author and publisher.

towns of Central Asia—Balkh, Samarqand, Bukhara, and Ferghana—and would soon be meeting Chinese armies face-to-face. To the south, Muslim navies sailed to the coasts of western India where in 711 they conquered and occupied the densely populated Hindu-Buddhist society of Sind. Thus began the long and eventful encounter between Islamic and Indic civilizations, during which time Islamic culture would penetrate deep into India's economy, political systems, and religious structure.

While Arab rule in Sind was being consolidated, other Arab armies continued the overland drive eastward. Requested by Turkish tribes to intervene in conflicts with their Chinese overlords, Arab armies in 751 marched to the westernmost fringes of the Tang Empire and engaged Chinese forces on the banks of the Talas River. The Arabs' crushing victory there, one of the most important battles in the history of Central Asia, probably determined the subsequent cultural evolution of the Turkish peoples of that region, who thereafter adopted Muslim and not Chinese civilization. Although Muslims would never dominate the heartland of China or penetrate Chinese civilization as they would India, their influence in Central Asia gave them access to the Silk Route, which for centuries to come served as a conduit for Chinese civilization into the Muslim world. Moreover, Muslim Arabs had already established maritime contact with China, having begun trading along the Chinese coast in the late seventh century.

Traditional Theories Explaining Islamic Expansion

Thus within 130 years of Islam's birth, Arab armies and navies had conquered a broad swath of the known world from Gibraltar to the Indus delta, and had penetrated both China and Europe by land and sea. But how to explain it? Whence came the energy that had propelled Arab Muslims out of the Arabian peninsula, laying the groundwork for the establishment first of an Arab empire and then of a world civilization? Traditionalist Muslim sources generally accounted for these momentous events in terms of a miraculous manifestation of Allah's favor with his community, an interpretation consonant with Islamic understandings of the relationship between divine will and the historical process, but one that tells us more of Islamic theology than of Islamic history. Theories of the Muslim conquests advanced by many nineteenth- and early twentieth-century European Islamicists are hardly more helpful. The general tone is captured in the following lines penned in 1898 by Sir William Muir, a Scot,[2] whose interpretation of the Arab conquests sounds rather like the screenplay for a Cecil B. deMille film production, complete with technicolor, panoramic vision, and stereophonic soundtrack:

> It was the scent of war that now turned the sullen temper of the Arab tribes into eager loyalty. . . . Warrior after warrior, column after column, whole tribes in endless succession with their women and children, issued forth to fight. And ever, at the marvellous tale of cities conquered; of rapine rich beyond compute; of maidens parted on the very field of battle "to every man a damsel or two". . . fresh tribes arose and went. Onward and still onward, like swarms from the hive, or flights of locusts darkening the land, tribe after tribe issued forth and hastening northward, spread in great masses to the East and to the West.

In the end, though, after the thundering hooves have passed and the dust has settled, in attempting to explain the conquests, Muir leaves us with little of substance, apart from simply asserting the Arabs' fondness for the "scent of war," their love of "rapine," or the promise of "a damsel or two." Muir's vision of a militant, resurgent Islam gone berserk reflected, in addition to the old European stereotypes, colonial fears that Europe's own Muslim subjects might, in just such a locustlike manner, rise up in revolt and drive the Europeans back to Europe. Sir William, after all, was himself a senior British official in colonial India as well as an aggressive activist for the Christian mission there. But his was no fringe school concerning the rise of Islam or the subsequent conquests; indeed, his understanding dominated for decades

2. in *The Caliphate, Its Rise, Decline, and Fall*

to follow and, like the traditionalist Muslim interpretation, tells us more about the narrator than of the subject itself.

In the early twentieth century, scholars introduced the thesis that around the time of the Prophet's death, Arabia's grazing lands had suffered from a severe, short-term desiccation that drove the nomadic Arabs to search, literally, for greener pastures. Although it lacked convincing evidence, this theory found plenty of advocates then as it continues to today. Variations on the desiccation theory, also lacking firm evidence, held that poverty, overpopulation, or other such social miseries had driven the Arabs out of their homeland. Still other historians shifted attention from the Arabs themselves to Byzantine Rome and Sasanian Persia, the two great empires of western Asia, whose domains included, respectively, Syria and Iraq. These empires were portrayed as "exhausted" from several hundred years of mutual warfare, thus enabling the more "vigorous" Arabs to walk over both with ease. But this thesis likewise lacked empirical evidence, and, above all, failed to account for the Arabs' continued expansion into lands far beyond the domain of either empire. Meanwhile, the notion of the Arabs' supposed militancy, legitimized by the religious doctrine of *jihâd* or holy war, generally still informs popular sentiment about Muslims and has continued to find its way into history textbooks to the present day, though in a somewhat less lurid version than Muir's portrayal.

Recent Theories Explaining Islamic Expansion

Whereas older theories saw the invasions as a random or unorganized influx of ragtag hordes pushed out of the peninsula by population pressure or drawn by the love of rapine, recent research has revealed methodically planned and well-executed military maneuvers directed by a central command in Medina and undertaken for quite rational purposes. There was the economic need to provide the growing community with material support—accomplished by the movement's capture of lucrative trade routes and new surplus-producing regions—which the relatively meager economic resources of Arabia could not provide. And there was the political need to contain and channel the tremendous energies released by the Prophet's socioreligious revolution. In this latter sense, the initial Arab conquests resemble the French or Russian revolutions, in which socioideological energies generated in the process of consolidating the original movement proved so intense that they could not be contained geographically and spilled over into adjacent regions.

Jihad

The concept of jihad, *or holy war, has provided one explanation for the rapid expansion of Islam. Verses 74 and 75 of the fourth sura, or chapter, of the Koran explain the purpose of* jihad.

Let those who would exchange the life of this world for the hereafter, fight for the cause of God; whoever fights for the cause of God, whether he dies or triumphs, We shall richly reward him.

And how should you not fight for the cause of God, and for the helpless old men, women, and children [in Mecca] who say: 'Deliver us, Lord, from this city of wrongdoers; send forth to us a guardian from Your presence; send to us from Your presence one that will help us'?

The true believers fight for the cause of God, but the infidels fight for the devil. Fight then against the friends of Satan. Satan's cunning is weak indeed.

N.J. Dawood, translator, *The Koran: With a Parallel Arabic Text.* New York: Viking, 1990.

Above all, what is missing from earlier explanations is any mention of Islam itself. One does occasionally come across references to the lure of an Islamic paradise filled with dark-eyed beauties awaiting the frenzied believer who would martyr himself in battle, but such romantic allusions appear to be holdovers from older stereotypes associating Islam with sex and violence. By and large, Western historians of the nineteenth and early twentieth centuries displayed a chronic inability to accept the possibility that the religion itself could have played a fundamental, as opposed to supportive, role in the movement. In recent years, however, there has been an effort to bring religion back into the discussion by focusing on the Muslim community's social fragility during the earliest years of its formation, and especially the volatility of divine revelation as the basis of its authority. Thus the death of Muhammad in 632 confronted the community of believers, then confined to the population of western Arabia, with their first genuine crisis: How would the charismatic authority of the Prophet, who for ten years had provided both spiritual and political leadership to the growing *umma*, be sustained or channeled when he was no longer present? Some tribes, apparently supposing that with the loss of the Prophet the continuing authority of revelation had ended, simply withdrew from the community altogether. Others began following rival prophets—at least two men and one woman sprang up in the Arabian interior—who claimed to be receiving continuing revelations from God.

The Strategy of Abu Bakr, Muhammad's First Successor

With both the political and the religious basis of the fledgling community thus threatened, Muhammad's first successor as leader of the community, Abu Bakr, moved vigorously to hold the volatile movement together. First, he forbade any tribe to leave the community once having joined; and second, in order to prevent the movement from splintering into rival communities around rival prophets, he declared that Muhammad had been the last prophet of God. These moves amounted, in effect, to a declaration of war against those tribes who had abandoned the *umma* or subscribed to other self-proclaimed prophets. Thus the initial burst of Muslim expansion after the Prophet's death was directed not against non-Muslims, but against just such Arab tribes within the peninsula. In the process of suppressing these rebellions, however, Abu Bakr made alliances with tribes on the southern fringes of Iraq and Syria, and as the circle of such alliances widened, Muslim Arabs soon clashed with client tribes of the Sasanians and Byzantines, and eventually with Sasanian and Byzantine imperial forces themselves.

Once launched, the movement continued to be driven by

powerful religious forces. Islam had derived its initial power from Muhammad's ability to articulate the collectivization of Arabia's deities into a single supreme God, together with the collectivization of its tribes into the single, corporate *umma* under the direct authority of God. After the Prophet's death, these movements gained momentum as the masses of Arab soldiery participating in the expansion came to regard the movement's social ideals as immediately attainable. Hence for them the distribution of the riches of conquered lands among members of the community, which looked to the rest of the world like senseless plunder, served to actualize the ideal, preached by the Prophet, of attaining socioeconomic equality among all believers. The importance of this factor is underscored by the fact that one of the first and most serious dissident movements in Islam, the Kharajite movement, was spearheaded in conquered Iraq by men of piety whose military stipends had just been reduced. Leaders of the revolt, which resulted in the assassination of the Caliph[3] Uthman in 656, justified their actions by emphasizing the radical egalitarianism, including social equality for women, that had been preached by the Prophet. In short, recent explanations of the early Arab conquests, unlike earlier European theories, have focused on social processes rather than social stereotypes, and on the internal dynamics of early Muslim society and religion.

3. a successor of Muhammad, as leader of the Islamic Community

Political Growth of the Islamic Empire

Richard C. Martin

Richard C. Martin explains Islam's classical age, during which caliphs—temporal successors of Muhammad—ruled the Islamic empire from a single location. According to Martin, after the Mongols destroyed the caliphate in Baghdad in 1258, four centers of power emerged to govern the vast Islamic world. Richard C. Martin has taught at the University of Arizona. He is the author of *Islamic Studies: A History of Religions.*

Arabia dramatically entered the stage of world history in the seventh century, although it had been playing a regional role for several thousand years. South Arabia had once been well known as the Kingdom of Sheba, and it became a source of frankincense and myrrh and other spices and exotica from the East, destined for Mediterranean markets. Less important on the larger world scene was the nomadic population of central Arabia. Its main city, Mecca, was barely known to the rest of the world until just before the time of the Prophet. Yet it was from central and not South Arabia that the Islamic Empire was launched across North Africa and the Middle East.

The occasion for the early seventh-century outpouring of Arabs into Syria, Iraq, Persia, and later into Egypt and North Africa was a new vision of monotheistic religion inspired by the Prophet Muhammad. Born of humble circumstances in the city of Mecca late in the sixth century, in about A.D. 610 Muhammad began to preach a message that at-

Excerpted from *Islam: A Cultural Perspective*, by Richard C. Martin, ©1982. Reprinted by permission of Prentice-Hall, Inc., Upper Saddle River, N.J.

tacked the tribal provincialism, social injustice, and polytheistic paganism that had differentiated the Arabs from their more urbanized and cosmopolitan neighbors in Byzantium and Persia, and the settled peoples of Syria and Iraq. Although Muhammad died before the Arab armies were to expand their control significantly to lands outside of Arabia, the message he recited in the form of Revelation accompanied his most trusted companions and generals, thus taking root where they established political control throughout the Middle East. The history of Islam, then, begins properly with the Prophet Muhammad and the Revelation recited by him to the peoples of Mecca and Medina. . . .

A Tradition of Migration

It may be useful to think of the outpouring of Arabs from the Arabian Peninsula in the seventh century as a *Völkerwanderung*, a mass migration of people not unlike earlier migrations in the Middle East. For example, late in the third millennium B.C. a migration of Semitic peoples had moved into Mesopotamia and had established the ancient Babylonian Empire. The Biblical story of Abraham's migration from Ur of the Chaldees (Babylonia) to Haran and then to Palestine corresponds to what we know of such a *Völkerwanderung* from Mesopotamia to Palestine ca. 2000 B.C. The conquest of Canaan (Palestine) by the Hebrew people several centuries later was part of a large pattern of migration which included the Philistines and other newcomers to that area. Migrations such as these inevitably involved wars and conquests. They also brought new ideas as Semites, Persians, and other peoples encountered one another and established new civilizations on top of older ones. The older civilizations were not always destroyed in the process; each new conquering people took command but absorbed much of the culture of the previous landlords, adding new ideas and developing distinctive forms. Thus, power in the Middle East had already changed hands many times prior to the Arab conquests in the seventh century. A successful economy of agriculture and trade had existed for nearly four millennia, and in this context cultural achievements in writing, literature, monumental architecture, and legal institutions had left a rich heritage on which the Arabs and the people they conquered could now build an Islamic Empire.

Two great empires gave way to the Arab conquests. The troops of Byzantium, the Orthodox Christian Empire with its capital in Constantinople, were pushed out of Syria and Iraq by Muslim armies. Centuries of Christian and Jewish presence in these lands was not greatly affected by the changing of the guard. Many became Muslim, but the existing culture was left more or less intact. Byzantium retained its strength in Anatolia (modern Turkey) until the fifteenth century, when the Ottoman Turkish Muslims successfully marched on Constantinople. During the eight centuries of coexistence between Islam and Byzantium, the occasional military clashes did not prevent important cultural exchanges.

The Sassanian Persian Empire fared less well when the Arab armies made their march across the Middle East. The Persians had already played out their resources after centuries of conflict with the Byzantine Empire. By the middle of the seventh century the last Persian king was assassinated, and the once great Persian Empire fell to the Arabs. The political and cultural implications of this change of balance in Middle Eastern powers was considerable. Henceforth the ethnic and cultural composition of the Abode of Islam was a mixture of Arab, Persian, Turkish, Armenian, and other Middle Eastern peoples.

The Classical Age of Caliphate Rule

From the seventh to the thirteenth centuries, Islam formed an empire dominated by the caliphate. . . .

The Rashidun (632–661). Following Muhammad's demise, the first caliphs ruled from Medina in Arabia. They were known as the Rashidun or "rightly guided" caliphs because they had been companions of the Prophet. By the end of the Age of the Rashidun, Medina proved to be an impractical command post for the growing empire.

The Umayyads (661–750). The next period of the caliphate was under an Arab dynasty that ruled in Damascus, Syria. Known as the Umayyad caliphate, this was the period of the consolidation of Arab rule and gradual growth of Arabic and Arab influence over the still existing languages and institutions of previous civilizations. The religion of the Muslim conquerors was adopted by many of the conquered peoples, and a mode of coexistence was worked out with several of the religious communities that did not convert to Islam. In culture, the Arabic language expanded beyond local Arabian *oral* traditions of poetry and Islamic worship to become an important *literary* language. The Arabic Koran played a key role in this development. Soon literature about the Prophet and various aspects of Islamic religion appeared. Muslim scholars sought to broaden the base of the language by consulting pure Bedouin usage and by writing grammars and dictionaries. The works of earlier Greek philologists appear to have been fundamental to this enterprise. In art, the field of architecture dominated as the Muslim conquerors continued the ancient Middle Eastern mode of cultural expression through monumental architecture. One of the signal achievements of the Umayyad Age was the Dome of the Rock mosque in Jerusalem, built by Caliph Abd al-Malik in 691.

Spain. In the year 711, Umayyad forces crossed the Straits of Gibraltar and established a branch of the Umayyad caliphate in Spain. Al-Andalus, as the Arabs called it (Andalusia in English) remained in Muslim hands until the Christian *Reconquista* in the thirteenth century. During five centuries of Islamic rule, culture flourished under the Spanish Muslims (Moors), and al-Andalus served as an important point of contact between Christendom and the Islamic world. In literature, philosophy, and architecture, the Spanish Muslims made several notable achievements that have survived to this day. An example is the richly decorative design of the Alhambra.[1] The writings of the Moorish philosopher Averroës inspired considerable philosophical discussion in later Medieval Europe. The Spanish language itself bears witness to the Islamic heritage, for it has served as a conduit of many Arabic words into other Western languages.

---

1. a fortress and palace built on a hill overlooking Granada, Spain; a fine example of Moorish architecture

The Abbasids (750–1258). In 750 the Umayyad caliphate in Damascus fell to another Arab family, the Abbasids. The Abbasid caliphate established its own capital, Baghdad, along the banks of the Tigris River in Mesopotamia. Under Abbasid rule, Arab hegemony[2] gave way to increasing influence from other elements within the Islamic population. At first the Abbasid caliphs were able to coordinate successfully and productively the tensions between Sunni and Shi'ite Muslims, Arabs, Persians, Turks, and other ethnic groups, and the various social and professional classes of the older civilizations still living in the Middle East. But such diversity within the vast Islamic Empire had a centrifugal effect, and the caliphate in Baghdad started losing control over people and lands that were distant from the capital.

Eventually the centrifugal effect also became centripetal. Turkish and Persian Muslim dynasties grew independently powerful enough to make demands upon Baghdad. A radical Shi'ite dynasty known as the Fatimids ruled first in North Africa, then Syria and Egypt from 909 to 1171. Under the Fatimids, Cairo became an important political capital; its institutions of learning and culture rivaled those of Baghdad. Today in Cairo, Muslim students from all over the world attend al-Azhar University, built by the Fatimids nearly a thousand years ago, two centuries before universities were established in Medieval Europe. Originally Shi'ite, al-Azhar is now a Sunni university.

Although the Abbasid caliphate remained the central symbol of political authority throughout these upheavals, first the Persian Shi'ite dynasty known as the Buyids (945–1055) and then the Turkish Sunni dynasty known as the Seljuqs (1055–1258) brought the Abbasid caliphate under their respective controls. Throughout the Abbasid Age, regardless of these political shifts, the level of cultural achievement remained high. It was during this period that ancient Persian reemerged as a Middle Eastern vernacular language, using the Arabic script and absorbing many Arabic words. Persian became a potent medium not only of Islamic religious literature

2. predominant influence of one state over others

along with Arabic, but also of several distinctively Persian genres of *belles-lettres*[3] and poetry. Chiefly in Baghdad, classic governmental, educational, and religious institutions such as hospitals, academies of science, schools called *madrasas*, and commercial ventures were established and thrived.

The Abbasid Age was also the period in which the classic schools of Islamic law and theology flourished. Disciplines that studied the four roots of the Shari'a[4] branched out into the four orthodox schools that are accepted in Sunni Islam. The Shi'ites formed schools or traditional interpretations of their own. The important oral tradition of sayings (*ḥadīth*) attributed to the Prophet Muhammad was written down and codified. Since the Abbasid Age there have been six orthodox collections, the best known of which is the *Authentic* by al-Bukhari (d. 870). Traditional religious disciplines such as law, Koranic studies, and studies of the prophetic traditions went on mainly in mosque schools. Late in the Abbasid Age enlightened patrons separately established academies known as *madrasas*. Well-known professors were appointed to the faculties of these institutions and were paid salaries, replacing the more informal arrangements of the earlier mosque schools.

Rule of the Islamic Empire After the Caliphate

With the invasion of the central Islamic lands by Mongol warriors, the Classic Age of the caliphate came to an end. We can only imagine what those decades of invasion and destruction must have been like for the Persians, Turks, Arabs, and other Muslims who lived and died in the path of the Mongol hordes. Originating in Eastern Siberia, the Mongols swept through Russia, China, Central Asia, and finally to the Middle East under the brilliant command of Chingiz Khan. His son, Hūlāgu, captured Baghdad in 1258. The Abbasid caliphate and its Seljuq lords were destroyed. But ironically, in just a few decades the Mongol lords who occupied the Abode of Islam themselves became Muslims, and the general shape of Islamic civilization remained remarkably

---

3. literature valued for its literary and artistic qualities   4. Arabic term for law derived from the Koran

stable without the caliphate as its central political symbol.

The Mamluks (1250–1517). Not all of the Abode of Islam fell to the Mongols. In Egypt and Syria an independent Islamic government had been set up that was able to resist Mongol pressures. The leaders of this regime were called the Mamluks. Originally Turkish slaves (*mamlūk* means "owned"), they were strict Sunni Muslims. In art and literary scholarship, the Mamluk period was productive. Culture was supported by royal patronage. The religious notables or Ulema were allowed complete authority over Islamic faith and practice. To this end the Mamluks maintained the fiction of a caliphate by permitting figurehead caliphs to sit in Cairo for a while. The most impressive literary achievements were in historical writing. One scholar of the period, Jalal al-Din al-Suyuti (1445–1505), wrote histories of Islam and scholarly studies of the Koran that soon gained great prestige throughout the Islamic world. In less scholarly circles some of the popular romances and tales of *The Thousand and One Nights* were generated in the Mamluk period.

The Ottoman Turks (1412–1918). The Muslims known to most Europeans after the sixteenth century were called Saracens. In fact they were the Ottoman Turks, a Sunni Islamic empire that lasted until the beginning of the present century. At the height of their power, the Ottomans took possession of much of the western portions of the Abode of Islam and marched as far as Austria in Europe before they were repulsed. Alarm over the Saracen threat appears in the writings of such figures as Martin Luther, signaling the serious military and psychological threat posed by the Ottomans. Basing themselves mainly in Anatolia (modern Turkey), they took possession of Syria, Egypt, and North Africa. Through the use of a highly trained paramilitary force known as the Janissaries, and of hand guns and artillery, the Ottoman sultans were able to capture and control large territories with relatively small forces. Their greatest prize was Constantinople, captured from the ailing Byzantine Empire in 1453. Renaming it Istanbul, the Ottomans made it their capital, adding to its many architectural treasures splendid monuments of their own. During the latter period of Ottoman rule, the Islamic lands paying tribute to the sultans in Istanbul were rewarded with serious neglect, causing cultural stagnation in the eastern and southern Mediterranean regions. The present century has seen a remarkable reversal of this trend.

The Safavids of Persia (1500–1779). At the same time that the Ottomans were establishing hegemony in western Islam, a Shi'ite dynasty gained control of Persia. Known as the Safavids, they established their capital in Isfahan, making it one of the most beautiful cities in the Islamic world. They retained power until the mid–eighteenth century, when they were overthrown by Muslim warlords from Afghanistan. Mistrustful of Ottoman intentions with good reason, the Safavid kings or *shahs* established diplomatic and economic ties with European powers. In art and architecture a distinctively Persian expression of Islamic culture developed. An outstanding example may be seen in the magnificent buildings erected by Shah Abbas (1587–1628).

The Mughals of India (1526–1730). While the Ottomans and Safavids were carving out their empires, Turkish and Afghani warlords moved into India to establish the Islamic empire of the Mughals (a form of the word *Mongol).* Sunni in religious persuasion, the Mughal rulers made Delhi their capital. There and elsewhere they built impressive royal palaces and mosques. The best known of these is the Taj Mahal. The Mughal emperors ruled an Indian population of which the vast majority was Hindu, not Muslim. The remarkable growth of Islam within this context was due not so much to the Sunni religious commitments of the rulers but rather to the Sufis or mystics, whose modes of piety were particularly at home in the Indian environment. . . .

From India, Muslim missionaries went to Malaysia and Indonesia, where Islam has grown with amazing vitality. Today Islam is quite strong throughout Southeast Asia, a fact that Westerners often overlook, so strong is the association of Islam with the Middle East. Another area of vital growth for Islam is the continent of Africa. South of the Sahara, where Islam had not penetrated in the initial push across North Africa to Spain, Islam is now growing rapidly as black tribal groups confront the twentieth century.

The Western Extent of Islam in Spain and France

Will Durant

Will Durant speculates that the Muslim defeat at the French city of Tours in A.D. 732 determined that European countries remained Christian rather than becoming Islamic cultures. Durant argues that the conflicts between the Umayyad and Abbasid rulers during this period diverted attention from France and Spain, weakened the army, and allowed Abd-er-Radman I and his successors to build in southern Spain some of the richest and most civilized cities in the world. Will Durant was a journalist and a professor of Latin, French, and philosophy. He and his wife, Ariel Durant, popularized history with the multivolume work, *The Story of Civilization*, which covers 110 centuries of world history.

It was at first the Moors,[1] not the Arabs, who conquered Spain. Tariq was a Berber, and his army had 7000 Berbers to 300 Arabs. His name is embedded in the rock at whose foot his forces landed; the Moors came to call it Gebel al-Tariq, the Mountain of Tariq, which Europe compressed into Gibraltar. Tariq had been sent to Spain by Musa ibn Nusayr, Arab governor of North Africa. In 712 Musa crossed with 10,000 Arabs and 8000 Moors; besieged and captured Seville and Merida; rebuked Tariq for exceeding orders, struck him with a whip, and cast him into prison. The Caliph Walid recalled Musa and freed Tariq, who resumed his conquests. . . .

1. northern African Muslims of Arab and Berber descent; Berbers were tribes from North Africa

The Spread of Islam Is Blocked

The victors treated the conquered leniently, confiscated the lands only of those who had actively resisted, exacted no greater tax than had been levied by the Visigothic[2] kings, and gave to religious worship a freedom rare in Spain. Having established their position in the peninsula, the Moslems scaled the Pyrenees and entered Gaul,[3] intent upon making Europe a province of Damascus. Between Tours and Poitiers, a thousand miles north of Gibraltar, they were met by the united forces of Eudes, Duke of Aquitaine, and Charles, Duke of Austrasia. After seven days of fighting, the Moslems were defeated in one of the most crucial battles of history (732); again the faith of countless millions was determined by the chances of war. . . .

The caliphs of Damascus undervalued Spain; till 756 it was merely "the district of Andalusia," and was governed from Qairwan. But in 755 a romantic figure landed in Spain, armed only with royal blood, and destined to establish a dynasty that would rival in wealth and glory the caliphs of Baghdad. When, in 750, the triumphant Abbasids ordered all princes of the Umayyad family slain, Abd-er-Rahman, grandson of the Caliph Hisham, was the only Umayyad who escaped. Hunted from village to village, he swam the broad Euphrates, crossed into Palestine, Egypt and Africa, and finally reached Morocco. News of the Abbasid revolution had intensified the factional rivalry of Arabs, Syrians, Persians, and Moors in Spain; an Arab group loyal to the Umayyads, fearing that the Abbasid caliph might question their titles to lands given them by Umayyad governors, invited Abd-er-Rahman to join and lead them. He came, and was made emir of Cordova (756). He defeated an army commissioned by the Caliph al-Mansur to unseat him, and sent the head of its general to be hung before a palace in Mecca.

Perhaps it was these events that saved Europe from worshiping Mohammed: Moslem Spain, weakened with civil war

2. Western Goths who invaded the Roman Empire and established a monarchy lasting from the fourth to the eighth century   3. an ancient region comprising modern-day France

and deprived of external aid, ceased to conquer, and withdrew even from northern Spain. From the ninth to the eleventh century the peninsula was divided into Moslem and Christian by a line running from Coimbra through Saragossa and along the Ebro River. The Moslem south, finally pacified by Abd-er-Rahman I and his successors, blossomed into riches, poetry, and art. Abd-er-Rahman II (822–52) enjoyed the fruits of this prosperity. Amid border wars with the Christians, rebellions among his subjects, and Norman raids on his coasts, he found time to beautify Cordova with palaces and mosques, rewarded poets handsomely, and forgave offenders with an amiable lenience that may have shared in producing the social disorder that followed his reign.

Abd-er-Rahman III (912–61) is the culminating figure of this Umayyad dynasty in Spain. Coming to power at twenty-one, he found "Andaluz" torn by racial faction, religious animosity, sporadic brigandage, and the efforts of Seville and Toledo to establish their independence of Cordova. Though a man of refinement, famous for generosity and courtesy, he laid a firm hand upon the situation, quelled the rebellious cities, and subdued the Arab aristocrats who wished, like their French contemporaries, to enjoy a feudal sovereignty on their rich estates. He invited to his councils men of diverse faiths, adjusted his alliances to maintain a balance of power among his neighbors and his enemies, and administered the government with Napoleonic industry and attention to detail. He planned the campaigns of his generals, often took the field in person, repulsed the invasions of Sancho of Navarre, captured and destroyed Sancho's capital, and discouraged further Christian forays during his reign. In 929, knowing himself as powerful as any ruler of his time, and realizing that the caliph of Baghdad had become a puppet of Turkish guards, he assumed the caliphal title—Commander of the Faithful and Defender of the Faith. When he died he left behind him, in his own handwriting, a modest estimate of human life:

> I have now reigned above fifty [Mohammedan] years in victory or peace. . . . Riches and honors, powers and pleasures,

have waited on my call; nor does any earthly blessing appear to have been wanting to my felicity. In this situation I have diligently numbered the days of pure and genuine happiness which have fallen to my lot. They amount to fourteen. O man! place not thy confidence in this present world!

Developments in the Southern Spanish City of Cordova

. . . Gleaming cupolas and gilded minarets marked the thousand cities or towns that made Moslem Spain in the tenth century the most urban country in Europe, probably in the world. Cordova under al-Mansur was a civilized city, second only to Baghdad and Constantinople. Here, says al-Maqqari [in *History of Mohammedan Dynasties in Spain*], were 200,077 houses, 60,300 palaces, 600 mosques, and 700 public baths; the statistics are slightly Oriental. Visitors marveled at the wealth of the upper classes, and at what seemed to them an extraordinary general prosperity; every family could afford a donkey; only beggars could not ride. Streets were paved, had raised sidewalks, and were lighted at night; one could travel for ten miles by the light of street lamps, and along an uninterrupted series of buildings. Over the quiet Guadalquivir Arab engineers threw a great stone bridge of seventeen arches, each fifty spans in width. One of the earliest undertakings of Abd-er-Rahman I was an aqueduct that brought to Cordova an abundance of fresh water for homes, gardens, fountains, and baths. The city was famous for its pleasure gardens and promenades.

Abd-er-Rahman I, lonesome for his boyhood haunts, planted in Cordova a great garden like that of the villa in which he had spent his boyhood near Damascus, and built in it his "Palace of the Rissafah." Later caliphs added other structures, to which Moslem fancy gave florid names: Palace of the Flowers . . . of the Lovers . . . of Contentment . . . of the Diadem. Cordova, like later Seville, had its Alcazar (*al-qasr*; castle, from the Latin *castrum*), a combination of palace and fortress. Moslem historians describe these mansions as equaling in luxury and beauty those of Nero's Rome: majestic portals, marble columns, mosaic floors, gilded ceilings, and such refined decoration as only Moslem art could give. The palaces of the royal family, the lords and magnates of land and trade, lined for miles the banks of the stately stream. A concubine of Abd-er-Rahman III left him a large fortune; he proposed to spend it ransoming such of his soldiers as had been captured in war; proud searchers claimed they could find none; whereupon the Caliph's favorite wife, Zahra, proposed that he build a suburb and palace to commemorate her name. For twenty-five years (936–61) 10,000 workmen and 1500 beasts toiled to realize her dream. The royal palace of al-Zahra that rose three miles southwest of Cordova was lavishly designed and equipped; 1200 marble columns sustained it; its harem could accommodate 6000 women; its hall of audience had ceiling and walls of marble and gold, eight doors inlaid with ebony, ivory, and precious stones, and a basin of quicksilver whose undulating surface reflected the dancing rays of the sun. Al-Zahra became the residential center of an aristocracy renowned for the grace and polish of its manners, the refinement of its tastes, and the breadth of its intellectual interests. At the opposite end of the city al-Mansur constructed (978) a rival palace, al-Zahira, which also gathered about it a suburb of lords, servants, minstrels, poets, and courtesans. Both suburbs were burned to the ground in the revolution of 1010.

The Extravagant Blue Mosque

Normally the people forgave the luxury of their princes if these would raise to Allah shrines exceeding their palaces in splendor and scope. The Romans had built in Cordova a temple to Janus; the Christians had replaced it with a cathedral; Abd-er-Rahman I paid the Christians for the site, demolished the church, and replaced it with the Blue Mosque; in 1238 the *reconquista*[4] would turn the mosque into a cathedral; so the good, the true, and the beautiful fluctuate with the fortunes of war. The project became the consolation of Abd-er-Rahman's troubled years; he left his suburban for his city home to superintend the operations, and hoped that he

4. reconquering

might before his death lead the congregation in grateful prayer in this new and majestic mosque. He died in 788, two years after laying the foundation; his son al-Hisham continued the work; each caliph, for two centuries, added a part, till in al-Mansur's time it covered an area 742 by 472 feet. The exterior showed a battlemented wall of brick and stone, with irregular towers, and a massive minaret that surpassed in size and beauty all the minarets of the time, so that it too was numbered among the innumerable "wonders of the world." Nineteen portals, surmounted by horseshoe arches elegantly carved with floral and geometrical decoration in stone, led into the Court of Ablutions, now the Patio de los Naranjos, or Court of Oranges. In this rectangle, paved with colored tiles, stood four fountains, each cut from a block of solid marble so large that seventy oxen had been needed to haul it from the quarry to the site. The mosque proper was a forest of 1290 columns, dividing the interior into eleven naves and twenty-one aisles. From the column capitals sprang a variety of arches—some semicircular, some pointed, some in horseshoe form, most of them with voussoirs, or wedge stones, alternately red or white. The columns of jasper, porphyry, alabaster, or marble, snatched from the ruins of Roman or Visigothic Spain, gave by their number the impression of limitless and bewildering space. The wooden ceiling was carved into cartouches[5] bearing Koranic and other inscriptions. From it hung 200 chandeliers holding 7000 cups of scented oil, fed from reservoirs of oil in inverted Christian bells also suspended from the roof. Floor and walls were adorned with mosaics; some of these were of enameled glass, baked in rich colors, and often containing silver or gold; after a thousand years of wear these dados[6] still sparkle like jewels in the cathedral walls. One section was marked off as a sanctuary; it was paved with silver and enameled tiles, guarded with ornate doors, decorated with mosaics, roofed with three domes, and marked off with a wooden screen of exquisite design. Within this sanctuary were built the mihrab

5. an oval shield or oblong scroll used as an architectural ornament to bear an inscription   6. lower portion of a wall, decorated differently from the upper part

and *minbar*, upon which the artists lavished their maturest skill. The mihrab itself was an heptagonal recess walled with gold; brilliantly ornamented with enameled mosaics, marble tracery,[7] and gold inscriptions on a ground of crimson and blue; and crowned by a tier of slender columns and trefoil[8] arches as lovely as anything in Gothic art. The pulpit was considered the finest of its kind; it consisted of 37,000 little panels of ivory and precious woods—ebony, citron, aloe, red and yellow sandal, all joined by gold or silver nails, and inlaid with gems. On this *minbar*, in a jeweled box covered with gold-threaded crimson silk, rested a copy of the Koran written by the Caliph Othman and stained with his dying blood. To us, who prefer to adorn our theaters with gilt and brass rather than clothe our cathedrals in jewelry and gold, the decoration of the Blue Mosque seems extravagant; the walls encrusted with the blood of exploited generations, the columns confusingly numerous, the horseshoe arch as structurally weak and aesthetically offensive as obesity on bow legs. Others, however, have judged differently: al-Maqqari (1591–1632) thought this mosque "unequaled in size, or beauty of design, or tasteful arrangement of its ornaments, or boldness of execution"; and even its diminished Christian form is ranked as "by universal consent the most beautiful Moslem temple in the world."

Intellectual Developments in Spanish Cities

It was a common saying in Moorish Spain that "when a musician dies at Cordova, and his instruments are to be sold, they are sent to Seville; when a rich man dies at Seville, and his library is to be sold, it is sent to Cordova" [according to A.F. Calvert in *Cordova*]. For Cordova in the tenth century was the focus and summit of Spanish intellectual life, though Toledo, Granada, and Seville shared actively in the mental exhilaration of the time. Moslem historians picture the Moorish cities as beehives of poets, scholars, jurists, physicians, and scientists; al-Maqqari fills sixty pages with their

---

7. ornamental work of interlaced and branching lines   8. an architectural form appearing like a leaf

names. Primary schools were numerous, but charged tuition; Hakam II added twenty-seven schools for the free instruction of the poor. Girls as well as boys went to school; several Moorish ladies became prominent in literature or art. Higher education was provided by independent lecturers in the mosques; their courses constituted the loosely organized University of Cordova, which in the tenth and eleventh centuries was second in renown only to similar institutions in Cairo and Baghdad. Colleges were established also at Granada, Toledo, Seville, Murcia, Almeria, Valencia, Cadiz. The technique of paper making was brought in from Baghdad, and books increased and multiplied. Moslem Spain had seventy libraries; rich men displayed their Morocco bindings, and bibliophiles collected rare or beautifully illuminated books. The scholar al-Hadram, at an auction in Cordova, found himself persistently outbid for a book he desired, until the price offered far exceeded the value of the volume. The successful bidder explained that there was a vacant place in his library, into which this book would precisely fit. "I was so vexed," adds al-Hadram, "that I could not help saying to him, 'He gets the nut who has no teeth.'"

Scholars were held in awesome repute in Moslem Spain, and were consulted in simple faith that learning and wisdom are one. Theologians and grammarians could be had by the hundred; rhetoricians, philologists, lexicographers, anthologists, historians, biographers, were legion. Abu Muhammad Ali ibn Hazm (994–1064), besides serving as vizier to the last Umayyads, was a theologian and historian of great erudition. His *Book of Religions and Sects*, discussing Judaism, Zoroastrianism, Christianity, and the principal varieties of Mohammedanism, is one of the world's earliest essays in comparative religion. If we wish to know what an educated Moslem thought of medieval Christianity we need only read one of his paragraphs:

> Human superstition need never excite our astonishment. The most numerous and civilized nations are thralls to it. . . . So great is the multitude of Christians that God alone can number them, and they can boast of sagacious princes and il-

lustrious philosophers. Nevertheless they believe that one is three and three are one; that one of the three is the Father, the other the Son, and the third the Spirit; that the Father is the Son and is not the Son; that a man is God and not God; that the Messiah has existed from all eternity, and yet was created. A sect of theirs, the Monophysites, numbered by hundreds of thousands, believes that the Creator was scourged, buffeted, crucified, and that for three days the universe was without a ruler.

Ibn Hazm, for his part, believed that every word of the Koran was literally true. Science and philosophy, in Moslem Spain, were largely frustrated by the fear that they would damage the people's faith.

Islamic Laws Affect Agriculture and the Environment

Xavier de Planhol

Xavier de Planhol discusses the effects of Islamic laws banning the consumption of wine, pork, and dog meat. According to de Planhol, with the spread of Islam, Mediterranean vineyards all but disappeared, and much land was deforested as sheep and goat grazing replaced the raising of swine. Though the consumption of dog meat is still practiced in northern Africa, de Planhol believes the spread of Islam reduced the number of dogs and discouraged their consumption. Based on his experience and preliminary research, Xavier de Planhol launched a study of the relationship of geography and religion and called for geographers to conduct systematic studies of human geography in Muslim countries. He is the author of *An Historical Geography of France*.

Islam is a city dweller's religion. Mohammed belonged to the commercial, urban aristocracy of Mecca. Working the soil about oases was by definition a servile occupation. After the conquest in the lands newly annexed to Islam the countryside remained for a long time under the control of unbelievers, whereas the cities were centers of the faith. These circumstances may be seen in all the teachings of the Prophet. In the Koran the growth of crops is never viewed as the consequence of human labor but as the simple expression of divine will (for example, XXVI, 33–36, or LVI, 64–65—God is the true sower of seeds). The so-called "Oral Traditions" of

Reprinted from Xavier de Planhol, *The World of Islam*. Copyright ©1959 by Cornell University. Used by permission of the publisher, Cornell University Press.

Islam are filled with a spirit hostile to the peasantry. Seeing a plowshare, the Prophet is said to have remarked, "That never enters into the house of a believer without degrading it.". . . .

The Effect of Laws Banning Wine

Islam's ban on alcoholic drinks as a whole and on wine in particular (only the Hanafites[1] tolerate alcohol in any form; they limit the ban to wine) has had noteworthy effects on the agricultural countryside of the Mediterranean areas conquered by the Moslems. It has pushed toward the northwestern part of the Mediterranean the winegrowing industries that had previously been localized in the eastern part. As late as the high Middle Ages, the Syrian wines of Gaza and Zarephath exported by native merchants were much sought after in Merovingian[2] Gaul. The ban on alcohol did not originally extend to the cultivation of vines, and the falling off in grape production was gradual. Yet it was very notable. Only in Moslem Spain, it would seem, did the growing of vines remain important. In Persia too the growing of grapes lingered long, and wine was sung by the Persian poet Hafiz. The Shiite heresy encouraged the continued drinking of wine in Persia, but in Azerbaijan, Shiraz and Isfahan, Khurasan and Teheran, the making of wines has always been almost entirely in the hands of Jews and Armenians. In 1889 a monopoly on the trade was conceded by the shah to Europeans, and it soon passed into the hands of some Belgians organized under the veiled name of "The General Society of Commerce and Industry in Persia." In Sicily, despite the Arab poetry in praise of wine which has come down to us, the decay of the trade was rapid, and before long the island had to import its wine from Naples. In Asia Minor wine production was almost entirely limited to Christian, Greek, and Armenian villages. In Crete the wine trade was completely destroyed by the Turkish conquest and by the partial Islamization of the populace. The Moslem invasion of the second half of the sixteenth century is popu-

---

1. Muslims following one of the various schools of Muslim law   2. a dynasty ruling Gaul after the fifth century

larly supposed to have ruined grape growing in Ethiopia. In Syria and North Africa the grapevine became a decorative garden plant. . . .

Taxes on Non-Muslims

Even among Christian peoples the growing of wine grapes was ruined by the imposition of excessive taxes. The most remarkable example is that of Cyprus, where at the time the British took over the winegrowers were staggering under a veritable torrent of special taxes. There were a tax on the grape harvest, a tax on the amount of wine produced, a surtax on transportation, and a tax of 10 per cent ad valorem[3] after the product of the whole district had been assessed. In addition, the long waiting periods at the government office at Limassol where the wine was to be weighed ultimately gave it the taste of goatskin, which rendered it all but unfit for exportation. Under these circumstances it was barely possible to make a profit. For reasons like these men abandoned the growing of grapes on the high rugged meadows on the southern slope of Troodos, where the vine was practically the only thing that could be grown at all. In fact all regions under the political control of Islam saw their winemaking industries disappear, and the vine became a plant grown only in the mountains, more or less integrated with the Mediterranean flora and the local way of life, but never capable of supplying even a reasonable export demand. From the plains the vine retreated to the mountains, from the open fields to the gardens. . . .

Exceptions to the Wine-Banning Law

In this gloomy picture of Islamic grape growing a touch of color is furnished by the little urban vineyards of western Algeria. There in the neighborhood of the principal cities of the mountainous interior (such as Mascara and Miliana) one might find, long before the French occupation, genuine vineyards, with the plants ranged properly in order, and private wineries belonging to individual citizens. The mingling

3. in proportion to the value

of strains, generally exotic ones, gave them a rather special bouquet, almost riotous in its richness, but there was a quality about them which was altogether extraordinary in Islamic countries, something inherited from Rome and the Andalusian tradition but reconstituted under the aegis of Islam after the destruction of the wine trade under the Arab invasions. (To be sure the Arabs had treated vines no worse than they did other fruit-bearing plants.) These were wines of a new atmosphere, quite different from those of the great domains of antiquity. But they were far from adequate to quench even the local thirst of the Barbary Coast, where, in defiance of religious law, renegades and pirates drank generously from stocks of wine imported from Spain, Italy, and Provence.

A second interesting circumstance is the recent revival of vine growing in Asia Minor. During the last years of the Ottoman Empire the industry was essentially a concern of the fiscal office, which was preoccupied with increasing the yield of the tax on alcohol and therefore lent its influence to reconstituting vineyards in several Christian villages. After the war of independence and the expulsion of the Greeks the Turkish immigrants who replaced them either neglected the vineyards or uprooted the vines. But the government did not wish to be deprived of substantial revenues and so intervened. For the first time in an Islamic country the state itself turned vintner; the new immigrants did not make wine themselves but grew grapes which they sold to the state liquor monopoly, which completed the process. The end product was exported, chiefly to Scandinavian countries; local consumption remained very slight. Today the wine-growing industry of Anatolia is completely artificial; it produces only for sale and has no roots in the peasantry's way of life or civilization; it is actually a relic. . . .

The Effects of Laws Banning Pork

Much more important in its consequences has been Islam's ban on pork, an old Near Eastern custom followed by Egyptians, Semites, and Libyans, and transmitted by them to Islam. It is a rule much better observed in Islamic countries than the rule against alcoholic beverages. Here again the exceptions to the rule are found on the frontiers of Islam. The clearest example of frontier tolerance is furnished by the Far East. In Indonesia, where conversion to Islam is often superficial, the tolerance of swine's flesh is universal. In China the greatest possible indulgence is common. Appearances are saved by the simple process of christening the pork "mutton." This hypocrisy is very general elsewhere, if one believes the proverb according to which "a Moslem traveling alone gets fat, two Moslems traveling together get thin" (because the solitary traveler does not scruple to eat pork when he is out of sight of his coreligionists). Another proverb declares, even more sharply, "One Moslem is no Moslem; two Moslems are half a Moslem; three Moslems are one Moslem." In Moslem lodginghouses and hotels pork is almost always served to non-Moslems. . . .

However, the ban on pork, like that on alcohol, is making progress. Several tribes which used to eat ass's flesh have given it up on purely philological[4] grounds; the same word in their language (*m'bam*) designates both ass and pig. In certain Balkan areas where Islam had long been established, feeling in the matter reached a point where it influenced the Christians, some of whom refused to eat pork. Aside from these exceptions on the borders of Islam the only peoples who eat pork within the zone of Islam's influence are primitive tribes, half converted and considered impure. What is more, they are always hunters, and the problem centers on their eating of wild hogs, not domestic swine. . . .

The geographical effects of this ban on pork have been considerable. The rule against pork has thrown open the wooded ranges to sheep and goats and thus indirectly brought about a catastrophic deforestation. This is one of the basic reasons for the sparse landscape particularly evident in the Mediterranean districts of Islamic countries. On the borders of Moslem rule, in Albania, for example, the amount of wooded countryside becomes much greater immediately as one crosses into the Christian cantons, where pork is raised.

4. pertaining to the study of words

Islam has also made its contribution to a decrease in the practice of cynophagy, or dog eating, which is an old Libyan and Berber custom. The dog was a domestic animal of the ancient Libyans and was deliberately cultivated as food; it is still part of the alimentary picture in a broad zone of the Sahara reaching from North Africa (above all Derna in Tripolitania, Sfax in Tunisia, Gabès in the Fezzan, Chott Djerid, Souf, Touat, and Mzab) as far as Bahrein in the Orient. Dog's flesh is eaten not only in case of famine but also as a remedy against fever and as a fattening diet (the dogs are first stuffed with dates). Especially at Djerba[5] is this diet customary for young ladies who wish to acquire the *embonpoint*[6] so much admired by their future husbands. Although certain jurists seem to tolerate the practice, Islam clearly denounces the eating of dog's flesh. The ban derives no doubt from the fact that the animal is thought impure (the impurity of the Nimadi is linked in part to the fact that these professional hunters live in such intimacy with their dogs) as well as from the fact that, even though impure, the dog enjoys a certain consideration. Islam has reduced the prevalence of this typically Saharan custom, so that today it is scarcely more than a curiosity. On another level Islam rebukes the possessor of dogs that do not have an obvious practical value (as watchdogs, hunters, or progenitors of improved breeds), and in this way it has considerably reduced the number of dogs kept for pleasure and for display. . . .

With respect to the positive influences of Islam on the working of the soil, the most obvious influence is certainly in the realm of the sheepherder. Says the Koran: "It is equally glorious to lead the flocks to their fold or into the pastures" (XVI, 6). Carried as it was by nomads or by sheepraising peoples, Islam has spread its favored animal species across entire continents and in the wake of its conquests has converted great areas from crops to pasture. The spread of nomadism across cultivable plains, reinforced by the aversion of Islam to pork and by the sacred character of the sheep in Islam (every Moslem must sacrifice a goat, sheep, or

---

5. an island, part of Tunisia   6. the condition of being plump; stout

other animal when he makes his pilgrimage and another each year at the sacrificial feast which marks the ending of Ramadan), accounts for the density of sheep in Islamic countries, and of their companions the goats as well; and to these close grazers the upland forests have been sacrificed. In China the Moslems have a practical monopoly of the sheep-growing trade. The Islamic conquests introduced new strains of sheep into Spain from North Africa.

Chapter 3

The Spread of Islamic Art and Thought

Turning Points

IN WORLD HISTORY

Islamic Contributions to Science and Mathematics

John B. Christopher

John B. Christopher explains the major medical, scientific, and mathematical contributions of Islamic scholars to the wider intellectual world. Despite their scientific approach to infectious diseases and the invention of the zero for simpler mathematical computation, ancient Islamic scholars retained outdated beliefs in astrology and alchemy. John B. Christopher has been a professor of history at the University of Rochester in New York and a research analyst for the Department of State. He is the author of *The Middle East: National Growing Pains* and *Lebanon: Yesterday and Today*.

Several of the great names in Islamic philosophy—ar-Razi, al-Farabi, Avicenna—also figure prominently in the history of Islamic science. Scientists, too, built on the work of older civilizations, Greek, Persian, Hindu, and even Chinese (it is possible that the Arabic word *alchemy* is derived from the Chinese for *gold-extracting juice*). . . .

The linguistic preeminence of Arabic and the relative ease of travel across the length and breadth of the medieval Islamic world permitted the development of important scientific centers all the way from Spain and Morocco to Samarkand in Central Asia, capital of the conqueror Tamerlane, who established a great school there at the close of the Middle Ages. In the first two Muslim centuries the major scientific center was the city of Jundishapur in southwestern

Persia, founded by the Sasanid emperor Shapur, who defeated the legions of Rome in the third century A.D. Renowned for its hospital and its medical and scientific academies, Jundishapur attracted many Nestorian refugees from Byzantine persecution. Under the early Abbasid caliphs leadership passed to Baghdad, where the caliphs' House of Wisdom established a vigorous intellectual tradition continued by the city's schools and hospitals. In the tenth and eleventh centuries the energy of the Ismaili[1] movement and the patronage of the Fatimid[2] caliphs, particularly in establishing a great library, brought Cairo to the first rank. It remained there during many later political vicissitudes thanks to the continuity provided by institutions such as its famous hospitals and the university of al-Azhar.

Medicine

In the medieval Islamic world the medical profession was established and recognized to a degree unknown in Catholic Europe. Reputable physicians were on the whole highly esteemed and well paid; an outstanding doctor such as Avicenna served Persian princes not only as a physician but also as a political counsellor. The starting point of Islamic medicine was the legacy of Hindu and Persian medical lore preserved at Jundishapur, supplemented by the Arabic translation of the Greek physician Galen, who had summarized the medical legacy of the ancient Mediterranean world in the second century A.D.

Past authorities did not necessarily command uncritical deference from Muslim physicians. For example, ar-Razi, who flourished about A.D. 900, cited Greek, Syriac, Persian, and Hindu opinions on a given question and then presented his own views. This independent attitude enabled ar-Razi to make some important discoveries, above all to distinguish for the first time the differences between smallpox and measles. Here is an excerpt from his monograph on these two diseases:

The outbreak of small-pox is preceded by continuous fever,

1. a branch of Shiism that follows a divinely inspired successor to the Prophet   2. a Muslim dynasty descending from Muhammad's daughter

aching in the back, itching in the nose and shivering during sleep. The main symptoms of its presence are: back-ache with fever, stinging pain in the whole body, congestion of the face, sometimes shrinkage, violent redness of the cheeks and eyes, a sense of pressure in the body, creeping of the flesh, pain in the throat and breast accompanied by difficulty of respiration and coughing, dryness of the mouth, thick salivation, hoarseness of the voice, headache and pressure in the head, excitement, anxiety, nausea and unrest. Excitement, nausea and unrest are more pronounced in measles than in small-pox, whilst the aching in the back is more severe in small-pox than in measles.

Through careful detailed observation, ar-Razi added much to the store of clinical data about infectious diseases that had been accumulating since the pioneering work of Hippocrates[3] 1300 years earlier.

Special Contributions of ar-Razi and Avicenna

Ar-Razi's contribution to Islamic medicine was the more remarkable because he only began his studies in middle age, when he already had many other intellectual irons in the fire. He directed a hospital in his native Rayy, then another at Baghdad, and wrote more than fifty clinical studies in addition to more ambitious general works. The latter included the *Comprehensive Book*, the longest medical work in the Arabic language (over eighteen volumes in an incomplete modern edition), which Renaissance Europeans much respected in its Latin translation. In the present century ar-Razi has attracted attention because of his *Spiritual Physick* and other original works on the psychological and sociological aspects of medicine. A few pertinent titles are: *On the Fact That Even Skillful Physicians Cannot Heal All Diseases; Why Frightened Patients Easily Forsake Even the Skilled Physician; Why People Prefer Quacks and Charlatans.*

A hundred years later, Avicenna also placed considerable stress on psychosomatic medicine and reportedly was able to

---

3. the Greek physician who laid the foundation of scientific medicine, called "the father of medicine"

cure a prince suffering from a severe depression. The patient imagined himself to be a cow, made lowing noises, and demanded to be butchered and converted into stew beef; Avi-

Resignation of a Scientist and Poet

Besides his achievements in astronomy and mathematics, Omar Khayyám wrote poetry, expressing his views of the world in the Rubaiyat, *meaning quatrains. In the following lines, Khayyám resigns himself never knowing the purpose of his existence on earth.*

Ah, make the most of what we yet may spend,
Before we too into the Dust descend;
    Dust into Dust, and under Dust to lie,
Sans Wine, sans Song, sans Singer, and—sans End!

Alike for those who for TODAY prepare
And those that after some TOMORROW stare,
    A Muezzin from the Tower of Darkness cries,
"Fools! your Reward is neither Here nor There."

Why, all the Saints and Sages who discuss'd
Of the Two Worlds so wisely—they are thrust
    Like foolish Prophets forth; their Words to Scorn
Are scatter'd, and their Mouths are stopt with Dust.

Myself when young did eagerly frequent
Doctor and Saint, and heard great argument
    About it and about: but evermore
Came out by the same door where in I went.

With them the seed of Wisdom did I sow,
And with mine own hand wrought to make it grow;
    And this was all the Harvest that I reap'd—
"I came like Water, and like Wind I go."

Into this Universe, and *Why* not knowing
Nor *Whence*, like Water willy-nilly flowing;
    And out of it, as Wind along the Waste,
I know not *Whither*, willy-nilly blowing.

Robert Warnock and George K. Anderson, eds., *The World in Literature*. Vol 1. Chicago: Scott, Foresman, 1950.

cenna, posing as a cheerful butcher, refused to oblige, claiming that the intended victim was too scrawny and needed to be fattened up; whereupon the patient began eating heartily and eventually recovered his health. Avicenna compiled an encyclopedia, *The Canon of Medicine*, which was more systematic than Razi's *Comprehensive Book* and was widely consulted in the Arab world down to the last century and in Western Europe until the 1600s. Avicenna appears to have been the first doctor to describe and identify meningitis and the first to recommend alcohol as a disinfectant.

The more scholars examine the sources, the more "firsts" can be claimed for Islamic medicine. The work of Avicenna and others on eye diseases, very prevalent in the Middle East, and on the nature of vision helped to found the study of optics. These studies also made possible rather complicated operations on the eye. Muslim surgeons used opium for anesthesia and attempted experimental operations, including the extraction of teeth and their replacement by ones made from animal bones, the removal of kidney stones lodged in the bladder, and possibly even colostomy (opening of an artificial anus after removal of cancerous tissue).

However, it is important to keep a proper perspective on Islamic medical achievements and not to magnify them unduly. Mortality among surgical patients appears to have been very high, because doctors knew little about either antiseptic measures or the details of anatomy. Muslim tradition forbade dissecting corpses, though a little clandestine dissection may have occurred, mainly in Spain. Some scholars, therefore, discount reports that a thirteenth-century Egyptian physician discovered the existence of the pulmonary circulation, which accounts for the passage of the blood from one chamber of the heart to another via the lungs. He may have advanced this theory three centuries before it was confirmed by European scientists; but it was a purely speculative hypothesis, untested clinically or experimentally.

Mathematics

To describe certain procedures mathematicians borrowed from the vocabulary of surgery the term *al-jabr*, meaning restoration or reestablishment of something broken (Spaniards still call a bone-setter an *algebrista*). Islamic algebra was built on Greek and Hindu foundations and closely linked to geometry; its principal architects were the ninth-century Zoroastrian, al-Khuwarizmi, and the twelfth-century Persian, Omar Khayyam. Al-Khuwarizmi, who worked at the House of Wisdom in Baghdad, wrote a very influential book on algebra and also contributed to the development of trigonometry. He described an angle by an Arabic word meaning *pocket* or *pouch*, which was translated into the Latin *sinus*—whence our *sine*. Omar Khayyam,[4] who was also a poet and a Sufi as well as an astronomer, is an excellent instance of the Muslim who sought both the rationalist and the gnostic[5] paths to truth. Indeed, many Islamic mathematicians, like the Pythagoreans of ancient Greece, believed that through numbers men could ascend beyond the world of bewildering phenomena into a higher realm of abstractions and eternal verities. Because the science of numbers was regarded as "the tongue which speaks of unity and transcendence," it was appropriate to use as charms magic squares based on the numerical value of some of the ninety-nine names of God.

To the average Westerner, Arabic numbers have the merit of great simplicity, in contrast to the cumbersome Roman system based on letters. The simplicity of the Arabic system, however, is somewhat deceptive. The numerals used in the West, except for 1 and 9, do not look much like those used today by Arabs and Persians: their numerals are derived from those used in medieval Iraq, whereas ours come through medieval Spain. All of them, except for zero, almost certainly go back ultimately to the Hindus. The most revolutionary innovation of Arabic numbers was not their greater convenience, valuable and time-saving though this was; it lay in the Arabs' use of a dot to indicate an empty column, ten, for example, being 1·, one hundred one 1·1, and one million and one 1·····1. The dot was called *sifr*

---

4. author of the famous poem *Rubaiyat*, translated into English by British writer Edward Fitzgerald 5. spiritual; knowledge revealed by God

("empty"), whence our *cipher* and, through an Italian translation, our *zero*. This system made possible a whole new world of arithmetical operations.

Physical Sciences

Islamic mathematicians opened new worlds to science, or at least freshened understanding of older worlds. Increased knowledge of geometry and algebra aided the development of optics. The tables compiled by observers systematically recording their findings were utilized by later astronomers both in the Islamic world and in Europe. Islamic advances in trigonometry allowed computations that refined the picture of the earth-centered universe drawn by Ptolemy, the Greco-Egyptian astronomer of the second century A.D. One such refinement disclosed the eccentric behavior of Venus, which would have been easier to explain if the planet had been viewed as orbiting around the sun rather than around the earth. But, as in the medieval West, acceptance of the Ptolemaic system[6] was too ingrained to countenance such a radical innovation as the heliocentric universe.

In certain instances theoretical science was turned to practical account. Astronomical tables enabled the faithful to determine the direction of Mecca and to schedule the five daily prayers and fix the annual festivals and holy days of the lunar calendar. Astronomy and geography facilitated navigation of the monsoon-swept Indian ocean, and mathematics and physics encouraged improvement of water clocks and of water wheels and other irrigation apparatus. Mechanical devices were sometimes remarkably ingenious, as in this thirteenth-century clock consisting of an elephant and a fantastic contrivance mounted on its back, [described by Richard Ettinghausen in *Arab Painting*],

> Every half-hour the bird on top of the cupola whistles and turns while the mahout hits the elephant with his pick-axe and sounds a tattoo with his drumstick. In addition, the little man who seems to be looking out of a window . . . moves his

6. the astronomical system of Ptolemy, in which the earth is at the center of the universe with the sun, moon, planets, and stars revolving about it

arms and legs to induce the falcon below to release a pellet. This moving downward, makes the dragon turn until it is finally ejected into the little vase on the elephant's back. From there it drops into the animal, hits a gong, and finally comes to rest in a little bowl where the observer can establish the half-hours passed by counting the number of little balls collected there.

Astrology and Alchemy

Modern Westerners, who are amused by the talent expended on such fanciful gadgets, are uneasy when they learn that many Islamic astronomers were also astrologers and that a pioneer psychologist and physician such as ar-Razi could also be an alchemist. Astrology is based on the belief that the universe is, as the name suggests, a totality in which the stars do determine and indeed predestine activities on earth. Alchemy is based on the theory that there is a hierarchy of metals, from the base to the pure; if man can find the magical philosopher's stone or elixir, he will be able to change one to the other, iron to gold, or lead to silver, and perhaps also to make glass or quartz into emeralds or some other precious stone.

To us today all this seems an unfortunate confusion between true science and occult or pseudo science; our medieval forebears accepted the occult as a matter of course. Ancient traditions, together with the gnostic elements present in both Christianity and Islam, nourished the widely held conviction that there were other pathways to truth beside the one that we call rationalist or scientific. The more radical Shiites, especially the Ismailis with their concern for discovering the hidden message of the Koran, endeavored to unlock the secrets of nature by esoteric means as well as by scientific ones. The Sufis strove to release themselves from the physical restraints of body and mind to enable the soul to penetrate the veils concealing God.

A modern Persian scholar [Seyyed Hossein Nasr], familiar both with the history of science and with the Shii and Sufi traditions, advances this explanation for the popularity of alchemy:

We must remember that ancient and medieval man did not

separate the material order from the psychological and spiritual in the categorical manner that has become customary today. There was a "naiveness" in the mentality of premodern man which made it possible for him . . . to see a deeper significance in physical phenomena than just plain facts. . . . The basic symbols and principles of alchemy stem from the earliest periods of history and convey through their very concreteness the primordial character of this point of view. Ancient man, during the millennia before recorded history, considered metals to be a special class of beings, which did not belong to the natural environment of the "Adamic race." The earliest iron probably came from meteorites which, in falling from the heavens, gave that metal special virtues and powers.

Although this hypothesis is controversial, there seems little doubt that alchemy was regarded as a quasi-religious pursuit. It has been argued that, just as the alchemist sought to transmute baser metals into gold, so he also sought a kind of transmutation of the soul, which would release it from the sin imposed by the fall of Adam from Eden and allow it to reach a nobler state. The alchemist has likewise been compared to a Sufi sheik, guiding his disciples on their way to God, and to the Christian priest, celebrating the miracle of the mass, which transforms the bread and wine into the body and blood of Christ.

Astrology and alchemy were, in effect, the face and obverse of the same coin, the one turned toward the heavens and the other toward the earth. The seven metals of the alchemist were the earthly symbols of the astrologer's seven planets—gold symbolized the sun, silver the moon, quicksilver Mercury, copper Venus, iron Mars, tin Jupiter, and lead Saturn. From the ancient Greeks Islamic alchemists borrowed the concept of four fundamental elements—fire, air, earth, and water. Each of these, they argued, combined two of the four fundamental characteristics or qualities of nature, heat, cold, dryness, and wetness: fire was hot and dry, air hot and wet, earth cold and dry, and water cold and wet.

Islamic physicians, also borrowing from the Greeks, put the four humors of the human body into this pattern, noting that each produced a characteristic temperament. Yellow bile, which was hot and dry, made a man fiery or choleric; blood, which was hot and wet, made him sanguine or cheerful; black bile, which was cold and dry, made him melancholy; and phlegm, cold and wet, made him phlegmatic. When the humors were reasonably balanced, the individual was in good health. In illness, the balance was destroyed; and treatment consisted in prescribing for the patient drugs and a diet that would supply the humors in which he was deficient until his normal balance was restored.

The doctrines of astrology and alchemy did not win universal approval in the medieval Islamic world. The ulema proclaimed them contrary to the faith, and several distinguished philosophers rejected them as contrary to reason. Ibn-Khaldun concluded:

> The worthlessness of astrology from the point of view of the religious law, as well as the weakness of its achievements from the rational point of view, are evident. In addition, astrology does harm to human civilization. It hurts the faith of the common people when an astrological judgment occasionally happens to come true. . . . Ignorant people are taken in by that and suppose that all the other astrological judgments must be true.

And Avicenna flatly denied the possibility of physical transmutation:

> As to the claims of the alchemists, it must be clearly understood that it is not in their power to bring about any true change of species. They can, however, produce excellent imitations, dyeing the red metal white so that it resembles silver, or dyeing it yellow so that it closely resembles gold. They can, too, dye the white metal with any colour they desire, until it bears a close resemblance to gold or copper; and they can free the leads from most of their defects and impurities. Yet in these dyed metals the essential nature remains unchanged.

This last passage nevertheless suggests how the Arabic *al-kimiya* was to furnish modern chemistry both with its name and with some of its techniques and apparatus. In addition to being expert dyers, the alchemists developed methods of refining metals and of applying varnish to protect iron or waterproof cloth. They employed such chemical processes as distillation, evaporation, sublimation, crystallization, and filtration. Ar-Razi, in his writings on alchemy, describes vials, beakers, mortars and pestles, flasks, smelters, and other items of equipment. A modern scholar [A. Mieli] has compared the power attributed to the elusive philosopher's stone with that actually present in a chemical catalyst.

Islamic Literature and Art

Mervyn Hiskett

Mervyn Hiskett explains the *qasida*, a form of poetry that developed in ancient Arabia, and identifies two prose forms that emerged in the centuries after Muhammad. According to Hiskett, since painting and sculpture were forbidden, scribes and artists perfected forms of calligraphy to produce beautiful editions of the Koran and to enhance the decor of Islamic buildings; the mosque of Muhammad in Medina became the standard architectural style for religious buildings and palaces. Mervyn Hiskett has extensively researched Islamic art, science, and education. He is the author of *A History of Hausa Islamic Verse* and a frequent contributor to scholarly journals.

The Muslims started at some disadvantage. They had little cultural heritage of their own. Yet they were not wholly bereft of cultural antecedents. . . .

Verse is one of the very few developed art forms that existed among the Arabs in the "Time of Ignorance", the immediate pre-Islamic period.

The South-Arabian kingdoms of the more remote past— the Minaeans, the Sabaeans, who may have been the Ishmaelites of Genesis 37:25,

> . . . and behold, a company of Ishmaelites came forth from Gilead with their camels bearing spicery and balm and myrrh, going to carry it down to Egypt,

and the Himyarites,[1] achieved a high level of material skills,

1. an ancient tribe of southwest Arabia who spoke Semitic

including, it would seem, some civil engineering and architectural competence. . . .

With one exception, little of cultural significance was passed on to the Arabians of the north. At the moment when Islam was revealed, they possessed only a simple desert culture which boasted nothing architecturally more complex than mud building and skin tents. But they did have the Arabian *qasida*. Whether this reached them from southern Arabia, or whether it arose spontaneously out of their desert environment, is open to question.

The *Qasida*, an Ode

The *qasida* is an elaborately structured ode, with an amatory prelude or love song:

> T'was then her beauties first enslaved my heart—
> Those glittering pearls and ruby lips, whose kiss
> Was sweeter far than honey to the taste.
> As when the merchant opes a precious box
> Of perfume, such an odour from her breath
> Came toward thee, harbinger of her approach;
> Or like an untouched meadow, where the rain
> Hath fallen freshly on the fragrant herb
> That carpet all its pure untrodden soil.

. . . Some believe such amatory preludes to be the first source of the chivalric love songs of the medieval European troubadors, introduced by the crusaders.

The amatory prelude led into the main body of the poem, which was taken up with tales of heroic deeds, praise of the author's horse or camel, or hunting scenes that portray the desert environment:

> She, the white cow, shone there through the dark night, luminous,
> Like a pearl of deep seas, freed from the string of it.
> Thus till morn, till day-dawn folded back night's canopy,
> Then she fled bewildered, sliding the feet of her . . .
> Voices now she hears, human tones, they startle her, though to her eyes naught is.

Man! He, the bane of her!
Seeketh a safe issue, the forenoon through, listening, now
in front, behind now, fearing her enemy.
And they failed, the archers. Loosed they then to deal with
her fine-trained hounds, the lop-eared, slender the sides
of them.
These outran her lightly. Turned she swift her horns on
them, like twin spears of Samhar, sharp-set the points of
them . . .

The *qasida* was capable of being composed in at least six-teen different metres, all of considerable complexity, and gov-erned by intricate rules. It was also subject to a strict prosody.[2] Some have suggested that these metres mimic the gaits of the camel—certainly an attractive theory for those who have de-lighted in the rhythmic grace of these magnificent beasts. Be that as it may, the elaborate structure of the *qasida*, and its so-phisticated conventions bespeak ancient origins.

The language of the *qasida* was also the language of the Meccan Arabs. It thus became the language of the Koran. This, in turn, became what we now recognise as "classical" Arabic, in distinction from the several regional dialects of Arabic that also exist.

The pre-Islamic *qasida*, with its amatory prelude, survived intact into the first Islamic century. But then, as Islamic reli-giosity took hold, it began to be modified to suit the attitudes of the *'ulama'*.[3] The prelude then became praise, not of a fe-male beloved but of the Prophet. This was later extended to become full-scale panegyric[4] in its own right. The body of the poem, instead of being devoted to hunting scenes, was given over to Islamic themes, often of an instructional kind. Indeed, the Muslims make a distinction between "poetry" (*shi'r*) and "versification" (*nazm*). They shun the secular, emotional and sensuous implications of the former; but they have taken over the latter with enthusiasm and use it for didactic purposes which avoid the undesirable non-Islamic associations.

---

2. the theory and principles of versification, particularly as they refer to rhythm, ac-cent, and stanza   3. learned elders; the senior religious officials   4. a formal com-position expressing praise

Especially popular in late medieval Islam, and even to the present day, were, and are, versified accounts of divine punishment and reward. These portray the delights of the Islamic Paradise and the condign[5] punishment of sinners and unbelievers in the seven Islamic hells. By this time, of course, Arabic was not the only vehicle for such verse. Many other languages, including Turkish, Urdu, Hausa and Swahili had become the languages of Islam. The following is taken from a nineteenth-century Hausa verse account of hell:

> [The sinners] are told: The little pleasure you enjoyed has
>   brought upon you
> Torment without end, for you failed to exercise restraint.
> Their top lip shall stretch to the cranium,
> The bottom lip to the navel, it is not a pleasant sight!
> They are taken to enclosed places for the torment of stoning,
> They are taken to the town of extreme cold, they all
>   grimace in pain,
> They return to the Fire, they are brought back into the
>   intense cold,
> . . .
> The fiends of Hell who bind their arms behind their
>   shoulders,
> Are of such a size you would think them a hundred years
>   old!
> Seventy thousand cudgels they carry on one shoulder
> And on the other seventy thousand hatchets!

These monstrous lips, which occur again and again in Islamic eschatological[6] verse, may be the origin of the gargoyles on many medieval Christian cathedrals and churches.

The same composer goes on to describe the joys of Paradise:

> Fine clothes will be brought and laid out for the Believers
> that they may mount horses and camels, clothes of silk, our
> saddles will be of gold, each with wings, We shall alight in
> Paradise, our fording place the heavenly river,

---

5. deserved 6. referring to the theology concerned with the end of the earth or of humankind

. . .

The young men of the seven cities of Paradise shall have
   their fill of the dark-eyed maidens,
Seventy becoming gowns shall clothe the virgin,
She shall have ten thousand slaves to do her bidding,
As often as she desires to embrace her spouse,
They will embrace for a full seventy years.

It was by attaching such sensuous imagery to such essentially
Islamic themes as Paradise that the Muslim versifiers
avoided the stigma of wandering, self indulgently among the
deviators in every valley. For such passages as the above offered a means of expressing carnality in a way that was acceptable within Islamic conventions. The ultimate source of
such imagery is of course the Koran. . . .

Islamic Prose

The whole scope of Islamic prose literature is too vast to be
encompassed here. But two especially notable fictional categories stand out. First, the telling and retelling of the major
Middle Eastern folklore cycles in their Islamic forms. Thus
there are endless recensions of the Alexander cycle (Iskandar
in Arabic), of his search for the Well of Life; of the Seven
Sleepers; of Gog and Magog and even of the Cid who, *mu-
tatis mutandis*,[7] was common to both the Spanish Christians
and their Moorish Muslim opponents. All these folkloric
themes were adapted by the Muslims. They were usually
given a Koranic background; and were also made to conform
to the particular traditions of the locality in which they cir-
culated. Such material began as oral literature and was later
written down. It was certainly not confined to the Arabic
language, but was taken up in all Islamic languages—Turkish, Urdu, Hausa and other Islamic tongues.

The second major Islamic fictional genre is that of *maqa-
mat*, the "frame story". . . . The "novel", as this is understood
in the West, is a very new introduction in the Islamic world.
It is to be found mainly in Egypt and Lebanon. The folkloric

7. the necessary changes having been made

themes and the frame story still hold pride of place in the literature of more traditional Islamic areas. . . .

Calligraphy

The cursive writing we now know as Arabic derives from an ancient South Arabian alphabet that, superficially, looks quite unlike it. Nonetheless, expert opinion has it that it is the source from which the later northern Arabic script was developed. This cursive, flowing hand was known in seventh-century Mecca. Although literacy in it appears to have been restricted, it was apparently used by certain merchants to keep their books. It was also used for recording some of the *qasidas* described above. At this time it lacked the vowel marks and certain other diacritics[8] and was therefore a somewhat rough and ready means of recording language.

With the revelation of the Koran, this script became of central importance to a religion which, from the start, set great store by literacy. Its dissemination and development quickly took on greater impetus. The need to record the Koran accurately, as it was revealed to the Prophet Muhammad, and passed on by him to his Companions, is self evident. This was at first done haphazardly, on "ribs of palm leaves and tablets of white stone" as well as on the blade bones of domestic animals. The text was essentially established in the reign of the Caliph 'Uthman (A.D. 644–56) but not finally fixed until A.D. 933. With the wider use of parchment and paper, innumerable copies were produced, lovingly inscribed in the Arabic script which in the process, acquired its final, standardised form. This included the vowel marks and diacritics it now displays. This elegant script became not only a means of recording language, but also a form of decoration for the greater glory of Allah's Word. Certain verses of the Koran are held to give more than a mere utilitarian value to it: "By the inkstand and the pen and that which they write" and:

Read, and thy Lord is most generous,

---

8. accent marks to indicate pronunciation

Who taught with the pen,
Taught man what he knew not.

Such verses were taken to enjoin the practice of calligraphy as a work of piety, as well as art.

Two main styles then emerged. *Naskhi*, the flowing, cursive script, which is to be seen in its finest decorative expression in the exquisite stucco lacework of Koran verses inscribed on the walls of the Alhambra Palace, in Granada.

Another, more angular style also developed. It was equally pleasing, but more stylised. It became known as *kufi*, since it originated among the Koran scribes of the city of Kufa. It can be seen on the Dome of the Rock, in Jerusalem; and in the mosque of Ibn Tulun, in Cairo. It lacks the flowing quality of *naskhi* but has a fine, geometrical intricacy of its own. Both styles are to be seen in numerous Arabic manuscripts, many of them illuminated with fine colouring. They are also frequently used to decorate ceramics.

Undoubtedly calligraphy largely took the place of painting in Islam, as a channel for expressing Muslim aestheticism. Drawing, painting and sculpture are normally banned in Islamic schools for reasons explained below. But calligraphy is taught in its stead. I have often seen examples of decorative calligraphy adorning the walls of schools in Islamic areas, in the same way that our own schools display their pupils' art work. The Arabic script has been adapted for the writing of a number of other Islamic languages, including Turkish, Urdu and Hausa. . . .

Islamic Attitudes Toward Art

The Koranic condemnation of anything that smacks of idolatry is no doubt well known:

> So coin not similitudes for Allah. Surely Allah knows and ye know not (16:74).

This and a number of similar verses are the basis of this condemnation. They have been taken to ban all forms of art and sculptory representing animate creatures, from an early date. Thus there could be no representation, in painting, wood, stone or other materials, of the human form or, strictly speaking, animal forms. It is true that the prohibition was imperfectly observed as is obvious from a glance at most Islamic art collections. In eastern Islam, where Persian and Indian influences prevailed, such representational art did occur quite frequently, though it tended to be stylised and formalistic; and never of such substance as to cast a shadow. It occurred, too, in Western Islam but more often than not it was executed by non-Muslims, usually Christian artists, not by the Muslims themselves. Many Muslims seem to have taken the view that, while they ought not to produce such art with their own hands, if it was produced by non-Muslims, they could legitimately enjoy it. One typical and charming example of this easy-going attitude is to be found in the Alhambra Palace, at Granada. Amidst the wealth of arabesque decoration in this lovely Islamic building, one wall alcove is to be found, out of sight of any but the deliberate observer. It bears a fine mural portrait of several white-bearded, chubby-cheeked old gentlemen who obviously represent the sultan's counsellors. It is entirely natural and life like and there is no attempt to disguise it with stylisation. The story goes that this group portrait was painted by a Christian craftsman in the sultan's employment. The old gentlemen were wont to retire to the alcove to enjoy their sherbet and rose water and admire their portraits!

Nonetheless, the Koranic ban on representational art was real. It influenced the development of Islamic art profoundly. It accounts for the characteristically geometric, foliated and scrolled style of that art, which is generally referred to as "arabesque.". . .

Islamic Architecture

The ban extended to mural decoration; and it is this arabesque style that will be found, to the virtual exclusion of all other styles, in Islamic buildings, especially mosques. . . . The prototype of mosque architecture is the Prophet's mosque in Madina, which derives from the Arabian urban dwelling of his day. This was an unroofed rectangular courtyard enclosed by four walls, along the inside of which were built cloisters. These were then roofed over and divided into chambers to function as living quarters, store rooms, granaries and shelter for domestic animals. At one end of this traditional building the Prophet placed his *minbar*, "pulpit", from which he delivered the address to the congregation assembled for prayer. It has continued to be used for this purpose by the *imam*, "prayer leader", ever since. Most typical of this pristine style is the mosque of Kairouan, in Tunisia, which is readily accessible to tourists in North Africa. It is of particular interest since it was built out of the debris of Byzantine basilicas and the like, that the seventh-century Muslim invaders of North Africa found at their disposal—or may perhaps have created. Thus Byzantine columns support the fabric that surrounds the open courtyard of the Kairouan mosque. . . . The same phenomenon—the plundering of Byzantine ruins for material to build mosques—is commonplace all over former Byzantine territories annexed to the Islamic empire.

Later, probably under the influence of Byzantine church architecture, mosques became domed over and also acquired towers. A fine example of this more developed type of western-Islamic mosque is the Blue Mosque, in present Istanbul.

In those areas of the Islamic world where Persian influences prevailed, mosque architecture reflected this. Spiral towers, staged towers or *ziggurat*, and other Asiatic features are in evidence, as in the Great Mosque at Samarra.

The mosque builders reached a high level of proficiency in the use of light and shadow, and in the creation of currents of air within the building, to provide natural air conditioning. Developing building techniques went hand in hand with increasingly elaborate decorative skills. These made use of glazed tiling and faience[9] work, using the calligraphy and geometrical painting described above.

Domestic architecture, apart from palace building, which largely followed mosque styles, usually remained unpretentious. It followed the basic north-Arabian pattern described

---

9. earthenware decorated with colorful glazes

above—that is an unroofed rectangular walled compound, with covered quarters, etc., within. In the more traditional areas of the Islamic world, such as northern Nigeria, this pattern is still widely adhered to even in the case of new buildings; although in more remote areas of that country, where mud building still predominates, circular walled compounds are sometimes met with, and the walls surround individual circular thatched, mud huts, which take the place of the cloisters. Great privacy surrounds the Muslim dwelling, since part of its purpose is to preserve the seclusion of the women folk. With rare exceptions, only members of the extended family enter the inner compound. Other visitors are met and entertained by the head of the family in a porch or entrance hut designed for this purpose. . . .

Ceramics and Handicrafts

Calligraphy was particularly apt to the decoration of ceramics of all kinds. Decorated tile work was introduced from Persia and the Muslims became experts in the enamelling and gilding of pottery.

Carpet weaving and the production of fabrics were also highly developed among the Muslims of the Middle Ages, as indeed they are today. No coach load of tourists in North Africa or Istanbul is likely to miss a visit to a carpet workshop, where exquisite carpets are still produced by the women, using traditional hand looms.

These carpets and fabrics of Islamic origin were highly prized in Christian Europe during the Middle Ages and the Renaissance period. They were exported to Europe in considerable quantities. Indeed, the word "fustian", which describes a thick, dyed cotton twill widely popular during the Middle Ages, derives its name from al-Fustat, an early Arabic name for Cairo, where it was originally made.

Transmission of Learning from Islam to Western Christendom

The transmission of learning, much of which was based on the Greek and Roman heritage but became deeply coloured by Islamic ideas and attitudes, to western Christendom, took place mainly from Moorish Spain and from Sicily, which was briefly in Muslim hands from the ninth century until its reconquest by the Normans in the eleventh century. But even after that event, Sicily continued for many generations to be a centre of Islamic culture and a source of Islamic influence in Europe, by way of the Italian peninsula.

According to [historian Philip K.] Hitti, the main route by which such influences travelled, carried by scholars and merchants, went by way of Toledo, across the Pyrenees to Provence, then across the Alpine passes to Lorraine. From there it passed to Germany and was diffused across western and central Europe, including Britain. The medieval universities of Oxford, Paris, Bologna and Naples were main centres where the theological, mathematical, philosophical and scientific gifts of Islam were received and worked on. Such outstanding Christian doctors as Robert of Chester, Thomas Aquinas, Duns Scotus, Roger Bacon, among others, were among its beneficiaries. But as Hitti says:

> By the close of the thirteenth century Arab science had been transmitted to Europe, and Spain's work as an intermediary was done.

Perhaps this postulates too abrupt a severance of influences that surely continued, in some measure, beyond that point. Nonetheless, it is true that Islamic intellectual activity of a creative kind, in Spain as elsewhere, gradually diminished after A.D. 1300.

Religious Inspiration Through Story and Art

John Renard

John Renard traces the development of Islamic religious and inspirational teaching from the oral tradition to the written form and explains the graphic arts that accompany various stages. Renard notes that while stories uniformly feature exemplary heroes as subject matter, art forms vary from realistic to abstract, from folk art to the illuminated manuscripts of trained artists. John Renard's research has focused primarily on Islamic religion and art. He is the author of *Letters on the Sufi Path*.

Books have long been powerful tools for exhorting people to strive for lofty ideals, but mass literacy is a relatively recent development in most of the world. Over the centuries the vast majority of Muslims have learned their tradition's values without reading. What they have learned first from their families has been reinforced by listening to people with a gift for bringing the past to life, and by looking at the vivid renditions of Islam's models, fashioned by artists both popular and sophisticated.

Storytellers Bring Exemplary Figures to Life

In the ancient arts of stylized, recitative storytelling, as well as in the more elaborate musical narrative forms, exemplary figures continue to come alive for communities of Muslims all over the world. . . .

In *The Book of Professional Storytellers*, Ibn al-Jawzi describes the important role storytellers have played in Muslim societies. Any group that exercises such influence can, he admits, fall prey to various problems. Ibn al-Jawzi deals with those difficulties head-on in an attempt to make it clear that, for all their human failings, storytellers perform an essential service. He lists six reasons why earlier generations of Muslims had criticized and hated storytellers. Muslims, he notes, have traditionally been careful not to introduce practices not sanctioned by the Prophet himself. Early Muslims even questioned the writing down of the Qur'an, because Muhammad had not done so. Another reason is that many popular stories about the peoples of old, especially those about the children of Israel, were often unreliable—in contrast to the total authenticity of the Qur'anic revelation. . . . Ibn al-Jawzi sums up the remaining reasons:

> The fourth reason is that there were stories in the Qur'an and exhortations among the traditions of the Prophet which rendered superfluous stories whose authenticity was not certain. The fifth reason is that some people who introduced into religion that which did not belong there told stories. Furthermore, they inserted into their stories elements which corrupted the minds of the masses. The sixth and final reason is that the majority of *qussas*[1] did not search out what was true, nor were they on their guard against error by reason of the meagerness of their knowledge and their lack of fear of God. And so, therefore, those who despised these excesses came to despise storytelling. However, when the learned man gave exhortation, and those who knew the difference between what was authentic and what was corrupt narrated stories, there was no loathing.

In other words, Ibn al-Jawzi is convinced that the benefits of the storyteller's art outweigh the dangers, assuming that the storyteller is a person of integrity, and that listeners exercise good judgment as they absorb the tales. The principal virtue for the professional storyteller is sincerity: one must always practice what one preaches. One must not succumb to the lure of popularity and put on airs as a result of this impor-

---

1. professional storytellers, especially during medieval times

tant vocation and the gifts that support it. Storytellers must remain ever conscious of their origins among the people. Their task is to keep alive in the minds and hearts of a broad public the words and deeds of Islam's religious heroes, for the power of example in ethical formation is enormous.

Pictures Used for Education

Pictures created to illustrate a live story performance have a long history in various cultures across the Islamic world. They have taken the form of scrolls or posters big enough for a small crowd to see but small enough to be portable, and have been used extensively in Iran. From a functional perspective these images form a bridge between narrative as public entertainment and reading stories for personal enjoyment and edification. I make a distinction between folk and popular arts on the one hand, and the more elite arts on the other; and I use the term *folk art* to characterize artifacts produced by individuals not formally schooled in their art, usually constructed of basic natural materials and often of unpolished execution, such as the domestic pilgrimage murals. . . . Popular arts, objects of broad appeal and accessibility, are often produced by highly skilled individuals rigorously schooled in an artistic medium. These works include the murals painted on structures used for the ta'ziya[2] ritual.

Multimedia presentations are hardly a modern invention. Muslim storytellers have often used visual aids, notwithstanding the widespread impression—even among Muslims—that Islamic tradition forbids images of human beings. An excellent example of a tradition of popular art still alive especially in the Arab Middle East and North Africa is that of under-glass painting. Themes for most of these paintings come from the vast repertoire of heroic lore and epic saga that has continued to form the kernel of much popular storytelling the world over. Most of the characters are folk heroes, such as 'Antar, Abu Zayd al-Hilali, 'Abdallah ibn Ja'far, and such famous female counterparts as 'Abla and Yamina.

2. "consolation," the Shi'i passion play that commemorates the martyrdom of Husayn at Karbala

Many paintings in this genre, however, come from stories of religious figures, including Muhammad; 'Ali and his two sons, Hasan and Husayn; and the widely popular Friend of God 'Abd al-Qadir al-Jilani. Among these works, three types are distinct: images of religious heroes; representations of some attribute or character intimately connected with the personage's story; and symbolic, nonrepresentational images, sometimes utilizing calligraphic designs, that are associated with a particular religious figure.

Images of Religious Heroes

Pictures of 'Ali engaged in combat against the demon of woeful countenance known as Ra's al-Ghul are among the most prominent North African examples of the first type. Here Muhammad's son-in-law displays the essential trait of the religious hero, willingness to engage the forces of evil and injustice. 'Ali usually dispatches the demon with a stroke of his forked sword, Dhu 'l-Faqar (the cleaver), which he inherited from Muhammad. The sword provides a natural iconographic clue to the hero's identity.

Images of 'Ali and his sons, Hasan and Husayn, have been particularly significant for Shi'i Muslims; but they have received special attention also within the Sunni community in various regions. North African tradition, particularly in Tunisia, regards 'Ali as a high exemplar for youth. He was "the first adolescent to have embraced the new religion without ever having previously bowed to any idol or worshipped a deity other than God." 'Ali is moreover the father of two sons who model ideal behavior for young people. Before they were martyrs, Hasan and Husayn were children of a heroic father. And as youthful martyrs, the two embody innocence and purity standing firm in the face of evil. On lacquered mirrors and boxes from Iran, as well as on under-glass paintings from further west, the trio often appear seated frontally, with 'Ali in the middle holding his sword across his lap.

The renowned Friend of God 'Abd al-Qadir al-Jilani also appears in under-glass paintings. A favorite episode depicts the hero taming a wild lion. More than mere fable, the scene speaks to its viewers of the power (baraka) of a holy person over brute force. In addition, and perhaps more important, the victory of the Friend of God over the lion models the crucial theme of the Greater Jihad, the struggle against one's own baser tendencies and passions. The lower self, or *nafs*, is sometimes likened to a wild beast.

Stylized Representations and Symbols

In the second category stylized and abstract representations of objects or beings are often associated with some religious hero's story. All over the Islamic world one finds pictures of Buraq, the winged human-faced quadruped upon which Muhammad made his Night Journey from Mecca to Jerusalem and his Ascension from Jerusalem through the seven heavens and the netherworld. The image itself recalls the story of the Prophet's wondrous adventure; but it often functions also as a protective device. Such talismanic functions are often difficult to separate neatly from those of devotional ritual and spiritual edification.

The term *pictograph* has been used to describe some of the objects in the third category, because it uses calligraphy to outline an animal or plant. For example, calligraphic texts referring to 'Ali as "Our Master, the victorious Lion of God" are molded, like wire-frame images, into the shape of a lion. Such calligraphic forms appear in media other than under-glass painting all over the Islamic world.

Abstract symbolic designs intimately associated with the Prophet are related to pictographs. Actual images of Muhammad do not appear in the under-glass paintings, but one fascinating symbol of the Prophet's life and presence has maintained some popularity: the image of his sandals, and that image is in turn associated with footprints. Sometimes occurring in under-glass painting and in other media, such as manuscript painting, the sandals function both as talismanic devices and as reminders of the whole of the Prophet's exemplary life story. The Arabic word *sira* (used earlier to refer to Muhammad's earliest literary biography) derives from a root whose literal meaning is "progress or journey," a notion the image of a sandal or a footprint readily recalls.

Many mosques and shrines, especially in south Asia, claim to possess footprints of Muhammad.

Poster and Calendar Art

Another genre of popular imagery occurs in the form of revolutionary poster art. The most prominent examples thus far studied as a group come from Iran during the Khomeini era (especially through the 1970s). Some emulate the style of classic Persian miniatures but are blown up to a size suitable for posting on walls in public places. The posters draw their fundamental themes from Qur'anic and postscriptural stories of the prophets. . . . These visual productions clearly serve a predominantly political purpose, but they use evocative religious imagery to bolster their claims to political legitimacy and to undermine that of the incumbent regime—in this instance, that of Muhammad Riza Shah Pahlavi.

Many of the posters juxtapose images of Ayatollah Khomeini with images of a deposed shah in such a way that the Iranian Muslim viewer cannot escape certain scriptural associations. For example, Khomeini is a modern-day Moses; the shah, a new Pharaoh. The staff of the new Moses has become a fire-breathing dragon about to scorch and devour the godless monarch. Although visual materials of this genre do not inspire in the same way that, for example, biographies of prophets and holy persons do, they nevertheless belong on a continuum with those life stories. Both provide vivid examples of the conviction that a provident God has sent spiritual models and exemplary leaders in timely fashion throughout history. The posters depict Iran's recent revolution [according to William L. Hanaway Jr.] "as an Iranian and Islamic event, and its context is Iranian history in its sweep from the legendary past to today. It is taking place in a God-centered society in which the rules are divinely given and men are governed by a regent of God."

Finally, a type of calendar art popular especially in south Asia recalls the exemplary role of prophets and Friends of God in two ways. Some actually depict the holy persons, either individually or in groups—sometimes gathering in a single image personalities from far-separated times and places. Others suggest the ongoing presence of these paradigmatic figures indirectly by showing pictures of the holy sites associated with them.

Illustrated Books

The media and forms change at a different level of artistic production and patronage, but there is a great deal of functional continuity. In this category one encounters a wide range of illustrated manuscripts, objects that are both expensive to produce and of limited availability. Many . . . have inspired patrons and painters to create marvelous visual accompaniment, but the purpose of the images is not always easy to determine. One aspect of their function is fairly clear from the outset. Images in expensive books enhance and beautify the written text; they are not substitutes for it. Pictures produced in glass or on murals, or even to a great extent as poster art, do not presuppose a written text at all. They speak for themselves through symbolism or recall a whole story with a set of powerful associations or illustrate a dramatic performance. Although the theme of an image may be obviously religious, its function is not necessarily sacred. Furthermore, an important difference exists between the function of devotion and that of inspiration and edification. The life story of Muhammad and other works dedicated entirely to the stories of exemplary figures may be illustrated; however, mirrors for princes are illustrated very rarely, if ever.

One of the most extraordinary illustrated manuscripts produced anywhere by a Muslim is the sixteenth-century Turkish *Life of the Prophet* (*Si-yar-i nabi*). The six-volume version of the fourteenth-century text includes over eight hundred illustrations, most of which depict a veiled Muhammad entirely surrounded in a flaming nimbus.[3] Its story begins with the signs and portents attending the announcement and expectation of Muhammad's birth, and proceeds visually through dozens of events in his life. . . .

One cycle of stories from Muhammad's life has received

---

3. a radiant light that appears about or over the head in the representation of a god, demigod, saint, or sacred person

special attention in an early fifteenth-century manuscript of the *Book of the Ascension* (*Mi'rajnama*), from Herat (in what is now Afghanistan). Approximately four dozen charming miniatures show Muhammad, face unveiled and wearing his emblematic green robe, moving through the various key moments in the experience of Night Journey and Ascension. In Jerusalem he accepts the invitation of the various prophets assembled at the al-Aqsa Mosque to lead them in prayer. As he makes his way through the various strata of heaven, he meets each prophet in his assigned level. He witnesses in amazement such wondrous phenomena as the cosmic rooster, the ultimate arbiter of the timely call to prayer, a creature so huge that its feet protrude beyond the bottom edge of the miniature's frame. The images of the torments of the damned in hell are exceedingly vivid; lovers of European painting may find them reminiscent of works by Hieronymous Bosch.[4] As for the influence of the stories themselves, one scholar has theorized that their imagery is so similar to that of Dante's Divine Comedy that one can hardly resist suggesting that the Islamic material may have fueled the fourteenth-century Italian's imagination.

Many images of religious themes adorn the pages of various versions of the genre of stories of the prophets. Among the frequently depicted figures are Adam, Noah, Abraham, Moses, Joseph, Solomon, and Jonah. Adam usually appears with Eve, either as the two are expelled from the Garden or arranged across the page with their progeny. Noah and the ark are often shown, and I know of no other scene in which Noah appears. Abraham's two most important scenes are his victory over the fire into which the evil king Nimrod threw him, and his preparation to sacrifice his son just as God intervenes by angelic messenger.

Moses plays a number of visual roles, occasionally from the episodes of his encounter with Pharaoh, but more often in peripheral scenes—encountering an infidel, berating a shepherd—whose ancient textual antecedents are difficult to

---

4. fifteenth-century Dutch painter whose religious works are characterized by grotesque, fantastic creatures mingling with human figures

trace. Joseph appears in perhaps more images than any other prophet. Solomon usually sits on his throne, often side by side with Bilqis, the queen of Sheba, but almost always surrounded by the jinn (creatures of smokeless fire) and by members of all the animal kingdoms, whose languages the king speaks. The fabled encounter with a whale provides virtually the only visual setting for Jonah. The Arabian prophet Salih, extruding a camel miraculously from a mountain, occasionally appears; David makes chain mail as his ravishing song (the Psalms) renders the iron soft to his touch; and Jesus is depicted as a child with Mary, or raising Lazarus.

A pattern has begun to emerge. What begins in oral form (Qur'an and Hadith, forms of prayer, stories) is soon written down for the sake of accuracy and preservation. Then over a period of perhaps centuries, a layer of commentary on the written sources (tafsir,[5] manuals of prayer and ritual, elite literature on heroic figures) appears in order to reinterpret the tradition for changing circumstances. As the written commentary becomes more elaborate and less accessible to the average person, parallel forms of oral and visual commentary (popular preaching and the folk arts) continue to make the tradition available to a broader public.

5. explanation, commentary

Chapter 4

The Spread of Factions Within Islam

Turning|Points

IN WORLD HISTORY

The Historical Development of Islamic Sects

Edward Mortimer

Edward Mortimer argues that movements to restore the true doctrine of Islam and to overthrow existing political orders are common patterns in Islamic history. Mortimer explains how various sects—the Kharijites, the Shi'a, the Twelvers, the Mu'tazilites, and the Sufis—fit these historical patterns. Edward Mortimer, a journalist, was employed by the Carnegie Endowment for International Peace to research Islamic politics. He is the author of *Faith and Power: The Politics of Islam, The Rise of the French Communist Party*, and *France and the Africans, 1944–1960; a Political History*.

The Koran is full of injunctions to the believers to 'struggle in the way of God'. In the context, of course, the struggle (*jihād*) in question was against unbelievers. But was it not logical to suppose that such a struggle would be equally necessary later against those corrupt Muslims who introduced into the Muslim community those very evils of arrogance, selfishness, injustice, etc., which the Koran had denounced in the pagan society of Muhammad's time?

Not surprisingly, it has seemed so to successive generations of Muslim reformers and malcontents. The history of Islam, especially its first few centuries, is full of movements that sought simultaneously to restore what they saw as the true doctrine of Islam and to overthrow the existing political order. Again, it is unlikely that in their own minds the leaders of these movements made any distinction between these two objectives. Many of these movements gave birth to sects that still exist in some form today; and even those Muslims who do not adhere to such sects are indirectly affected by them, since it was in the course of these early conflicts that the Sunna—the Beaten Path or tradition which the majority of Muslims follow—was defined. . . .

Khārijism and Shi'ism, the two great tendencies that split off from the main body of Islam early in its life, both have their origin in events that occurred within a generation after Muhammad's death, as his successors struggled to cope with the unexpected problems of managing an enormous empire. The third caliph, Uthmān, who succeeded in A.D. 644, came from the Umayya, one of the old ruling families of Mecca. He antagonized many of the soldiers in the conquering Arab armies by appointing his own relatives to provincial governorships and reserving for them a share in the spoils, and also by making the first attempt to impose religious uniformity on the Muslim community: after issuing an authorized version of the Koran he ordered the destruction of all variant copies, thereby imposing his own authority on the provincial preachers. In A.D. 656 a group of mutinous soldiers returned to Medina and killed him. Muhammad's cousin Alī, who had been passed over when Uthman was elected, was then acclaimed as caliph by the Muslims present in Medina. Ali's failure to take action against those responsible for Uthman's murder, some of whom were his own supporters, led to risings against him and the first civil war between Muslims.

The most serious rising was that of the governor of Syria, Mu'āwīya, a relative of Uthman, who refused to acknowledge Ali as caliph and fought an inconclusive battle against him at Siffin (between Syria and Iraq) in A.D. 658. After this Ali agreed to let the dispute be judged by two arbitrators 'according to the Koran'. But this compromise was rejected by a group of Ali's more fanatical supporters, who now turned against him, proclaiming 'there is no judgement but God's'. (The implication was that Uthman's murder had been just punishment for his errors as caliph.)

These people became known as Khārijites, from an Arabic word meaning 'to go out'—implying both secession and rebellion. They were the first distinct sect to appear in Islam. As with almost all subsequent sects, their separation was self-imposed. It was they who proclaimed that all who did not follow them were outlaws and unbelievers. By contrast, the mainstream community of Sunni Muslims (those who follow the Sunna) has always been willing to accept a great diversity of opinions, drawing the line only at those which appear to deny either the oneness of God or the finality of the revelation to Muhammad.

The Kharijites maintained that a grave sinner no longer remains a Muslim, and they therefore proclaimed *jihad* against the rest of the community and particularly its leaders, seeking to bring about political change through violence and assassination—of which Ali himself was an early victim in A.D. 661. They were absolute and uncompromising egalitarians, arguing that all men were equal in the sight of God and equally accountable to Him, and therefore rejecting any notion of privilege, whether for the family of Muhammad, for the Meccan tribe of Quraish from which he sprang, or for the Arabs in general. The only criterion of virtue was of faith. The test of faith was good works, therefore any conspicuous sinner was disqualified. The true believers were instructed by the Koran to 'commend good and forbid evil'. This gave them both the right and the duty to overthrow an unjust caliph, and in his place to choose any one of themselves who was morally and religiously irreproachable, 'even if he were a black slave'. . . .

As far as most Muslims are concerned, the Kharijites put themselves beyond the pale of respectability by their fanaticism and violence against fellow Muslims, and therefore most Muslim movements of today would strongly disclaim any connection with them. Yet in a sense they were the prototype of all subsequent Muslim revival movements, and especially those which are today called 'fundamentalist'.

The Shī'a: The Party of Ali

Kharijite influence on later Islam has been mainly indirect. But the other great sect, the Shī'a, still has numerous adherents in many parts of the Islamic world, and in Iran it is the official religion of the state. From this tradition came the ideology of the Iranian revolution.

At the time of Ali's death in A.D. 661 the *Shī'at Alī*, or party of Ali, was probably no more than that: a party or tendency of people supporting Ali's claim to the caliphate. That claim was based on Ali's closeness to Muhammad as a member of his immediate family—his first cousin, in some sense his adoptive brother, the husband of his favourite daughter Fātima and father of his favourite grandsons. (Muhammad had no surviving sons.) Ali was felt to be a more authentic representative of what Muhammad had stood for than the wealthy and worldly Umayyads. His personal piety and virtue may indeed have compared favourably with theirs; but in the minds of his followers this fact was clearly connected with the close blood relationship between the two men.

After Ali's death the leadership of this school of thought passed naturally to his two sons, Hasan and Husain, who were also Muhammad's grandsons. Although they were not strong enough to prevent Mu'awiya from establishing himself as caliph and so founding the Umayyad dynasty, Ali's descendants became an important focus of opposition to that dynasty. The notion spread that rightful leadership of the Muslim community belonged to Muhammad's family, who enjoyed a special sanctity. Only when the rule of Muhammad's rightful heir was established would the tyranny and injustice of the existing order be replaced by good government in accordance with the Koran and the example (Sunna) of the Prophet. This heir would be the Mahdi, a leader directly guided by God. . . .

The essential belief of the Shi'a is that the historic caliphs were merely *de facto*[1] rulers, while the rightful leadership of Islam passed through a kind of apostolic succession of Imāms,[2] starting with Ali and carrying on down in the male line. The Imam may or may not be in a position to exercise political power, but his spiritual authority is seen as an essential ingredient of Islam. . . . Thus Shi'ism accepts the notion of spiritual

---

1. actually exercising power, but not legally or officially established   2. divinely inspired successors to the Prophet

authority in a sense that Sunni Islam does not, and it makes a distinction, even if it is a *de facto* rather than a *de jure*[3] one, between spiritual and temporal authority. The Christian notion of a church, and of relations between church and state, is therefore more closely paralleled in Shi'ism than elsewhere.

Islam in general sanctifies political action. Sunni Islam is the doctrine of power and achievement. Shi'a Islam is the doctrine of opposition. The starting point of Shi'ism is defeat: the defeat of Ali and his house by the Umayyads. Its primary appeal is therefore to the defeated and the oppressed. That is why it has so often been the rallying cry of the underdogs in the Muslim world. Central to Shi'ism's appeal, especially for the poor and dispossessed, is the theme of suffering and martyrdom—a theme reminiscent at times of Christianity. . . .

The Twelvers: Today's Main Branch of the Shi'a

The main branch of the Shi'a surviving today is known as that of the 'Twelvers' because it traces the line of Imams from Ali down to the twelfth, after which it comes to a stop. The twelfth Imam is believed to be not dead but hidden, and will one day return as Mahdi to purify the world. This is the Shi'ism that has been the official doctrine of the Persian state since the sixteenth century, and is today followed by about 80 per cent of the population of Iran, by the majority of the Arabs in neighbouring Iraq and by substantial minorities in Turkey, India, Pakistan, Lebanon and the Arab Gulf states, including Saudi Arabia.

In all these countries, except Iran, political power has usually been in the hands of Sunnis. That Twelver Shi'ism has survived so successfully under Sunni rule is mainly due to the fact that historically it was the least politically activist, if not non-political, party within the Shi'a. The nine Imams after Husain were people who escaped repression by the caliphs of their time precisely because they did not put themselves forward as claimants to political power, but were content with providing spiritual guidance to their followers. In time, at least

3. according to law; by right

an implicit connection came to be made between the virtue and piety of Ali and his sons and their lack of political success: they were seen as unworldly, even self-effacing men. . . .

According to Twelver doctrine, the Imams did not abandon their claim to leadership of the community. They simply chose not to assert it politically in unfavourable circumstances. Rather than legitimizing the existing government, they authorized their followers to obey it. . . .

The Mu'tazilites, or Neutralists

By no means all the early disputes within Islam resulted in formal schisms or the creation of separate sects. More often rival schools of thought coexisted for a time until one or other of them was condemned by the consensus of the *ulama*[4] and petered out, but even then some of its ideas would usually live on, sometimes synthesized with those of its opponents into a new version of orthodoxy.

Muslim theology as such lies outside the scope of this book. But one or two of the early schools of thought need to be mentioned because their ideas continue to play a part in the struggles of today. Of particular importance in this respect are the Mu'tazilites, or neutralists—so-called probably because they adopted an intermediate position between the Kharijites, who regarded a grave sinner as an outright infidel, and the main body of Muslims who considered him a 'sinner-Muslim'. Their importance lies in the fact that they were the first to attempt a justification of Islam in rational and philosophical terms. This led them to argue that reason was an equal source, with divine revelation, of moral truth. They argued that reason was an aspect of the inherent justice of God, and that God could not, by definition, do that which was unreasonable or unjust. Therefore, God could not be held responsible for human acts: human beings enjoy free will and are responsible for their own actions.

The Mu'tazilites' concept of God was a highly abstract one. They explained away all anthropomorphic[5] descriptions

4. learned elders; the senior religious officials of a Muslim community   5. giving human qualities to a nonhuman being

of Him in the Koran or the Tradition as mere figures of speech. Rejecting the notion that the Koran was the eternal, 'uncreated' Word of God, they insisted that He had created it in a specific time and place, for a specific purpose. These ideas have proved very attractive to Islamic modernists of the nineteenth and twentieth centuries, who have found in them a basis for reconciling Islam with some modern Western ideas, including political liberalism. . . .

The Sufis, or Mystics

Far more important for the future of Islam as a whole was the development of Sufism. The original Sūfīs (probably so called in allusion to their simple woollen garments—*sūf* is the Arabic for wool) were essentially mystics: pious Muslims who believed that through meditation and self-discipline they had attained a direct personal experience of God. There is nothing un-Islamic about this; indeed, Muhammad himself was clearly a mystic in this sense, at least in the early part of his career. But Sufism did provide a kind of corrective to the predominant emphasis of the first century of Islam, which was on the expansion and organization of the Muslim community rather than the spiritual development of the individual soul, and on the omnipotence and transcendence of God rather than His immanence and accessibility to direct human knowledge.

As time went on, Sufism itself became gradually institutionalized. Individual mystics attracted groups of followers who learned to imitate their 'path' (*tarīqa*)—a series of mental and sometimes physical exercises leading up to communion with God. In time the word *tariqa* came to mean a group of people following a particular Sufi *shaikh* (old man, teacher), and these groups took on a quasi-monastic organization—sometimes actually living together in a monastery, sometimes travelling, preaching and teaching, rather like the friars of medieval Europe. Thus, one can speak of Sufi 'orders' or 'brotherhoods' (*turuq*), some of which have existed from the twelfth or thirteenth century A.D. until the present day (usually undergoing many changes and revivals) and can be found in many different countries.

The Sufi preachers developed an approach to Islam based on personal piety, which was often easier for simple people to accept than the somewhat arid, scholastic and legalistic approach of the *ulama*. Through Sufism, Islam was able to absorb many religious beliefs and practices that were non-Islamic in origin but deeply rooted in the culture of the peoples who were converted to Islam. Islam thus adapted itself to widely differing cultures, and after the first generation of Arab military conquest the Sufis became its most effective missionaries. Sufi leaders came to be venerated as local saints and credited with miracles, especially after their deaths, when their tombs often became centres of pilgrimage. They also emerged, at various times and places, as champions of the masses against a corrupt or aristocratic establishment with which the *ulama* had become too closely associated.

Many of the early Sufis were strongly influenced by Shi'ite ideas, at a time when the Shi'a was still more a school of thought than a clearly distinct sect. One such idea, which was to be of great political importance, was that of the Mahdi, the divinely guided leader who would appear at the end of time and restore the supremacy of justice and Islam over ungodly forces. This idea never became a formal doctrine for Sunni Muslims, as it did for the Twelver Shi'ites, but thanks to the Sufi preachers it gained a strong hold on the imagination of many ordinary Muslims who considered themselves orthodox Sunnis, and though not positively endorsed, neither is it condemned by the consensus of Sunni *ulama*.

The *ulama* in general have been suspicious of various aspects of Sufism—essentially those which seemed to encourage superstition—but have been astute enough to try and exercise some control over it rather than condemn it outright. . . .

Properly understood, therefore, Sufism was not a challenge to the Shari'a,[6] but a way of strengthening and deepening one's allegiance to it. The main flock of Sufis thus passed within the fold of Sunni orthodoxy, though there continued to be lost sheep from time to time.

---

6. the code of laws and rules governing the life and behavior of Muslims

Common Themes and Divergent Interpretations Among Muslims

John Obert Voll

John Obert Voll first describes elements of belief common to all Muslims and then explains the diverse interpretations that have developed within Islam since the original unity under Muhammad. Voll identifies the diversity within the major faction, the Sunnis; the alternative vision of the Shi'ites; and the practices and values of the masses of Islamic peasants and workers. According to Voll, all factions demonstrate a variety of styles of adherence to Muslim beliefs. John Obert Voll has taught history at the University of New Hampshire. In 1991 he received the Presidential Medal from President Hosni Mubarak of Egypt in recognition of his scholarship on Islam. He is the author of the *Historical Dictionary of the Sudan* and the coauthor of *The Contemporary Islamic Revival*.

Islam is a distinctively identifiable part of world history, but it is not monolithic. While the most visible aspect of the Islamic dimension is the experience of the Sunni-dominated community, as articulated by the political and cultural elites, it is not the totality of the experience of Muslims. Within the broad framework of the shared basic Islamic message, there is a luxuriant diversity. Part of the dynamism of the Islamic experience has been the continuous interaction between common themes and diverse interpretations and applications of those themes.

Excerpts from *Islam: Continuity and Change in the Modern World*, by John Obert Voll. Copyright ©1994 by Syracuse University Press. Reprinted by permission of the author and publisher.

Common Themes

All Muslims, regardless of their particular interpretations, accept certain common elements of faith. The first of these is symbolized in the acceptance of the statement that "there is no god but the one God." However it may be defined, Islam means submission to the divine, and that principle is expressed in a clear monotheism.

The full statement of Islamic belief that is accepted by all Muslims adds the affirmation, "and Muhammad is the messenger of the one God." This addition has two important corollaries. It means that God's revelation through Muhammad is the real word of God and that Muhammad is in some ways a significant person in the history of the world. . . .

The experience of the Quran [Koran] surrounds Muslims in a variety of ways. Its recitation is a common sound in the Islamic world; it is visually present in the decoration of buildings; and its phrases are a part of the long literary tradition. Indeed, its very syntax and grammar are the basis for linguistic study and usage. The Quran overrides sectarian and geographic divergences and is a vital element in the continuity of Islamic history.

The second corollary involves the definition of Muhammad's role. The revelation is in the word, not specifically in the person of the Prophet. The tone is set in the Quran by the statement: "And what is Muhammad, except simply a messenger? Before him there have been other messengers who have passed away." [Koran 5.144] The role of the messenger is, however, crucial when the message is from God. As a modern Arab writer notes, "recourse to testimony is one, if not the only, foundation of the Muslim religion; for the word of God is transmitted by a witness, the veracious Prophet."[1] Without a full acceptance of the integrity of Muhammad, the validity of the Quran would be suspect. . . .

Another common theme is the idea of unity (*tawhid*), which, on the most general level, is the principle of the unitary nature or oneness of God. In specific terms, there may be disagreement over the implications of *tawhid*, but Mus-

1. from Abdallah Laroui, *The Crisis of the Arab Intellectual*, trans. Diarmid Cammell

lims across a full spectrum of views see the principle as a key one in terms of human life. A modern Shi'i philosopher states, "To the Muslim, the idea of unity does not just mean the assertion that there is only one God sitting in heaven instead of two or three. . . . On the social plane Unity expresses itself in the integration of human society."[2] Similarly, a major Sunni fundamentalist thinker says that "*Tawhid* is that which gives Islamic civilization its identity, which binds all its constituents together and thus makes of them an integral, organic body which we call civilization."[3]

These common themes emphasize the moral and ethical dimensions of the revelation. Muslims are to build and work in a moral, divinely guided community, and the *ummah* (the Islamic "community") is an important focus of Muslim identity and loyalty. Although there are disagreements over specific aspects of the nature of the community, the moral dimension of Islam and the critical importance of the community of believers are common themes within the Islamic tradition.

The oneness of God, the Quran, the significance of Muhammad, and the community are basic elements in the continuity and unity of the Islamic dimension. Different perceptions of these elements and diverse historical experiences create varying manifestations of Islam. However, this diversity is more often expressed in local variations and overlapping interpretations than in formal schisms and sectarian distinctions.

Diversity Within the Sunni Tradition

The ideals and organizations of the majority of Muslims fit within the broad patterns of Sunni Islam. However, within these boundaries there is great scope for diversity of approach and emphasis. Even on the basic question of the meaning of the oneness of God, differing aspects of the divine are emphasized by different Sunni groups. Two poles of the interpretive spectrum are emphasis on the immanence[4] of God and emphasis on God's transcendence.[5] Although no

2. from Seyyed Hossein Nasr, *Ideals and Realities of Islam* 3. from Isma'il Raji al Faruqi, *Tawid: Its Implications for Thought and Life* 4. the belief that God lies within the world and the individual 5. the belief that God is supreme and lies beyond perception beyond the world and the individual

Muslim loses all sense of either aspect of God, there is a tendency to focus on one or the other. . . .

The life of Muhammad has received great attention in the Sunni tradition. Major efforts to collect the Traditions of the Prophet culminated in the ninth century when six great collections of *hadith*s were compiled and came to be accepted as the standard body of the Traditions. However, these collections are not canonical[6] and their authority comes from a flexible consensus in the community rather than an official institutional validation.

The information provided by the records of the early community is the basis for the Sunni definition of the just society. The early community is accepted by Sunni Muslims as being a special example of the way the *ummah* should be, and later Sunni revivalists have modeled their actions on those of the *salaf* ("pious ancestors"). This community provides a relatively concrete basis for the ideal even though great diversity in interpreting the experience is possible.

Sunni Muslims are in full agreement that the message of unity provides the foundation for social integration and that this means that the legal basis for society is Islam. However, as the Islamic legal system evolved, a number of accepted schools emerged rather than one single, authoritative statement of the law. By the time of the rule by sultans [in medieval times], four Sunni schools of law (*madhhab*s) had come to be accepted as equally authoritative, despite the disagreements among them. These schools are not separate "sects" or "denominations," but, rather, emphasize different moods and techniques of law and interpretation. . . .

The Importance of the Ruler in Shi'ism

The major division within Islam is between the Sunnis and the Shi'ites. At the heart of the split is disagreement over the nature of the *ummah* and the full meaning of the revelation. The Sunni majority tradition has the authority of being confirmed by the historical experience of the community, while the Shi'i Islamic tradition has often been at odds with the ac-

6. established by an official religious council

tual historical experience. The Shiʻi tradition developed as an alternative vision and, in the days of the caliphs, presented a basis for opposition to the emerging Sunni political and social establishments. When Abbasid unity crumbled in the tenth century, successful Shiʻi movements built the large Fatimid empire in Egypt and north Africa and a number of smaller states. However, the firm establishment of the sul-

Shiʻa Views of Christians and Jews

Alfred Guillaume explains the differing interpretations of Muslim law banning Jews and Christians from mosques. In Baghdad, Guillaume was warned not to enter the city's major mosque; in Jerusalem, less strict friends gave him a tour through their entire mosque.

We need not pause to look at the minor differences between Shīʻī and Sunnī law, though one matter on which they differ is of some importance to Western travellers in the east. The Shīʻīs take a much stricter view of ritual purity, so that to them all Christians and Jews come into the category of the unclean. Where this principle is rigidly adhered to Christians are not allowed to enter Shīʻī mosques. I was politely warned not to try to enter the Kazimayn mosque in Baghdad; and though it might have been possible to gain admission in the company of Shīʻīs of my acquaintance I decided against making the attempt against the prevailing hostility towards Christians. I could not but contrast this prejudice unfavourably with the kindness I received from friends in Jerusalem who devoted some hours to showing me everything in their beautiful mosque, and that too on the feast of Nabī Mūsā when the mosque was reserved for the worship of believers. To the strict Shīʻī the 'people of the scriptures' [Christians and Jews] are unclean, and they will not eat or drink from vessels they have used; but it is only fair to say that in most places where Europeans reside the prohibition is silently ignored. Still, under the surface the feeling that they are unclean (*najis*) persists.

Alfred Guillaume, *Islam*. London: Cassell, 1963.

tanate system was accompanied by a reassertion of Sunni dominance in most of the Islamic world.

In the framework of the great common themes, the Shi'ites tend to emphasize the immanent aspects of the divine, especially in terms of leadership for the community as being centered in the figure of the Imam.[7] In the Shi'ite view, Muhammad *did* designate a successor and that person was Ali. The validity of the succession of the first three caliphs was denied, and the community is believed to have been in error. The importance of a designated successor or Imam was explained in terms of the continuing human need for guidance in understanding and applying the revelation. "The interpretation of the divine revelation by the Imam . . . was regarded as the right guidance needed by the people at all times."[8]

For most Shi'ites, there was a line of twelve Imams who provided this guidance, even though none of the Imams gained significant political power. . . .

The Practices and Contributions of the Masses

The vibrant diversity of Islamic experience is not confined to the realms of the ulama[9] and the political elites. Underlying the visible movements of thought and social structure is the general faith of the masses. The application of the great common themes in daily life is influenced strongly by local customs and traditions. There is a lively interaction in Islamic history between the cosmopolitan literate tradition and the "popular religion" of the masses. "Popular Islam" is often defined in negative terms as Islamic experience that has been "diluted" by non-Islamic practices. Traditionally strict ulama as well as modern intellectuals tend to condemn what they see as magical practices and superstitions.

One dimension of popular faith is the role of specially respected local holy men. In all of the areas which became part of the Islamic world, there were customs built around the

7. in Shi'ite Islam, the title of the rightful, divinely guided ruler, believed to follow a line through Muhammad's son-in-law Ali   8. from Abdul aziz A. Sachedina, *The Just Ruler in Shi'ite Islam*   9. learned elders; the senior religious officials of a Muslim community

local religious leader, and the functions performed by those leaders were taken over by Muslim guides as the communities converted to Islam. Just as there are distinctive differences between the shamans[10] of central Asia and the village spiritual leaders in Africa, local Muslim leadership also presents a picture of diversity. In general terms these figures came to be explained in Islamic terms as *wali*s, or individuals who are especially close to God. . . .

A second major theme in popular religion is continuing messianic expectations. Although the achievements of the Islamic community have been great, life for the average peasant, worker, or nomad continues to be difficult. The revelation is seen by them as a promise for a better future, a world of justice without oppression. Islam was and is a vehicle for the expression of these hopes. It is widely accepted that at the end of the current age, God will send a rightly guided leader, the Mahdi, "who will fill the world with justice, as it had been filled with injustice.". . .

The more, too, the Muslim masses have felt themselves oppressed . . . the more fervent has been their longing for this ultimate restorer of the true Islam and the conqueror of the whole world for Islam. . . .

Popular Islam presents further elements of diversity within the Islamic community. The faith of the masses has been shaped by the broad, common themes of Islam and they have looked to the great leaders of the faith as well as their local leaders for guidance. At the same time, the vigor of popular faith has helped to maintain an awareness of the problems of daily life and the special visions of hope shaped by the expectations of the masses have influenced the thinking and practices of the intellectual and political elites.

Four Styles of Action

In this complex array of great themes, elements of diversity, and different moods and approaches, it is helpful to look for common patterns or styles of approach and action among

10. in tribal society, a member who mediates between the visible world and the spirit world and who practices magic for healing

Muslims. . . . In the experiences of coping with change and maintaining continuity, it is possible to define four styles of action. . . .

The first of these styles is the adaptationist, which represents a willingness to make adjustments to changing conditions in a pragmatic manner. This style is visible in the political realism of the early caliphs and sultans and is manifested in the intellectual traditions of those thinkers who adapted Greek philosophical traditions in explaining Islamic positions. The religious openness of Akbar in Moghul India and the flexibility of popular Sufi teachers are other examples of this style. . . .

The success of Islam brought achievements that are worth preserving, which is the motivation behind the second style, the conservative. As a great synthesis emerged, much of the learned community hoped to preserve the gains that had been made. From the very beginning, the perfection of the revelation has been seen by Muslims as requiring a reserved attitude about change that is too rapid. In this style, a mistrust of innovation tends to be the keynote. The efforts of the conservatives have served the Islamic community well in times of turmoil, and they have helped to keep the compromises of the adaptationists within the bounds of what has become accepted as Islamic. . . .

The third style is the fundamentalist. The scriptures of religions that accept the concept of recording divine revelations provide a basis for a permanent standard to use in judging existing conditions. In Islam, the Quran is this unchangeable standard, and the fundamentals of the faith as presented in the Quran have a universally accepted validity within the Islamic community. The fundamentalist style insists upon a rigorous adherence to the specific and general rules of the faith and presents a critique of existing conditions by calling for a return to the fundamentals of the faith. When additional elements are accepted as authoritative, they may also be included among the fundamentals. Thus, within Sunni Islam, the Sunnah [way or path] of the Prophet, as defined by the *hadith* literature, is also used as a basis for evaluating Muslim practices, as are the collections of the traditions of Ali and the Imams within Shi'i Islam. The distinction between the fundamentalist and conservative styles is important. Fundamentalists are unwilling to accept adaptations and are more often critics than defenders of existing conditions. They frequently are political activists, and they often are disturbing elements who upset social stability and oppose the conservative establishments of Muslim society. The fundamentalist style serves as a corrective adjustment mechanism. In the context of change and adaptation, fundamentalists work to keep the basic Islamic message in full view of the community. When adjustments to local conditions or the adoption of new ideas and techniques threaten to obliterate the unique and authentically Islamic elements, fundamentalist pressure begins to build. In one sense, the mission of Islamic fundamentalism is to keep adjustments to change within the range of those options that are clearly Islamic.

The fourth style places emphasis on the more personal and individual aspects of Islam. Although all Muslims recognize the communal implications of the revelation, there is a style which tends to subordinate legal structures and communal institutions to the personal aspects of piety and leadership by charismatic, divinely guided individuals. The Shi'i concept of the Imamate and the popular belief in the Mahdi are broad political manifestations of this style, and it is also visible in the Sufi tradition of personal piety and the importance of the local spiritual guide. This style of action permeates the whole Islamic experience, and in a general sense, the resistance of the Islamic tradition to the creation of a formal church structure and an ordained clergy is a product of this individualized spirit.

These styles are not formal, separate movements within the Islamic community but represent orientations for action within the broader Islamic experience as a whole. In any specific group or individual, the styles are combined with varying degrees of emphasis. The identification of these styles is for the purpose of providing an analytical framework for understanding the complex dynamics of the Islamic experience.

Islamic Mysticism and the Sufi Sect

Alfred Guillaume

Alfred Guillaume argues that the Koran contains verses identifying a mystical dimension in Islam that forms the basis for the Sufi sect. Guillaume explains the role of the Sufi masters, the *shaykhs*, who attract a large number of devoted followers or initiates, called the *darwishes*, or dervishes. Dervishes practice special exercises and methods to achieve a state of divine ecstasy. Alfred Guillaume has researched the history and traditions of Islam and translated Arabic texts into English, including the standard biography of the Prophet, *The Life of Muhammad*. He is the author of *The Traditions of Islam*.

In the Qurān, despite its preoccupation with battles, spoils, and women, and the heavenly orchard with large-eyed houris[1] and handsome boys, there is a strong note of other-worldliness and, to a lesser degree, of mysticism. The beautiful 'throne verse' [is here] cited

> [Allah: There is no God but He, the living, the ever-existent One. Neither slumber nor sleep taketh Him. His is what the heaven and earth contain. Who can intercede with Him save by His permission? He knows what is before and behind men. They can grasp only that part of His knowledge which He wills. His throne is as wide as heaven and earth and the preservation of them wearies Him not, and He is the Exalted, the Immense.]

1. voluptuous, alluring women; beautiful virgins of the Koranic paradise

and there are two other texts which have inspired Muslim mystics on countless occasions, namely, 'We are nearer to him [i.e., man] than the vein of his neck' and 'Wherever ye turn there is the face of God.' In the hearts of men longing for a deep and intimate knowledge of God, discussions of anthropomorphism[2] and pantheism[3] found no place. They concentrated on the text, 'A people whom He loveth and who love Him' (5:59). It was this text above all others which appealed to the Sūfīs, who sought to lose themselves in the divine love. Sūfī (from *sūf*, wool) was the nickname given to them by their countrymen because the early ascetics[4] wore a garment of undyed wool like Christian ascetics.

The First Sūfīs

There was a strong note of asceticism among the more serious of the early Muslims, who were disgusted at the widespread luxury and loose living which marked the Caliphates of Damascus and Baghdad. They enjoined austerity and prayer and gave themselves up to a life of contemplation and religious exercise. To what extent they were influenced by factors and forces outside Islam is of no moment. What is certain is that Islam itself with its doctrine, fasting, and litanies (*dhikr*), provided the authoritative background of their lives. These people were the non-militant counterparts of the puritan Khārijites who translated their disgust with worldliness into violent action. Ibrāhīm ibn Adham, prince of Balkh, whose conversion from a life of luxury and ease was brought about by a heavenly voice, is reported to have said of a man who was studying grammar: 'It would be better for him if he studied silence.' There is a simple restraint in the story of this man's call; his endeavour to evade it, his wholehearted response; and finally his life of utter poverty in devotion to God. While the Sūfīs could have such leaders they could not fail to attract the most devout men of their time.

Before the second century had ended the Sūfīs had already worked out a method of attaining the *gnosis* or mystic

2. attribution of human motivation, characteristics, or behavior   3. belief in and worship of all gods   4. those who renounce material comforts and lead a life of austere self-discipline, especially as an act of religious devotion

knowledge of God. Doubtless this method was the result of experience and observation. The Path by which their sects and leaders had ascended to an ecstatic union with God was the one that their followers must pursue. . . .

Sūfī Masters and Their Orders

From early days the Sūfīs recognized the necessity for a spiritual director to whom the novice owed blind obedience. He must no longer exercise his own judgement, but must be completely at the disposal of his *shaykh*[5] or *pir*. Such a state of affairs could be possible only in an organized association, and all over the Muslim world men renowned for their spiritual gifts were surrounded by scores of eager pupils. The members of the organization were known as *faqīrs* or *darwīshes*,[6] poor men or beggars. A solemn rite of initiation awaited a novice, and after that he remained with his *shaykh* until he graduated as a leader. The community was housed in buildings endowed by supporters, and there the dervishes could give themselves up to their life of devotion, meditation, and various physical exercises. From the twelfth century onwards these orders spread all over the Muslim world. There were a large number of different orders held together by a common aim of losing self in God, but vastly different in ritual and in their attitude to Islamic orthodoxy. As in the monastic orders in Christendom there were countless lay brothers who met to practice *dhikr*[7] and afterwards returned to their normal occupations in the outside world.

An extraordinary feature in some of the leaders was their religious indifference; for instance, Ibn 'Arabī could say that his heart was a temple for idols, a Ka'ba for pilgrims, the tablet of the Pentateuch[8] and the Qurān; love alone was his religion. One of his pupils said that the Qurān is polytheism *(shirk)*. The confession of the divine unity lay only in the speech of the Sūfīs. How deeply this thought of the all-embracing unity of the mystical approach to God was rooted

---

5. a term for "maturity" and "wisdom"; a teacher or Sūfī master   6. an initiate in a Muslim mystic brotherhood; in English, dervish   7. a Sūfī term for spiritual exercises that focus the consciousness on God; for example, remembering with the mind or mentioning with the tongue   8. the first five books of the Hebrew Scriptures

among the Sufis can be seen from the lines of one of Avicenna's friends written some two centuries earlier:

So long as mosque and school still stand
The dervish work lies still to hand.
While faith and unfaith stand apart
There is no Muslim true of heart.

It would be impossible to give an account of all the dervish orders, and only a few of the principal fraternities can be mentioned. One of the most attractive of these is the

---

Woman as a Metaphor for Divine Ecstasy

To the Persian Sufi master Rūzbihān, mystical ecstasy can be embodied or symbolized in the beauty of and love for a woman. An account of Rūzbihān recorded by Ibn 'Arabi in 1201 illustrates his idea. The story is told of Shaykh Rūzbihān that he was afflicted with the love of a woman singer; he fell ecstatically in love with her, and he cried much in his state of ecstasy before God, confounding the pilgrims at the Ka'ba during the time he resided there. He circumambulated on the roof terraces of the sanctuary, but his state was sincere. When he was afflicted by the love of this singer, no one knew of it, but his relationship with God was transferred to her. He realized that the people would imagine that his ecstasy was for God in its origin. So he went to the Sufis and took off his cloak, throwing it before them. He told his story to the people, saying, "I do not want to lie about my spiritual state." He then became like a servant to the singer. The woman was told of his state and his ecstasy over her, and she learned that he was one of the great saints of God. The woman became ashamed, and repented before God for the profession she had followed, by the blessing of his sincerity. She became like a servant to him. God removed that relationship with her from his heart, and he returned to the Sufis and put on his cloak. He was not seen to have lied to God about his state.

Carl W. Ernst, *Rūzbihān Baqli: Mysticism and the Rhetoric of Sainthood in Persian Sufism.* Richmond Surry, UK: Curzon, 1996.

Qādiriya, named after 'Abdal-Qādir al-Jīlanī (d. A.D. 1166).
He was a powerful preacher who is said to have converted
many criminals in Baghdad and organized relief for the poor
and needy. His biographers assert that he performed miracles from time to time. A volume of his sermons has been
published. They show a noble, religious, and philanthropic
spirit. In one of them he wishes that the gates of Hell could
be shut, and that the gates of Heaven could be opened to all
mankind. Undoubtedly he had great hypnotic powers, and
an immense number of people flocked to hear him preach. A
ribāt or monastery was built for him outside the city. The
head of the Qādirī order who is in charge of his tomb today
is said to be one of his direct descendants. The Qādirīs have
remained true to the example of their founder in that they
are tolerant, pious, and peace-loving men. They gave birth
to a great many offshoots. The Rifā'īya, founded by Jīlanī's
nephew, is notorious for its fanaticism and those practices
which are associated with dervishes in the popular European
mind, such as fire-walking, eating glass, handling snakes,
and so on.

In North Africa, still a stronghold of Sūfiism, Marabouts
enjoy great prestige. Their holy men are credited with magical powers, and their tombs are venerated and visited by
thousands. In Turkey a series of edicts has greatly reduced
the once enormous multitude of dervishes, and naturally
their influence has declined. In India, as would be suspected,
the dervish orders are permeated with Hindu influences, so
that even the caste system has found place among them.

Rituals and Practices of the Dervishes

Something must now be said about dervish ritual and practice. Among the Naqshabandī order the *shaykh* recites the
declaration of belief in Allah and his prophet while the
novice keeps his attention fixed by placing his heart opposite
that of the *shaykh*. He shuts his eyes and his mouth, pressing
his tongue against the roof of his mouth, and clenches his
teeth and holds his breath. Then with great force he recites
with his heart, but not with his tongue, the words of the
shaykh. He must hold his breath so that within one respira-

tion he can say the *dhikr* three times and so allow his heart to be impressed. Many travellers have described the dances and extravagances of the dervishes. Perhaps the best account is that given by Lane in his *Modern Egyptians:* he describes a great ring of devotees jumping and leaping into the air to the beat of tambourines, dancing wildly with no ordered movement until they are utterly exhausted. Lane saw one of them rush from the dance and put pieces of red-hot charcoal one after another into his mouth, chewing them and finally swallowing them; while another put a live coal into his mouth and inhaled until it was almost white-hot. As he let out his breath sparks flew out of his mouth. Lane says that though he watched them carefully he could not see any indication of pain on their faces. It used to be the practice in Cairo for the *shaykh* of one of the dervish orders to ride over the bodies of a number of followers who threw themselves in his path.

A more recent writer [D.B. Macdonald, *Aspects of Islam*] gives an account of a dervish *dhikr* in Cairo just before the first world war. It took place in a long room with benches on either side. In the middle was a carpeted space with a railing in the form of a horseshoe. The Shaykh took his place at the open end of the horseshoe with his back towards the wall. The dervishes, men who had just come in from the street, stood inside the railing. The *shaykh* knelt sitting back on his heels and repeated the first chapter of the Qurān. Then the devotees recited the confession of faith and other phrases, accompanied by gestures of head and body, with great attention to breathing. Gradually the recitation and movements grew faster, the breathing being so regulated that the utterances of the formula produced a strong emotional effect. The writer noticed that the effect on some was a pleasant hypnosis, and he says that he himself was strongly tempted to join in the movements. There was none of that disorderly outburst of shrieking and leaping which accompanied the celebrations attended by Lane. This writer mentions the regret which a converted Muslim felt at having to abandon these religious exercises. It is interesting to note that this particular man said that as a dervish he had developed unusual telepathic power, so that he knew what was going on at a distance and could even hear words that were spoken there. Claims to such powers are commonplace in Sūfī literature. Certainly stories one has heard from people of unimpeachable veracity confirm the existence of very remarkable powers, whatever the explanation of them may be.

However, these are but by-products of an unselfish mystical search for God which can be found in all religions worthy of the name. To Islam belongs the honour of having the richest and most variegated literature on this sublime subject.

To the question whether personality survives in the ultimate union with God the majority of Sūfīs would say that it does not. Despite the mystical union expressed in terms of love and marriage, the union with the world soul is the utmost imaginable bliss for mankind, and the Sūfī has a positive passion for losing himself in the infinity of the Godhead.

Oh, let me not exist! for non-existence
Proclaims in organ tones, 'To Him we shall return.'

Chapter 5

The Modern-Day Resurgence of Islam

The Modern Fundamentalist Movement

Dilip Hiro

Dilip Hiro defines Islamic fundamentalism as practiced in the Middle East today. He outlines the methods used by leaders to recruit a large following and gives an account of the status of fundamentalist groups in various countries. Dilip Hiro, born in Pakistan, is a journalist whose writings have appeared in the *New York Times*, the *Wall Street Journal*, and the *Washington Post*. He has also been a commentator on Islamic affairs on British and American radio and television. He is the author of *Inside the Middle East* and *Iran Under the Ayatollahs*.

Revival and reform have been recurring phenomena in Islamic history. And they manifest themselves differently in different circumstances.

Closely related to Islamic revival is the movement to return to the fundamental scriptures of the faith: the Quran and the practices of Prophet Muhammad as recorded in the Hadiths, which together form the Sharia, Divine Law. When it comes to applying the Sharia to the everyday life of Muslims, the choice is between taqlid[1]—that is, dependence on or imitation of the opinions and interpretations of the ulama[2] of the past—and ijtihad,[3] independent interpretation. . . .

Irrespective of their sectarian persuasion, fundamentalist reformers have been unanimous that what the Quran offers

1. the action of imitation; following precedents set by earlier thinkers; opposite of *ijtihad*   2. learned men in the Islamic tradition   3. the action of using informed, independent judgment in a legal or theological issue; a person who uses *ijtihad* is called a *mujtahid*

is final, unique and most authentic, and that in Islam there is no room whatsoever for synthesizing the Quranic message with any non-Islamic doctrine or practice.

Thus fundamentalist reform means returning to the Sharia, creative interpretation of the Divine Law in the context of changing circumstances, and rejection of non-Islamic accretions to Islam.

Conflicts That Fueled Fundamentalism

The dynamic of fundamentalism derives from the conflict that exists between the egalitarian message of the Quran and the exploitation and iniquity of the real world, between the demands of virtuous existence made on the believer by the Sharia and the actuality of life surrounded by temptation and vice.

It was their commitment to the Quran and pious living that drove the Shiat Ali, followers of Imam Ali,[4] to struggle against his enemies. In that sense Shias were the first fundamentalists. Later, the rise of the pragmatic, yet despotic, Ummayads[5] was seen by true believers to be an affront to the teachings of Islam, and to bring about their downfall became the prime objective of the fundamentalists. They succeeded.

In subsequent centuries the Islamic community became vast and complex due to the spread of the faith throughout much of Asia, Africa and Europe, the firming up of the Sunni-Shia divide, the codification of the Sharia into four Sunni and one Shia schools, and the emergence of sufism as a prime agent of popularizing Islam. . . . There was creative tension between popular Islam, as represented by sufi brotherhoods, and establishment Islam, as represented by the ulama. . . .

Once Islamic reformers had offered political and other interpretations of the Sharia which took into account contemporary circumstances, it was only a matter of time before the tools of propagation and implementation of ideas employed by them too followed suit.

4. son-in-law of Muhammad   5. caliphs—religious leaders—who moved the capital to Damascus (661–750); they pragmatically blended tradition with local practices

The Muslim Brotherhood

Hassan al Banna, for instance, went beyond pamphleteering and soliciting the support of the élites in Muslim countries, the techniques used by Afghani[6] and Abdu.[7] In tune with the times of mass participation in political movements, he engaged the attention and energies of ordinary Muslims and created in the late 1920s the Muslim Brotherhood, a popular party with a slogan which included the Quran, Prophet Muhammad, God, constitutional government and martyrdom. The timing was right too. The Muslim masses were feeling disheartened and bewildered at the disappearance of the thirteen-century-old caliphate, and the message disseminated by the Muslim Brotherhood gave them succour and hope. It also provided a countervailing force to the tide of secularism sweeping Egypt not only from the West but also from the post-caliphate Turkey of Kemal Ataturk.

But Banna did more than found a mass party. By insisting that every branch of the Brotherhood should have its own mosque, centre, school and club or home industry, he gave flesh to the idea that Islam is all pervasive. By so doing, he also offered an institution which helped its predominantly poor and lower-middle-class membership to overcome the spiritual and social alienation it felt in an environment dominated by secular, westernized classes.

Since then as economic development has accelerated in Islamic countries in the wake of political independence, and latterly a dramatic rise in the price of oil—a mineral found in many Muslim states—cities have attracted vast numbers of migrants from villages. They feel lost and rootless in their new environment. This reservoir of alienated masses packed into the poor quarters of urban centres provides a ready audience and recruiting ground for radical and revolutionary groups, secular and religious.

Muslim fundamentalists try to rally the alienated and underprivileged on the basis of Islam. They present it as a religion of justice and equity and decry the current ruling élite

6. the father of the modern Islamic reformist movement   7. disciple of Afghani; recognized parliamentary democracy, public opinion, and useful, workable practices

as unjust, unIslamic and corrupt which deserves to be over-thrown, or at the very least replaced non-violently, by true believers. The tactics used to achieve this objective vary: from setting up secret cells to addressing large congregations inside a mosque or outside, from bloody confrontations with the security forces to peaceful participation in elections, from carrying out terroristic actions to holding non-violent demonstrations, from subverting official institutions through infiltration to total withdrawal from society, from waging open warfare against an infidel state to conducting intelligent debate with secular adversaries.

As a rule large organizations tend to function openly and small ones clandestinely. One could argue that because certain bodies are not allowed to operate openly they remain small. On the other hand, a popular party such as the Muslim Brotherhood in Egypt had an underground apparatus even when it was permitted to function legally.

But whatever the size and structure of a fundamentalist organization, or the intensity of its commitment to the cause, its ultimate goal remains to install a truly Islamic regime in the country.

One way to accomplish this is by transforming social protest into a revolutionary movement, in stages, using Islamic symbols, language, customs and festivals. This is what happened in Iran, except that there was no Islamic party like the Muslim Brotherhood functioning there—but, more significantly, a general body of Shia ulama with its own independent economic base and widespread network. Another path to the goal of installing an Islamic regime is for a fundamentalist group to assassinate the ruler (like Sadat in Egypt) or capture an important urban centre (such as Hama in Syria) or holy shrine (like the Grand Mosque in Mecca), hoping that the incident will trigger an uprising against the state, enabling the fundamentalist forces to seize power.

But whatever method is used the key element is the loyalty or otherwise of the military. The regimes in Egypt, Syria and Saudi Arabia survived the severe blows struck by radical fundamentalists because they continued to retain the loyalty of the military. Only in Iran was Khomeini able to undermine the morale of the army, gradually, to the extent of making it an ineffective tool for restoring law and order. . . .

Among the case studies presented in this survey, Syria, Iran and Afghanistan fall in the category of a sustained struggle by the fundamentalists to overthrow a secular regime, and Egypt and Saudi Arabia in the category of 'one-off' attempts. . . .

All along, external factors were very much part of the struggle waged by the fundamentalists. They had sanctuaries in Iraq and Jordan, and received aid from Riyadh.[8] The other important external element was Israel. Indeed, what finally settled the issue in Assad's[9] favour was the Israeli invasion of Lebanon in June 1982, which led to the closing of Syrian ranks. . . .

Islamic Iran will argue that God has been bountiful to the Muslims of the area by bestowing the Gulf region with 55 per cent of the known world oil reserves, and that it is the duty of Gulf governments to co-ordinate their plans to exploit this precious resource in order to maximize the benefits to the Muslim masses and use the surplus earned to transform the region into a hub of industry and advanced technology. In other words, Iran would offer plans to its neighbours of an Islamic Common Market along the lines of the European Economic Community. This would be presented as the first stage of a wide plan to draw all Muslim countries into a single economic network and thus transform Islam into a global economic system on a par with capitalism and socialism.

This would strengthen further the hands of Islamists who have always taken for granted the moral and spiritual superiority of Islam over other social systems. One important element that provides evidence for such a notion is that the moral challenge which fundamentalist leaders like Khomeini and Qutb[10] throw at a secular, corrupt or repressive regime flows not from the socio-economic interest of certain segments of society with which they identify but from an unshakeable belief that they are acting out the will of Allah.

8. capital of and largest city in Saudi Arabia   9. king of Syria who survived fundamentalists' assassination attempt   10. an ideologue who proclaimed two categories of social order: Islam and Jahiliya (Ignorance)

Such behaviour defies analysis from a liberal or Marxist perspective, the two powerful analytical tools of the West.

The other conflict which impinges directly on the Islamic world is the Arab-Israeli dispute concerning Palestinian rights. Were the Israelis to return the West Bank and Gaza, and let it be constituted as a Palestinian state—a highly unlikely scenario—the radical leftist and Islamic forces would then press for a struggle to recover the rest of pre-1948 Palestine from the Israelis. Either because of this, or due to the continued refusal of the Israelis to vacate the occupied Palestinian territories, a war between Israel and Arabs could erupt. Defeat by Israel of one or more Arab states would heighten opposition to America and such pro-American regimes as the ones in Saudi Arabia and Egypt.

What happens in Egypt is crucial to the shape of things to come in the heartland of Islam. The overt signs of a rise of fundamentalism are unmistakable: a growing number of women wearing the veil and men growing beards, and a dramatic rise in the number of religious publications. But much depends on the military officer corps. . . .

In the civilian sphere moderate fundamentalists have been slowly but surely infiltrating professional syndicates and administrative organs of the state, thus preparing the ground for the day when Islamist leaders, civil and military, would occupy top official posts, possibly as a result of a peaceful election or probably through a military coup. . . . The rise of affluent Islamic investment companies, functioning on the fringe of the national economy and providing funds to fundamentalist organizations, is an unprecedented phenomenon, signalling the emergence of an independent, self-sustaining economic base for the Islamist forces of Egypt. . . .

One thing is certain. The emergence of a revolutionary fundamentalist Egypt, a strategically situated Sunni country, will shake the Muslim and non-Muslim worlds even more than did the 1979 Iranian revolution.

The Nature and Causes of the Current Islamic Revival

R. Hrair Dekmejian

R. Hrair Dekmejian argues that both Western and Muslim intellectuals failed to recognize the development of the current Islamic revival, and he predicts no moderation of fundamentalist extremism unless conditions change. Dekmejian analyzes the complex social and economic conditions that caused Muslim masses to turn to fundamentalist Islam to restore their lost hope. Though major voices of this revivalist movement differ, they agree on five major points, according to Dekmejian, including the necessary unity of church and state and the vehement rejection of Western cultural values. R. Hrair Dekmejian has taught political science at the University of Southern California in Los Angeles. He is the author of *Islam in Revolution* and many other publications.

The revival of the Islamic ethos is one of the most pervasive and deep-rooted phenomena affecting the Muslim world today. Evidence of a return to Islamic life-styles and to the fundamental precepts of the faith can be seen in virtually all Muslim societies, affecting culture, social relations, economic affairs, and political life. Only after its revolutionary intrusion into the realm of politics and international affairs did the world take notice of the Islamic wave. Beginning with the Iranian revolution in 1979, a succession of dramatic events made the term *Islamic fundamentalism* a part of the West's political, scholarly, and journalistic vocabulary. The

From "Islamic Revival: Catalysts, Categories, and Consequences," by R. Hrair Dekmejian, in *The Politics of Islamic Revivalism: Diversity and Unity*, edited by Shireen T. Hunter. Reprinted with the author's permission.

direct threat to Western interests posed by the militant or revolutionary brand of Islam was instrumental in attracting global attention. After belatedly perceiving some of the destabilizing implications of militant Islam, the Western world has now become obsessed with the subject. Yet this preoccupation has not produced objective prognostication or effective policy.

The Islamic Revival Surprised Westerners and Muslim Intellectuals Alike

The revival of the Islamic zeitgeist[1] had long preceded its violent manifestations in Iran and the Arab countries, although with rare exceptions it had gone unrecognized. . . . Armed with a plethora of materialist and other theories of social causality ranging from liberalism to neo-Marxism and structural functionalism, the Western social scientist was unprepared to consider the potency of religion as a revolutionary force. This conceptual myopia had also blinded the majority of American Middle East specialists who incessantly taught that "Islam is a way of life, not simply a religion," while anticipating its "inevitable" depoliticization and encapsulation in an increasingly secularized context, in keeping with the pattern followed by Western societies. Even more serious was the perceptual impotence of Arab and Muslim intellectuals, many of whom were shocked and surprised by the emerging revivalist phenomenon in their own societies. . . .

Revivalist Attitudes Range from Passive to Extremist

The revival of Islam has taken several forms. At the most general level, it represents a heightening of Islamic consciousness among the masses. This type of popular Islam is represented by the spread of benevolent societies and brotherhoods of Sufis (those who practice Sufism, a mystical interpretation of Islam) and the conspicuous observance of Islamic practices. Despite its pervasiveness and its social and spiritual effervescence, this fundamentalism is usually characterized

---

1. the spirit of the time; the outlook characteristic of a generation

by political passivity, except when there is an instigation from the government or an external hostile source. However, within this generally amorphous revivalist milieu, there are islands of religious activism consisting of militant Islamic groups and societies. These groups display a heightened Islamic political consciousness that is opposed to the state and its ruling elements and institutions. . . . The contemporary revivalist movement should be regarded as a dynamic continuum between passivist spiritualism and militancy.

Specifically, these gradations of revivalist activity are reflected in the Arabic vocabulary used to describe revivalist individuals and groups. Often the proponents of Islamic revivalism refer to themselves as *Islamiyyin*—Islamists—or *asliyyin*—the original or authentic ones. Also used are the terms *mu'min* (pl., *mu'minin*) and *mutadayyin* (pl., *mutadayyinin*)—the pious or devout—in sharp contrast to *muta'sib* (pl., *muta'sibin*)—zealot or fanatic. The word *muta'sib* is often used by nonrevivalists to describe the Islamic militants who are predisposed to the use of violence. A related label is

Table 1. Causes of Islamist Resurgence

Leader/Movement	Cause
'Umar II (d. 720)	Umayyad's moral degeneration
Ibn Hanbal (d. 855)	'Abbasid imposition of Mu'tazila doctrine/state repression
Ibn Hazm (d. 1064)	Umayyad decline and defeat in Spain
Ibn Taymiyya (d. 1328)	'Abbasid demise/Tatar conquest/moral and economic crisis
Ibn 'Abd al-Wahhab (d. 1791)	Ottoman decline/religious-moral crisis
Sanusiyya (1880s)	Religious-tribal crisis/Italian conquest
Mahdiyya (1880s)	Religious-tribal conflict/economic crisis/Anglo-Egyptian-Ottoman rule
Salafiyya (1890s)	European military, cultural and economic imperialism
Muslim Brotherhood (1930s)	Social-economic-political crisis and British imperial presence

mutatarrif (pl., *mutatarrifin*) meaning radical or extremist.
. . . The terms *fundamentalist, revivalist,* and *Islamist* are often used interchangeably in the scholarly literature, although *fundamentalism* has assumed a new connotation in the West, meaning radicalism.

Also instructive are the specific constructs used in Islamic terminology to describe the revivalist phenomenon. Proponents and sympathizers frequently use the expressions *al-ba'th al-Islami* (Islamic renaissance), *al-sahwa al-Islamiyya* (Islamic awakening), *ihya' ad-din* (religious revival), and *al-usuliyya al-Islamiyya* (Islamic fundamentalism). The most appropriate term is *al-usuliyya al-Islamiyya* since it connotes a search for the fundamentals of the faith, the foundations of the Islamic community and polity (*umma*), and the bases of legitimate authority (*shar'iyyat al-hukm*). Such a formulation emphasizes the political dimension of the Islamic movement. In terms of general usage in Islam the concept of *tajdid* refers to the periodic renewal of the faith, while *islah* means restoration or reform. . . .

Islam's History of Crisis and Revival

The recurrent waves of resurgence during periods of acute crisis have been a persistent pattern since the early years of Islam. Throughout its fourteen centuries, Islam has shown a unique capacity to renew and reassert itself against competing ideologies and social forces through its revivalist mode, an inbuilt, self-regenerating social mechanism that is triggered when the moral integrity or physical existence of the umma[2] is under threat. This cyclical dynamic of crisis and resurgence is discernible in various historical epochs.

The conceptualization of the incidence of Islamic revivalism as a response to crisis raises an important theoretical question: What types of social crisis trigger a revivalist response? The usual explanation advanced by Western and Marxist theorists is one that rests on economic determinism: religious revival is seen as mainly the consequence of economic crisis. Despite their considerable theoretical power,

2. the total community of believing Muslims, worldwide

materialistic conceptualizations appear to provide partial explanations for the complex phenomenon of Islamic revival. In examining major historical cases of Islamic crisis and revival, one is confronted with a considerable diversity of causes (Table 1).[3]. . .

Real Crisis Conditions Led to Feelings of Hopelessness

In view of the great social, political, cultural, and economic diversity of the Islamic world, substantial differences exist in the local conditions of the various Muslim countries. Yet the existence of significant cross-national similarities between the crisis conditions prevailing in different Muslim countries permits generalization. . . . These conditions include identity conflict, legitimacy crisis, political conflict, class conflict, culture crisis, and military impotence, which act as the catalysts of Islamic revivalist responses.

The validity of these crisis factors is reinforced by the self-view and world view of many Muslims, particularly the revivalists themselves. The latter's view of the Islamic condition is one of gloom and doom marked by internal degeneration, secularization, socioeconomic injustice, political repression, and military defeat. To a significant degree, these perceptions are the product of the objective conditions existing throughout the Islamic world. In the Sunni context, the breakup of the Ottoman Empire and the abolition of the Caliphate in 1924 by Turkish nationalists under Kemal Ataturk meant the ending of any pretense of Islamic unity and power. One major consequence of Islamic decline was the crisis of individual and collective identity among the Muslims. The task of finding substitute frameworks of identity was to prove difficult since Islam is an all-encompassing social system that includes religion (*din*), state (*dawla*), and law (*shari'a*). In the Middle East, three main indigenous nationalisms arose as substitute identities—Turkish, Iranian, and Arab/Egyptian. . . .

3. from R. Hrair Dekmejian "Fundamentalist Islam: Theories, Typologies, and Trends," *Middle East Review*, 28–33.

Throughout this dialectic[4] of shifting identities, the Islamic countries experimented with a plethora of socioeconomic systems ranging from socialism to capitalism and corporatism under a variety of regimes—monarchies, single-party oligarchies, military autocracies, and constitutional democracies. Despite periods of limited success, these countries' problems have remained unresolved. Ambitious developmental efforts have failed to produce large-scale economic betterment. There have been gross disparities of income distribution in the Muslim countries (Table 2).

Indications are that during the past decade these disparities have substantially increased. For example, in less than a decade, the percentage of Moroccans in absolute poverty has risen from 28 to 45. A similar trend has been observed in Egypt. In these situations, feelings of relative deprivation have generated political instability as the prospects of upward mobility have diminished. Economically, the Muslim countries' dependence on the industrialized countries has deepened.

Lack of socioeconomic justice combined with official corruption and failure of political elites to mold strong identities through socialization has produced a crisis of legitimacy, where the moral bases of authority are in question. The legitimacy crisis is further deepened by the frequent use of coercion against opposition elements and the continued military weakness of the Muslim states against the West, Israel, the Soviet Union, and other antagonists. The continuing Arab military inferiority with respect to Israel has had a debilitating impact on the Muslim psyche. These conditions are exacerbated by oil-wealth-generated consumerism and a crisis of culture resulting from the penetration of Muslim society by imported values and modern life-styles.

Multiple Crisis Conditions Shaped the Nature of this Revivalist Movement

The foregoing conditions of crisis constitute the incubational milieu that shapes the personalities, life-styles, and world view of revivalist Muslims. At the general level, most revival-

---

4. argument that weighs contradictory facts or ideas with a view to resolution

ists possess a strong sense of commitment to Islam and to the observance of its basic obligations. Within this larger revivalist collectivity of popular Islam are the militant groups, consisting of radicals who are acutely alienated from the social and political order, which they seek to destroy as prelude to the establishment of an Islamic polity. These militants often follow a rigid discipline and an austere life-style and express a readiness to sacrifice themselves for their ideals.

Coincidence and Culmination of Dialectics

A question that begs for an answer concerns the timing of the present revivalist surge. Why did revivalism appear during the seventh decade of the twentieth century? . . .

Several attributes of the present crisis set it apart from

Table 2. Income Distribution in Islamic Countries, Mid-1970s

	Income distribution (%)			
	Richest 5% of households	Poorest 20% of households	Poorest 40% of households	% Population in absolute poverty*
Bangladesh	16.7	7.9	20.0	23.0
Pakistan	17.3	8.4	16.5	18.0
Indonesia	33.7	6.6	16.1	61.0
Egypt	21.0	5.2	13.9	9.0
Sudan	20.9	5.1	14.5	40.0
Nigeria	—	—	13.0	43.0
Morocco	20.0	4.0	11.3	28.0
Tunisia	—	—	11.1	14.0
Turkey	28.0	3.5	9.1	19.0
Iraq	35.1	2.1	—	—
Iran	29.7	4.0	11.5	10.0
Malaysia	28.3	3.5	11.1	10.0

*Using official exchange rates.

Source: World Bank, *World Economic and Social Indicators*, July 1978; M.S. Ahluwalia, N.G. Carter, and H.B. Chenery, *Growth and Poverty in Developing Countries*, World Bank, September 1978; and G. Sheehan and M. Hopkins, *Basic Needs Performance: An Analysis of Some International Data*, ILO, January 1978.

earlier periods of crisis. Its most distinctive features are (1) pervasiveness—the crisis condition is not limited to certain countries, but is pervasive throughout the Islamic world; (2) comprehensiveness—the crisis situation is multifaceted, at once social, economic, political, cultural, psychological, and spiritual; and (3) cumulativeness—the crisis situation is cumulative, representing the culmination of unsuccessful efforts in nation-building, socioeconomic development, and military prowess. Indeed, the 1970s marked the end of an era of optimism for Islamic countries, an era in which they sought to achieve modernity by the emulation of Western and socialist models or a mix of their variants. The West's powerful technological and cultural impact had generated aspirations, hopes, and reluctant admiration for its economic and military achievements. By the 1970s these hopes had been dashed as the socioeconomic viability and moral integrity of Western civilization came under attack. Thus, the 1970s became the repository of failed dialectical processes—ideological, developmental, and political—which came together to create a situation of hopelessness and pessimism among Muslims, from which there appeared to be no exit. Hence the return to Islam as the only remaining haven of identity and authenticity. Still another distinctive feature is (4) xenophobism.[5] A sense of xenophobia pervades Muslim society, the feeling that Islam itself is facing a mortal threat. In the opinion of revivalist intellectuals, the very integrity of the Islamic culture and way of life is threatened by non-Islamic forces of secularism and modernity, encouraged by Muslim governments.

The crisis of the 1970s coincided with the end of Islam's fourteenth century. Traditionally, the culmination of a century is marked by popular feelings of expectancy for the arrival of a renewer of the faith and the Islamic community. The 1970s were no exception to this historical pattern, except that the popular sense of expectancy was fueled by the existing milieu of crisis.

---

5. fear or contempt for that which is foreign, especially of strangers or foreign peoples

Common Views Expressed by Revivalist Writers

The protracted crisis of Muslim society has brought to the fore the Islamic alternative. The mass revival of Islam has been accompanied by a withering attack from revivalist writers and preachers calling for radical change along Islamic lines. . . .

The points of view expressed by these writers are quite diverse, yet they are in substantial agreement on certain main tenets, which can be taken to represent the general ideological framework of contemporary Islamic revivalism:

1. *Din wa Dawla.* Islam is a total system of existence, universally applicable to all times and places. The separation of religion (*din*) and state (*dawla*) is inconceivable. Rulership (*hukm*) is inherent in Islam; the Qur'an gives the law, and the state enforces the law.

2. *Qur'an wa Sunna.* The foundations of Islam are the Qur'an and the Sunna—the Traditions of the Prophet Muhammad and of his pious companions. The Muslims are enjoined to return to the early roots of Islam and the puritanical practices of the Prophet's umma in the quest for authenticity and renewal. Unless the Muslims revert to the "correct path" of their pious ancestors, there will be no salvation. While Sunni revivalists revere the four Rightly Guided Caliphs, the Shi'a venerate 'Ali, Fatima, and their descendants.

3. *Puritanism and Social Justice.* The family is the cornerstone of society, where men are placed in a position of leadership and responsibility while women are the source of love and kindness. The mixing of the sexes should be controlled and women decently dressed to maintain dignity and avoid temptation. Western cultural values and mores are vehemently rejected as being alien to Islam. To this end, the mass media are enjoined to propagate Islamic values and practices instead of disseminating foreign cultural influences. The return to the correct path also requires the establishment of socioeconomic justice. All property belongs to society and ultimately to God; man only uses wealth earned through his labor. Islam recognizes the right to private property but limits it in accordance with the general welfare of the community. Wealth accumulated through monopoly, usury, and dis-

honesty is prohibited. The practice of *zakat* (a type of Islamic tax) coupled with state policy will promote social justice and ameliorate class antagonisms. In promoting economic development, Islamic societies should avoid falling into situations of dependency on the advanced industrial countries.

4. *Allah's Sovereignty and Rule under the Shari'a.* The ultimate aim of the Muslims should be the establishment of God's sovereignty on earth. It can only be accomplished by constituting an Islamic order—*nizam al-Islami*—where Allah's law (*Shari'a*) is supreme. The establishment of an Islamic community will guarantee the liberation of man from others and from his own desires. Thus, only through Islam can there be salvation for humanity.

5. *Jihad: The Sixth Pillar.* The good Muslim is enjoined to go beyond observing the Five Pillars or obligations of Islam and to commit himself to a life of action in building the ideal community under the Shari'a. To establish such a community, it is necessary to destroy the existing *jahiliyya*—the pre-Islamic society of ignorance and impiety—and to dispossess worldly rulers of their authority by waging *jihad* (holy war). The resort to jihad should not be "defensive"; it should aim at conquering all obstacles placed in the way of Islam's propagation throughout the world, including states, social systems, and alien traditions against which the *mujahidin* (holy warriors) will employ a "comprehensive" jihad, including violence. Since the obligation of jihad could involve martyrdom, Muslims should be ready to sacrifice themselves, for victory can only come with the mastery of "the art of death." Since the onset of the Islamic order in Iran, Iranian revivalists under Khumaini have shed the passivist tradition in Shiism, which eschews the waging of jihad until the appearance of the *Mahdi* (Messiah); hence the convergence of Shi'a and Sunni doctrines of jihad.

The foregoing five categories contain the basic elements of revivalist ideology on which there has been broad agreement among virtually all radical revivalists of the Islamic world. Beyond these basics, however, significant areas of diversity are discernible in the creeds and programs of the various revivalist societies and movements. These differences spring from these groups' varying interpretations of the Qur'an, the Prophet's Sunna, and early Islamic history. Other factors shaping ideological content include the nature of the crisis situation, peculiarities in social conditions, and the personal imprint of a leader on his society or movement. . . .

At this juncture, the Islamist movement continues to pursue narrowly defined policies that have generated apprehension among secularists, minorities, and many mainstream Muslims. Nor have the fundamentalist groups shown the capacity to project a sense of unity. . . . Today's fundamentalism, however, is still a polycentric movement, consisting of country-centered groups and societies working for the establishment of Islamic polities in their respective national settings. Despite the persistence of state repression, the militant societies and their larger fundamentalist milieu will continue to pose a threat to those in power as long as crisis conditions persist and there are no alternative means of protest and political action to change the status quo.

American Perceptions of Islamic Resurgence

Fred R. von der Mehden

Fred R. von der Mehden argues that Americans are poorly informed about Islam in general and misinformed about the Islamic resurgence in particular. He cites several sources for the misperceptions, including public school textbooks and coverage of Middle Eastern events in newspapers, news magazines, political cartoons, and on television. Mehden maintains, however, that private and governmental organizations have begun to provide Americans with more accurate information about Muslims and Islam. Fred R. von der Mehden has taught political science at Rice University in Houston, Texas. He is the author of *Religion and Modernization in Southeast Asia*.

There can be little doubt that the public's perceptions of Islam have tended to be characterized by ignorance, confusion, and misinformation. Until the national trauma of the Embassy hostage situation in Iran,[1] our knowledge of this religion of over 700 million adherents was weak on Islam's basic tenets, recent history, internal schisms, and regions of dominance. Although informed about the Crusades in school, the average citizen knows little of the Five Pillars, the expansion of Islam to Southeast Asia and Black Africa, differences among sects, and the basic fact that the majority of Muslims live outside the Arab world. Beyond this, Islam and its causes have generally not received a sympa-

1. on November 4, 1979

thetic hearing and have been the subject of considerable criticism. . . .

The fundamental ignorance and, at times, antipathy of Americans regarding Islam needs to be judged in the light of our history. It can be argued that past cultural and racial biases against Third World societies in general has clouded our views of Islam as well as other "foreign" belief systems. Thus, Muslims were just another target of a type of international "Jim Crowism." Some observers, such as Professor E.W. Said, have asserted that Islam has been singled out for abuse, in part due to the historical confrontation between Islam and Christianity. Without rejecting the accuracy of this latter view in terms of historical attitudes of Americans, it would appear that current perceptions of Islam rise out of a combination of ignorance of the religion and negative reactions against the rhetoric and activities of a minority of its adherents. . . .

Islam as Represented in American Public Education

Public education in the United States normally devotes to the non-Christian world a relatively small part of World Civilization courses. What data we have on teaching about Islam show that recent texts used at the high school level can be characterized by brevity and incidents of confusion and bias. One example of such short shrift is A. Mazour and J. Peoples's *Men and Nations: A World History.* In this 878-page text for high school students, fewer than 700 words are given to an explanation of Islam as a religion, and less than five pages are devoted to the religion, its spread, culture, and law. There is no reference to the fact that the Muslim religion is the faith of Islam's largest nation, Indonesia. In a study of twenty such texts, Gerald Perry found that, while they provided basically accurate definitions of the Five Pillars, many were weak on other aspects of the religion, such as the caliphate, *shariah*, and the Sunni-Shia schism. Even regarding the most essential Pillar, there was some confusion expressed about the characterization of Allah. Americans have generally lacked an understanding of the Muslim view of the Supreme Deity or the role of Muhammad and the Judeo-Christian heritage of Islam. In the texts a statement such as

"Allah is the Arabic word meaning God" was exceptional, while comments such as "Muslims worship a God called Allah" reinforced misconceptions that there were fundamental differences in interpretation of the Deity between Christians and Muslims. Regarding the caliphate, one particularly erroneous text, which kept referring to the caliphate in the present tense, asserted that:

> Moslems are also united under the Caliph and other religious leaders. One group of Moslems, who are trained in Islamic law and religion, make up the "Supreme Spiritual Committee of Islam." This group of high officials meets in Cairo.

As well, these books tended to picture Islam as an intolerant religion, lacking in gentleness. Finally, these texts were mixed as to their interpretations of the Arab-Israeli conflict, a factor in American attitudes toward Islam. . . .

Ethnic stereotypes were also present: Arabs were viewed as farmers or nomads, the Turks as cruel, and all dressed strangely, etc. Yet, as one Committee member commented, "The overall impression one gets from these textbooks is not willful bias and prejudice, but rather the lack of thorough knowledge and understanding of the Middle East, its multifaceted civilization, and the forces at work there today.". . .

To this data we can add Michael Suleiman's studies of high school teacher and student reactions in several states. He also finds a paucity of information provided American youth regarding Muslims. While not concentrating on Islam as such, he found that approximately two-fifths of those teaching world history and social studies devoted two weeks or less to the Middle East. As well, 37 percent of one sample of teachers found them skipping the Middle Eastern sections of their courses: always (3%), most of the time (8%), and frequently (28%). In contrast, 67 percent spent six weeks or more on Europe.

Suleiman further noted that in a sample of 520 high school teachers, their students saw Islam as "strange," leading to fear and hostility. "Thus, to some students Muslims are followers of a 'strange religion, peculiar religion, weird,' 'people with a funny religion,' 'stupid religion,' 'infidels.'

Furthermore, Muslims 'dress strangely and practice polygamy.'" He does not provide any percentages of such hostile opinions. Nor does he quantify the "frequent" remarks among teachers praising Islam for its contribution to science, the arts, and architecture. Teachers tended to be more favorably disposed than students toward Muslims. . . . We thus find that Americans start with a weak foundation in their knowledge of Islam. . . .

Events in the Middle East Influence American Attitudes

Issues not central to an understanding of Islam as a religion have helped to determine overall attitudes. It is hypothesized that Islam itself has not been the issue, but such factors as the Arab-Israeli conflict, the oil crisis, and Iran's Islamic Revolution have influenced our view of Islam. It is further argued that the media have reinforced these views.

The Arab-Israeli conflict has made objective assessments of Islam and its adherents difficult, in part because, as [respected journalist] James Reston once explained, "You may put it down as a matter of fact that any criticism of Israel will be met with the cry of anti-Semiticism." From the beginning of the formation of Israel, American opinion has displayed greater sympathy for its cause than for that of its Arab opponents, with only a small percentage showing pro-Arab attitudes. . . .

The activities of some Arab states have frequently not helped matters. Against the Israeli sensitivity to the media has more often been a seeming Arab unwillingness to open satisfactory communications with the West. . . . Some Arab groups turned to strong language, anomic[2] disturbances, and threats. Again, these reinforced views of what Muslims are like. . . .

We must note that a key element in the American stereotype of the Muslim relates to Middle Eastern events. To all too many, Arab equals Muslim, and vice versa, and OPEC (Organization of Petroleum Exporting Countries) equals Arabs and vice versa. The public does not perceive the difference between AOPEC[3] and OPEC, and the existence of

2. socially destabilizing   3. Arab Organization of Petroleum Exporting Countries

often hardline non-Arab members of the latter, such as Nigeria or Venezuela, goes by with little notice. The use of rich oil sheiks in political cartoons to exemplify OPEC readily gives credence to the general stereotype. Threats by Muslim states to use the boycott in the Arab-Israeli conflict, and the paramount role of the often traditionally dressed Wahhabi Saudis in oil negotiations, all lend further evidence to support these perceptions. And, as we shall see, that particular stereotype has not been attractive. At the same time, it would be incorrect to give too much emphasis to the energy issue. . . .

The Islamic Revolution in Iran has been a two-edged sword in the battle to increase American understanding of Islam. There is no question that the number of newspaper and magazine articles, editorials, and television spots covering Muslim-oriented subjects has increased tremendously since its inception. Even academics have been called upon by government, business, social organizations, television, and newspapers to clarify the situation. A perusal of the *Reader's Guide* to popular periodicals displayed an astounding growth in articles related to Islam and its adherents. During the year from March 1976 to February 1977, there were only half a dozen pieces on various Islamic subjects, while in the first six months after the taking of the American hostages, there were more than fifty. There were similar increases in articles on Islam in newspapers, and general media coverage grew dramatically. Without the hostage issue and what preceded it, Americans would probably have remained even more ignorant of differences between Shiites and Sunnis, as well as the rising Islamic "fundamentalist" revival. However, along with explanations of the meaning of Islam there came other articles less illuminating, such as those entitled "Khomeini's Contagion," "Portrait of an Ascetic Despot," and "A Regime of Fanatics."

This reaction to the perceived excesses of the Iranian Revolution is the negative side to the problem. Americans became extremely antagonistic toward the Iranians due to the hostage issue. A survey in March 1980 showed that on a +5 to −5 scale, 90 percent of the sample rated Iran from a −1 to –5, and 69 percent –4 and –5. No other country reached that low. Polls in the months immediately after the capture of the hostages found a large majority of the public supporting punishment of the Iranians in one form or another. Chanting in the streets by demonstrators declaring, "Kill the American dogs," and attacks on the U.S. Embassy in Pakistan and on American facilities elsewhere after the fighting in Mecca tended to color the public's view of Islam as a whole. Nor did the statements of Ayatullah Khomeini[4] aid friendly relations. The comments by historian Kemal Karpat that "Khomeini has done more to harm the Islamic image in one month than all the propaganda of the past 15 years" may be too strong, but to many Americans Khomeini came to symbolize fanaticism and atavism in Islam. . . .

While newspaper editorials following the hostage-taking and later attacks on U.S. posts were generally careful not to blame Islam as a whole, many of them added to the confusion about the role of the religion. The picture of Islam as intolerant, extremist, and reactionary was fostered in some editorials. Thus, the *Miami Herald* referred to "a maddened clique of Islamic clergy that draws its power from the frenzy of murderous slogans"; threats to try the Shah and Embassy hostages brought out statements of "so-called Islamic justice"; and the attacks on other American facilities often condemned "Moslem mobs" rather than the nationalism of the offenders. In sum, the Iranian Revolution and particularly the hostage issue, when combined with the rhetoric of Iranian Muslim leaders, imprinted upon the American mind a picture of excess, intolerance, and fanaticism which may be difficult to erase. . . .

The Role of Newspapers and Magazines

Assessing the role of the media on any issue that encompasses the Middle East immediately raises the dangers of paranoia. Let it be stated at the outset that I do not see a major Zionist conspiracy which controls our media, although I recognize full well the efforts of pro-Israeli inter-

4. the radical clergyman who led the 1979 Iranian revolution against the shah

ests to influence what Americans see and read. This does not mean, however, that there has not been an historic bias in favor of Israel and an unattractive stereotypic view of the Arab Muslim. . . . Against this background we find considerable evidence that the American media have not been entirely even-handed and have not expanded the public's knowledge greatly past the aforementioned school textbooks. Perhaps more recently newspapers are not as biased as some would believe, as seen in Robert Trice's analysis of editorials in our elite press (*New York Times, Washington Post, Chicago Tribune, Los Angeles Times, Denver Post, Atlanta Constitution, Christian Science Monitor, St. Louis Post-Dispatch, Wall Street Journal, Louisville Courier-Journal, Dallas Morning News*). In viewing editorials from 1966 to 1974, he found that both support and criticism of Israel and the Arab states were weaker than expected, and that Israel was constantly criticized over retaliatory raids and the annexation of Jerusalem. However, the Arab cause was never able to get much sympathy from the American press; only the *Christian Science Monitor* showed an overall positive view of the Arabs, and only the *Monitor* and *Post-Dispatch* had an overall negative assessment of Israel. . . .

However, another part of the editorial page—the political cartoon—has not aided American-Islamic understanding. While the Ayatullah may have been *Time*'s "Man of the Year," he has become the cartoonist's breadwinner. In pinpointing the oil issue, the symbol of the despised OPEC is invariably the caricature of a greedy, sinister Arab, perhaps with a minaret[5] in the background. PLO[6] members are broadly characterized as knife- and gun-wielding fanatics in many of the cartoons. Two ameliorating factors should be noted: these negative pictures do not attack Islam as such; and all political cartoonists are not biased on this matter. Again, the *Christian Science Monitor* stands out for its long-term fairness, and there has been a general move toward greater understanding, except in the case of the Iranian issue. In sum, while press stories have become more even-

---

5. the tall slender tower on a mosque   6. Palestine Liberation Organization

handed (particularly with the opening of Arab states to American reporters), and editorials less pro-Israeli, stereotypes are maintained through cartoonists and some of the perceived excesses of extremists.

The Role of Television

Insofar as the rest of the media is concerned, the April/May 1980 copy of the *Link*[7] provides an interesting, if committed, analysis of the stereotypic view of the Arab on American television. After strong comments by liberal journalist Nicholas Von Hoffman ("no religious, national, or cultural group . . . has been so massively and consistently vilified") and by Jonathan Raban ("Arab is a word that people learn to hate when they hear it on television"), author Jack Shaheen provides examples of stereotyping. He notes the tendency to picture the Arab at different times as extremely wealthy, cruel, stupid, oriented toward the use of terror, and generally unattractive. The stereotypic pattern which categorizes whole peoples has thus put the Arab and his religion in the role of villain. Regrettably, Erik Barnouw is probably correct when he states:

> Viewers feel that they understand, from television alone, what is going on in the world. They unconsciously look to it for guidance as to what is important, good, and desirable, and what is not. It has tended to displace or overwhelm other influences such as newspapers, school, church, grandma, and grandpa. It has become the definer and transmitter of society's values.

If this is true, we need to consider carefully Shaheen's argument in another piece that asserts, "A negative, unjustifiable, and erroneous image of the Arab and his life style is offered to American viewers on a continuing basis."

American television news has been particularly vulnerable to accusations of unbalanced reporting on matters dealing with Arabs and Israelis. In part the situation has been due to easier access to news sources in Israel, where direct satellite coverage is available. . . .

7. in "The Arab Stereotype on Television," by J. Shaheen

NBC's Steve Mallory asserted that the U.S. viewer is less interested in news about people with darker skins and "Arabs are the people you see wearing kaffiyehs[8] and riding camels, right? And those aren't your neighbors in California or Kansas." To the extent that these charges are true, they buttress the points made earlier regarding perceptions of Islam influenced by the Israeli issue and attitudes toward the Third World in general. . . .

American Perceptions of Islamic Resurgence

Against this background of general ignorance and preformed ideas, it is not surprising that the American public finds it difficult to understand the current Islamic resurgence that has manifested itself throughout the Muslim world. . . . We can see several elements come into the public perception of the resurgence:

1. To understand the American reaction to Islamic resurgence, it is necessary to recognize the images that have influenced its collective mind. Those who have appeared in the media professing one form or another of "Islamic resurgence" include many who are identified in unfavorable terms. Among them are Ayatullah Khomeini himself who has referred to Americans as "devils" and held their people hostage; Libya's Colonel Qaddafi, charged with assassination attempts on his opponents; those responsible for attacks on Mecca and U.S. facilities in Asia; those leading demonstrations against this country in Iran; and the alleged assassins of Anwar Sadat.[9]

2. There is little knowledge of the resurgence outside of Iran and perhaps Pakistan, although there is a vague understanding that it is taking place elsewhere. Certainly, the movement in Indonesia and Malaysia is totally unknown outside the academic and corporate communities. The preempting of the movement by Iran insofar as the media are concerned means that the Ayatullah Khomeini and militants tend to define the resurgence for the American people.

3. Comments by Khomeini and the rhetoric of his fol-

8. a cloth headdress fastened by a band around the crown   9. president of Egypt

lowers have led Americans to view the resurgence as fanatical or extremist, missing other elements in the movement.

4. There is a tendency to believe that the Islamic revival is reactionary in its entirety. Pictures of women in traditional dress, rhetoric attacking foreign investment and Western culture, and demands to cleanse elements of modern morality, all provide a picture that dominates the media. Americans are generally unaware of the complex mosaic of beliefs in the movement; particularly misunderstood is the desire of many "fundamentalists" to modernize within a religious context acceptable to the indigenous culture and not to launch a modern Islamicized Luddite[10] movement.

To conclude, this article has attempted to show that the average American's views of Islam arise out of a brief and at times inaccurate description of the religion and its adherents presented in the schools. Beyond this perhaps murky picture he is influenced not by definitions of what Islam as a religion preaches, but by what he sees acted out by groups and individuals identified as Muslim. Lacking sufficient keys from his history, education, and the media as to why these actions are taking place, the citizen reacts to events. Thus, he sees the cost of living rise due to what his government says are unreasonable OPEC (read Arab) price increases, the long Arab-Israeli conflict in which the Arabs are characterized as militarily incompetent and prone to terrorism, and, most recently, a self-declared Islamic Revolution which has imprisoned his diplomats, endangered his investments, and called his country criminal.

It would be improper to end with this bleak picture, for changes are apparent. . . . Arab Americans have launched a campaign to pressure the networks regarding Arab stereotypes; and, with it all, the Iranian Islamic Revolution made Americans more acutely aware, and to a degree more knowledgeable, of the role of Islam as a religion and as a political force. As well, a number of private and government organizations have stepped forward to attempt to educate the general public on the basics of Islam.

10. one who opposes technological change

Muslims in America

Sulayman S. Nyang

Sulayman S. Nyang analyzes problems and challenges facing the growing population of Muslim immigrants and converts in America. According to Nyang, Muslims employ a variety of practices in order to retain their Muslim identity and yet integrate themselves into the American economic and political systems. Sulayman S. Nyang chairs the Afro-American Studies Department at Howard University in Washington, D.C. He is the author of numerous articles on Muslims in the United States and coauthor of a book on the Muslim community.

Our attention is focused on the emerging American Muslim community, which is now estimated to be between 3 million and 5 million. The constituent elements of this community are immigrants from virtually all parts of the Muslim world and native-born Americans who converted to the faith of Islam (or as these American Muslims themselves like to put it, "they return to their natural religion [*fitra*]"). The history of the immigrant segment of the emerging Muslim community goes back to the last century, as does the rise of Islam among native-born Americans. But Islam among Americans became a national phenomenon only in the 1960s. . . .

Identity Issues for Muslim Immigrants in America

One of the most crucial elements in the history and development of a social group is the maintenance of its identity. American Muslims find themselves in a country where identification is defined politically, linguistically, culturally, and

Adapted from *The Muslims of America*, edited by Yvonne Haddad. Copyright ©1991 by Oxford University Press, Inc. Used by permission of Oxford University Press, Inc.

ethnically. An American Muslim is therefore, first of all, a U.S. citizen and for this reason carries an American passport that distinguishes him from nationals of other countries in the Muslim world. He is also looked on by his fellow Americans as a member of a racial group and is further classified culturally and religiously as a member of one of the multiple cultural and religious groups of America. . . .

One can argue that to define properly and maintain effectively a strong identity the American Muslim must recognize that he lives in four concentric circles. He is a U.S. citizen whose political loyalty is to these United States, and he affirms this, accepting all duties expected of citizens and asserting his rights guaranteed by the U.S. Constitution. The loyal response to any national call to serve in the armed forces and the bold assertion of the freedom of speech to do da'wa[1] for Islam are two critical examples of the acid test of the Muslim American identity.

But the American Muslim also lives in other circles of identification. . . . Muslim Americans are neither racially homogeneous nor ethnically monolithic. Because of this sociological fact, one challenge to Muslims is to attempt to build the bridges within the Muslim communities necessary to spare the Muslim Americans the racial divide that presently splits the other Abrahamic religions[2] into multiple ethnic/racial islands.

Since one's identity in American society is not only defined by common national origin and racial similarities, a third factor had developed among American Muslims called ethnic consciousness. This ethnic identity within the Muslim community provides a subtler form of differentiation among the immigrant Muslims. It manifests itself as the number of Muslims from abroad increases and the process of self-identification and self-differentiation begins to be felt. For example, as the number of Arabic-speaking members of a Muslim community increases, a natural segmentation or grouping along national lines begins to take place. The Syr-

1. call, missionary work   2. religions deriving from Abraham—Judaism, Christianity, and Islam

ians begin to branch off from the Egyptians, and the Saudis from the Moroccans. The same phenomenon is observable among the South Asians. The Bengalis may regroup themselves in distinction to other South Asians as their numbers increase. Although many Muslim observers of the American scene may argue that this splinterization process is an American phenomenon, it can be argued that it is a natural human tendency. Efforts by Muslim leadership need to be directed to the positive use of such ethnic islandization of the Muslim umma[3] through the creation of bridges between leaders and members of such groups.

Identity Issues for Muslim Converts in America

In the Muslim segment of the African-American community ethnicity is virtually synonymous with raciality. Because of this peculiar situation in the black community, two tendencies have developed among converts to Islam, which can be called the assimilationist and the simulationist tendencies toward Islamization. The assimilationist approach is what makes the American Muslim convert totally change his way of life to the point that he adopts an Islamic name, an Islamic code of dress to reflect the cultural origins of those who introduced him to Islam, an Islamic code of ethics, and an Islamic consciousness, which negates a great deal of what he was previously socialized to accept as American culture. The assimilationist African-American Muslim begins to see his membership in the Muslim community as an alternative, and sometimes superior, identity to his original ethnic identity. Such a person may come to feel that his Islamic identity is in conflict with his American identity. However, other types of assimilationist African-American Muslims are better able to reconcile their Islamic identity with the secular culture that American sociologists called "Americanity." Two other types can be identified here. One is the assimilationist who immerses himself in Islamic culture but still recognizes his African-American identity. Though he now sees himself as a part of a subculture within the African-American commu-

3. community

nity, he identifies totally with that community in matters that are not related to religion. Such a person usually has a Muslim name and is active in African-American community life. The other is the African-American Muslim who assimilates totally into the Islamic culture, but for a variety of reasons opts for the Americanization of his Islamic culture. This type of African-American Muslim, by virtue of his previous positive attitudes toward American culture and American constitutionalism, sees his new Muslim identity as a way of shedding what he perceives as negative characteristics of his past identity in American society that Islam has helped eliminate in his personal life. Such a person usually has a Muslim first name and an American last name.

In contrast to the assimilationists' identity are the simulationists who take a totally different view of Islam. Their decision to embrace the new religion is determined largely by utilitarian considerations. They usually see Islam as a political weapon, a strategy for physical and spiritual survival, and a way of life that can be effectively appropriated in their struggle for racial justice and ethnic freedom. . . .

Two types of simulationists can be identified. One redefines his African-American identity in such a way that his new religion makes him different and separate from both the Muslim community and his fellow African-Americans of non-Islamic faith. . . . The other simulationist group consists of those who embrace Islam as a religion while still insisting strongly on a black nationalism that calls for the unity of all black people regardless of religion. . . .

Economic Issues Facing American Muslims

In looking at the points of convergence and divergence within the Muslim community, one finds that the issue of Muslim economic activity in the United States has become a problem for some leaders. There is the issue of Muslim attitudes toward interest (*riba*).[4] There is the question of ownership of property and the need to remain faithful to the Is-

---

4. The Koran forbids usury, exorbitant interest rates for loans; Muslim fundamentalists take a strong stand against usury.

lamic precepts, which are likely to be subverted by Muslim involvement with the rules and practices of capitalist materialism. There is still the problem of trading in goods such as alcohol, pork, and other items considered forbidden (*haram*) to Muslims. Strict orthodox Muslims can easily find themselves condemned to a marginal existence in the current American social and economic system.

At least three areas can be identified as of mutual interest to the entire Muslim community in the United States. The first area is the collective desire of Muslims to survive as individuals, as families, and as a community, which demands that they participate in their different ways in the American economy. . . .

The second area of mutual interest is in the selling of Muslim products or merchandise useful to Muslims. Muslims have found in the creation of their own businesses the best avenues to self-protection and the reduction of cultural trauma from the encounter with American society. Evidence for this point of convergence between the foreign-born Muslims and their native brethren can be gleaned from the number and types of businesses established by these two subgroups in the Muslim community. All these Muslim groups have seen, in the creation of businesses, opportunities to assert themselves and to demonstrate their independence from the majority culture's power of hiring and firing.

The third point of convergence between the immigrants and locals is the common Muslim interest in increasing Muslim cultural presence in American society. This interest, in my view, is inextricably linked to the economic question. By asserting their cultural presence, Muslims hope to win over non-Muslim entrepreneurs to make concessions to their community by not trampling on their sensitivities. . . . These "neighborhood stores," in areas where Muslims are numerous, are definitely appreciated by Muslims, although only a few Muslims might entertain the illusion that they protect Muslims from the economic penetration of the capitalist market.

The Muslim community diverges on other economic questions. The problem of interest in financial transactions remains the great divide between the rigidly orthodox Muslims and their brethren who are willing to make adjustments to American society. Although it may be dangerous, without a proper sample, to generalize about Muslims all over the United States one can argue that most of the practicing immigrant Muslims from the Old World and a sizable number of strict orthodox African-American Muslims tend to view interest (*riba*) with suspicion. These Muslims differ from their more accommodating brethren in two ways. First, they disagree over whether to participate actively in the United States economy and to take or pay interest. Second, they differ in their perceptions of the American Dream. To the strictly orthodox, the American Dream is not defined exclusively in terms of owning creature comforts and material things considered status symbols in the larger society. The Dream, if it has any significant place in his mental horizon, is a symbolic encapsulation of divine blessing (*baraka*) bestowed on American society and its inhabitants by a generous God who grants this favor as a trial.

Muslims and the American Dream

The accommodationist Muslim embraces the American Dream unhesitatingly. Like his Christian or Jewish neighbors who adjust their religions to face up to the challenges of the secularization of society, he maintains his commitment to his faith but makes minor concessions that more rigidly orthodox coreligionists would not accept. The accommodationist sees his presence in American society as a God-given opportunity to better himself and family and to demonstrate to the larger society that American Muslims do belong, no matter what religious bigots or Muslim fanatics think of his relationship to the American Dream. . . .

Opposed to these are the simulationists. . . . Concerned with the maintenance of identity separate from the larger community, the simulationists and the rigidly orthodox Muslims share the common attitude of rejection or isolation from the mainstream of society. Though the simulationists may, in the realm of theological purity, be dismissed as heretical or heterodox, in the realm of economic life and activity they share the attitude toward the corporate economic system of the rigidly orthodox Muslim. Both groups believe that any deep and abiding interaction with the larger economic system erodes and undermines the pillars of their separate existence and identity—hence the attempts to promote economic independence through the creation of economic and business networks. . . .

Muslim Americans Enter Politics

Attitudes similar to those about the economy are manifest in the political arena. . . .

The mosques of the American Muslim Mission have created a platform for political education of Muslims interested in politics, and conferences dealing with political issues continue to be held in different locations in the country.

As a result of these changes in attitudes and perceptions, many African-American Muslims with political ambitions no longer hesitate to seek elective office within the American political system. Though the number of Muslim politicians within the larger black community is negligible, there is reason to believe that, as the attitude change becomes more and more deeply felt in Muslim African-America and in the larger Muslim community, some American politicians with Muslim names will begin to make the roster of U.S. elected officials. . . .

In analyzing the question of Muslim involvement in American politics, and the divergent positions taken by the numerous groups within the community, one must also note the changes in the Muslim population that resulted from the immigration of a large number of highly educated Muslims from various parts of the Muslim world and most particularly from the Middle East and South Asia. While the implications of this influx of new and better educated Muslims are not yet properly understood, we can identify some of the factors responsible for changes in attitudes toward the American political process. The first is the emergence of national Muslim organizations committed to the assertion of a Muslim American identity. . . .

Over the last five years, because of their growing self-confidence and the increase in anti-Muslim harassments and attacks in the media and in the larger American community, some members of the ISNA[5] leadership have now begun to take seriously the option of greater and more active Muslim involvement in the American political process. This option is now being pursued at both the national and local levels. At the national level, there is talk of a national Muslim Political Action Committee. . . .

Unity and Diversity in the American Muslim Community

The identity question is central to the Muslim presence in the United States. The American Muslim can maintain his identity only by holding steadfastly on to the rope of *tawhid* (unity of Allah). This is definitely not an easy task, because numerous forces are at work which are likely to make life difficult. Though Muslims differ on some of the burning issues of American society, however, their sense of unity is evident in their common faith in *tawhid*, in their collective practice of Muslim rituals and in the expression of solidarity on matters affecting all Muslims living in America. To put this another way, one could say that, though divergence exists in the realm of perceptions of and attitudes toward American society, convergence exists in the realm of rituals and fellow feelings toward one's coreligionists. . . .

Muslim economic structures are beginning to emerge, and their success is going to depend on the availability of capital within the Muslim community and on the attitudes of Muslim business people toward the American capitalist system. The divergent attitudes identified in our classification of different definitions of the Muslim identity in the United States will have significant effects on the future role of Muslims in the economy. Assimilationist Muslims will fare very much like assimilationist members of other religious traditions operating within the U.S. economy. They will develop intellectual justifications for dealing with banks that charge interest and with home-building companies that include interest in

5. the Islamic Society of North America

their mortgage rates. The simulationists, on the other hand, will in the coming years create economic structures that are faithful to Islamic economics and reassuring to those who believe in God and the Sunna of Prophet Muhammad.

The rise in Muslim self-confidence and the increase in the number of Muslims in the country will lead assimilationist Muslims to participate more and more in the American political system. Related to this is the fact that the trends in interreligious relations in America and the Muslim world could affect not only the image of Muslims in the United States, but also their self-perception in American society. The future of Muslim survival in American society is inextricably linked to the future of religious pluralism in this country. Any radical alteration in this pattern could threaten not only Muslim Americans but all other minorities who are targeted for discrimination. If the present and recent past are significant guides to the future, it is possible to hope that Islam as a minority religion has a promising future and Muslims will be as well adjusted in the coming years as any other religious minority. Their religion will join Christianity and Judaism as the third branch of the Abrahamic tradition. Were this to occur, [scholar of religion] Will Herberg's statement on American religion could be amended to read that being American means that one may be a member of the Christian, Jewish, Muslim, or any of the other religious traditions in American society.

A Portrait of an American Muslim Woman

Geraldine Brooks

Geraldine Brooks profiles Sharifa Alkhateeb, an American Muslim woman who lives in Great Falls, Virginia. Brooks describes Alkhateeb's active personal and professional life, her typical motherly concerns for her daughters, and her typical struggles to balance home and work responsibilities. Not typical, in Brooks's description, are Alkhateeb's Muslim approaches to food, spiritual life, and public education. Geraldine Brooks has extensive experience writing about women and Islam. Her forthcoming book is entitled *Foreign Correspondence*.

On a Saturday night in suburban Virginia, Sharifa Alkhateeb is putting on a purple head scarf before rushing out for a potluck dinner at the local mosque. Meanwhile, her 16-year-old daughter, nose pierced, baggy jeans dangling from her hips, hangs out with her non-Muslim girlfriends. Returning home after 10, Sharifa finds a note pinned to the living-room door.

"Mom, can I stay over at Jessie's, please? Use the pager—that's what it's for."

Sharifa tugs off her head scarf and sighs. "Sometimes I wonder if I'll survive her teens." Even more than most parents, she worries about her daughter staying out at night. Like many Muslims, she believes unmarried women shouldn't socialize with men outside the family, even the fathers and brothers of close friends. Still, she trusts her daughter. Despite her appearance, Nasreen is a committed Muslim who doesn't date.

When Americans think of Islam, their image is often of fundamentalists in faraway lands, not the Muslims at the local mall. But numbering about six million, Muslims are almost as numerous in the United States as Jews, with roughly half of American Muslims born here. A Muslim in the United States now is twice as likely to be African-American as Arab. Meanwhile, Muslims raised in repressive countries are opening up in the noisy forum of American free speech. They are protesting anti-Islamic stereotypes, asking for halal[1] meat in school cafeterias and developing a faith-based feminism that may ultimately prove to be American Muslims' biggest contribution to Islam.

The Alkhateeb family's blond brick colonial sits amid manicured boxwoods in Great Falls, Va., an affluent community where signs touting "estate" lots for sale sprout among horse barns about 15 miles northwest of Washington. But a calendar by the fridge reminds the Alkhateebs that they also live in the Ummah—the community of Islam—where the year is 1418.[2] Sharifa Alkhateeb, born in the United States, is an academic adviser to foreign graduate students and a part-time intercultural trainer for teachers in the Fairfax County school system. Her husband, Mejdi, is an Iraqi immigrant and computer scientist who runs his own company.

Their closest mosque, the All-Dulles Area Muslim Society, occupies an unmarked floor of a bland office building in Herndon, amid a typical Northern Virginia sprawl of tract homes and strip malls. At the mosque's Saturday potluck, Sharifa places a pan of cinnamon-spiced kebabs beside Malaysian glass noodles, Egyptian braised lamb, Pakistani chicken biriani and chocolate brownies baked by an African-American. Mejdi heads to one side of the room, to sit with the men, while Sharifa joins a women's table where the dress is as diverse as the food. Most wear some kind of head cover.

In 1990, Sharifa compiled a directory of mosques in the greater Washington area. There were nine. When she up-

---

1. meat slaughtered in the manner prescribed by Islamic law   2. The Islamic calendar is lunar, having 354 days per year. It dates from July 15, 622, the day of the *hijra* (migration) of the Prophet Muhammad from Mecca to Medina, and is denoted by A.H., after *Hijra*.

dated the booklet in 1994, there were 39, and at least 6 more have appeared since. While a few serve a single ethnic group and hold firmly to national traditions, the majority welcome all comers. And that usually means preaching an Islam all kinds of Muslims—Middle Easterners, Asians, Africans and American-born—can agree on. Harsh customs like obligatory face veils or female genital mutilation, which have crept into the religion in various Islamic lands, are virtually nonexistent.

At Sharifa's table, the talk is mostly about children: whether a teen-age son should be allowed to watch *Executive Decision*, a film that portrays Muslims as terrorists; how to get permission for a child to miss class on a Muslim holiday; whether a daughter can transfer out of a school with gangs and drugs. "Don't say you want to change schools because of gangs," counsels Sharifa, who has worked in education for 30 years. "The authorities can't admit they have a rotten school. Find some positives about the school you want to move her to—it's got a better music program, more language classes."

As vice president of the North American Council for Muslim Women, Sharifa often dispenses this sort of advice. This can involve anything from writing memos to the imams at local mosques urging them to preach against domestic violence, to exhorting a conference of Muslim women in Turkey to pass a resolution condemning Taliban repression in Afghanistan, to helping develop guidelines for Federal employees that allow them to read the Koran or cover their hair at work. She even advises brides-to-be on formulating Islamic wedding contracts (1,300-year-old precursors of modern prenuptial agreements) that protect their rights. "Muslim women are quite capable of speaking up for ourselves," Sharifa says. "We're not waiting for Western women to pour their loveliness into our heads."

While she fights for women's rights inside the mosque, she struggles for a greater Muslim role in the wider political debate. She thinks part of the problem is that Muslim immigrants often come from countries where saying the wrong thing could get them killed. They have to be introduced to the American notion that activism is expected rather than suspect.

At a recent meeting at the Herndon mosque, Sharifa

urges a roomful of parents to get involved in their children's education. She encourages them to volunteer any skills they may have—driving, editing, cooking, computer programming—to become more familiar with the school and gain more influence over what happens there. One mother tells how volunteering as a classroom aide allowed her to steer her daughter's end-of-year celebration from a dance, which she considered un-Islamic, to a sports carnival. From the back of the hall, a father raises his hand. Muslims, he says, have skills passed to them through the Koran; namely, God's rules on how to live. Why not offer to give a course on that? "I think the public school would think that's a theological way of looking at the world and wouldn't be interested in promoting that idea," replies Sharifa diplomatically. "When we volunteer in schools, we shouldn't wear our religion on our shoulder. We should be willing to be part of the whole spectrum of American society."

Sharifa Alkhateeb got to know part of the spectrum of American society during an unsettled childhood in Philadelphia. Every year, a delegation of nuns would come to see her Czech-born mother, who converted to Islam before she married a Yemeni. "They would beg her to leave us," she recalls. Instead, it was the children who left, in flight from the strictness of their father. Of five children, "everyone ran away except me," Sharifa says. She stayed, plunging deeper into Islam than any of her siblings.

At the Community College of Philadelphia and the University of Pennsylvania in the late 1960's and early 1970's, fellow students who were initially puzzled by her covered hair eventually came to call her "the guru." "They came to me for advice, I guess because I was the only one who wasn't on something." She was 22 years old when an Iraqi-born computer-science student heard her speak at a Muslim student's convention. He wrote to her and they met—chaperoned by an Egyptian couple. "I sat on the sofa next to the wife; Mejdi sat on the other side, next to the husband. And that was how we talked, for 10 days. On the 11th, we got married at Niagara Falls." They've been together 27 years.

They moved to Great Falls about 10 years ago, into an all-

American subdivision with Neighborhood Watch and July 4th fireworks on a nearby farm. The Irish-American neighbors are friendly, but Sharifa politely declines invitations to their St. Patrick's Day parties. "It's a holiday that's mostly about drinking, so what would we do there?" she says. The neighbors also have sons, and she doesn't want her daughters to become too closely acquainted with them.

Sharifa worries about her daughters. She worries that the eldest, a fashion-design student in New York, may want to marry a Saudi. "I'm not sure that most men raised in that culture would allow a woman enough room to grow," she says. She worries about her middle daughter, trying to balance a job as a diversity trainer with marriage and a toddler. But most of all, she worries about Nasreen, her youngest.

A picture on the kitchen wall shows Nasreen at 9, reading the Koran, her hair tucked away in a scarf. She was in Iraq with her father, visiting relatives, when the Persian Gulf war erupted. While her father contrived their exit, she posed as a mute for almost a month to conceal her nationality. But when she finally got home, her head scarf branded her an enemy to her schoolmates. "It was, 'Every Muslim is a terrorist, every Muslim is Arab,'" she says. "The kids in my school knew nothing about the world. I felt harassed, beaten up mentally." On the school bus, pupils taunted her as "scarf head" and tried to snatch the cloth from her hair. Nasreen abandoned the scarf when she began middle school. She says she'll put it back "sometime in the future," but she's not sure when. "I love my religion; I'm very proud of it," she says. "I just wish people in this country were more accepting of other cultures."

On a Friday evening, before heading out to a girlfriend's house, she sits with her mother and her eldest sister, who comes home most weekends, in a living room decorated with oriental carpets and Arabic calligraphy. Upstairs, her own room features Jim Morrison posters and pictures of fashion models. Nasreen loves art and would like to work in theatrical makeup. She demonstrates how easily she can change her own appearance, twisting her nose ring so that it sits out of sight and tucking strands of wavy hair over the ornaments studding her ears. "My conservative look," she declares.

Sharifa gives a rueful smile. "I raised my daughters to question everything—to weigh all opinions, including mine." Sometimes, she says, she wishes she hadn't taught them quite so well. "But I know that there's less chance of someone walking all over them, whether it's a male in his male-chauvinist way or a woman as they try to rise in their professions. You can't be a quiet person in this country and make it."

She is mad at Nasreen for piercing her body and disappointed that she doesn't wear a scarf. But she also wants the world to understand that a Muslim woman with a nose ring is just as Muslim as a woman in a veil. "The Koran says, 'Let there be no compulsion in religion,' and while covering is important, it's not the most important thing. The most important thing is that you feel connected to God."

Sharifa renews her own connection to God in the five daily prayers that mark the passing of each Muslim's day. But on Fridays, the Muslim holy day, she makes the connection public by attending communal prayers. The closest Friday prayers are just across the road at the Embassy of Saudi Arabia. But she can't get there soon enough to avoid walking past some men, which the Saudis forbid. So she must drive to George Washington University, where an auditorium is packed with students, professors and office workers, standing shoulder to shoulder in stocking feet. Sharifa takes her place with the women, behind a lattice at the rear of the auditorium. Sometimes, the lattice is covered by a sheet, to further segregate male from female worshipers. "It's an overzealous young Spanish convert who puts it up," Sharifa says. "I always take it down."

Afterward, in the corridor, Sharifa greets a young friend, Huma Abedin, office manager for Hillary Rodham Clinton. Downstairs, in the street, she looks around for a place to grab a quick lunch. The closest restaurant is a T.G.I.F.— Thank God It's Friday. Sharifa laughs. "Who says it's impossible to be American and Muslim?" Inside, she orders a virgin daiquiri and a club sandwich: "Hold the ham. And the bacon."

Appendix

Document 1: From the Koran

The Koran, the sacred book of Islam, records the words of Allah spoken through an angel to Muhammad. It instructs Muslims on the authenticity of the Koran, explains creation, describes the paradise or hell humans will experience in afterlife, and guides Muslims in war and daily conduct.

The Authenticity of the Koran

(3:1) God! There is no god but Him, the Living, the Ever-existent One.

He has revealed to you the Book with the Truth. . . .

(3:6) It is He who has revealed to you the Book. Some of its verses are precise in meaning—they are the foundation of the Book—and others ambiguous.

(6:19) 'This Koran has been revealed to me [Muhammad] that I may thereby warn you and all whom it may reach. Will you really testify there are other gods besides God?'

(15:1) These are the verses of the Book, a Glorious Koran:

The day will surely come when those who disbelieve will wish that they were Muslims. Let them feast and make merry; and let their hopes beguile them. They shall know.

Creation

(7:54) Your Lord is God, who created the heavens and the earth in six days and then ascended the throne. He throws the veil of night over the day. Swiftly they follow one another.

It was He who created the sun, the moon, and the stars, and made them subservient to His will. His is the creation, His the command. Blessed be God, Lord of the Universe! . . .

(15:23) We created man from dry clay, from black moulded loam, and before him Satan from smokeless fire. Your Lord said to the angels: 'I am creating man from dry clay, from black moulded loam. When I have fashioned him and breathed of My spirit into him, kneel down and prostrate yourselves before him.'

(6:91) It is God who splits the seed and the fruit-stone. He brings forth the living from the dead, and the dead from the living. Such is God. How then can you turn away?

He kindles the light of dawn. He has ordained the night for rest and the sun and the moon for reckoning. Such is the ordinance of the Mighty One, the All-knowing.

It is He that has created for you the stars, so that they may guide you in the darkness of land and sea. We have made plain Our revelations to men of sense.

It was He that created you from one being and furnished you with a dwelling and a resting-place. We have made plain Our revelations to men of understanding.

It is He who sends down water from the sky with which We bring forth the buds of every plant. From these We bring forth green foliage and close-growing grain, palm-trees laden with clusters of dates, vineyards and olive groves, and pomegranates alike and different. Behold their fruits when they ripen. Surely in these there are signs for true believers.

Paradise and Hell

(47:15) This is the Paradise which the righteous have been promised. There shall flow in it rivers of purest water, and rivers of milk for ever fresh; rivers of wine delectable to those that drink it, and rivers of clearest honey. They shall eat therein of every fruit and receive forgiveness from their Lord. Is this like the lot of those who shall abide in Hell for ever, and drink scalding water which will tear their bowels?

(55:41) The wrongdoers will be known by their looks; they shall be seized by their forelocks and their feet. Which of your Lord's blessings would you deny?

That is the Hell which the sinners deny. They shall wander between fire and water fiercely seething. Which of your Lord's blessings would you deny?

But for those that fear the majesty of their Lord there are two gardens (which of your Lord's blessings would you deny?) planted with shady trees. Which of your Lord's blessings would you deny?

Each is watered by a flowing spring. Which of your Lord's blessings would you deny?

Each bears every kind of fruit in pairs. Which of your Lord's blessings would you deny?

They shall recline on couches lined with thick brocade, and within reach will hang the fruits of both gardens. Which of your Lord's blessings would you deny?

Therein are bashful virgins whom neither man nor jinnee [a spirit in human form with supernatural power over people] will have touched before. Which of your Lord's blessings would you deny?

Virgins as fair as corals and rubies. Which of your Lord's blessings would you deny?

Shall the reward of goodness be anything but good? Which of your Lord's blessings would you deny?

And beside these there shall be two other gardens (which of your Lord's blessings would you deny?) of darkest green. Which of your Lord's blessings would you deny?

A gushing fountain shall flow in each. Which of your Lord's blessings would you deny?

(55:68) Each planted with fruit-trees, the palm and the pomegranate. Which of your Lord's blessings would you deny?

In each there shall be virgins chaste and fair. Which of your Lord's blessings would you deny?

Dark-eyed virgins sheltered in their tents (which of your Lord's blessings would you deny?) whom neither man nor jinnee will have touched before. Which of your Lord's blessings would you deny?

They shall recline on green cushions and fine carpets. Which of your Lord's blessings would you deny?

Blessed be the name of your Lord, the Lord of majesty and glory!

(56:16) Such are they that shall be brought near to their Lord in the gardens of delight: a whole multitude from the men of old, but only a few from the latter generations.

They shall recline on jewelled couches face to face, and there shall wait on them immortal youths with bowls and ewers and a cup of purest wine (that will neither pain their heads nor take away their reason); with fruits of their own choice and flesh of fowls that they relish. And theirs shall be the dark-eyed houris [alluring women], chaste as hidden pearls: a guerdon [reward] for their deeds.

There they shall hear no idle talk, no sinful speech, but only the greeting, 'Peace! Peace!'

Those on the right hand—happy shall be those on the right hand! They shall recline on couches raised on high in the shade of thornless sidrs and clusters of ṭalḥ [banana]; amidst gushing waters and abundant fruits, unforbidden, never-ending.

We created the houris and made them virgins, loving companions for those on the right hand: a multitude from the men of old, and a multitude from the latter generations.

As for those on the left hand (wretched shall be those on the left hand!) they shall dwell amidst scorching winds and seething water: in the shade of pitch-black smoke, neither cool nor refreshing. For they have lived in comfort and persisted in the heinous sin [of idolatry], saying: 'When we are once dead and turned to dust and bones, shall we be raised to life? And our forefathers, too?'. . .

(56:51) 'As for you sinners who deny the truth, you shall eat the fruit of the Zaqqūm tree and fill your bellies with it. You shall drink scalding water: yet you shall drink it as the thirsty camel drinks.'

Such shall be their fare on the Day of Reckoning.

Jihad

(47:3) When you meet the unbelievers in the battlefield strike off their heads and, when you have laid them low, bind your captives firmly. Then grant them their freedom or take ransom from them, until War shall lay down her burdens.

Thus shall you do. Had God willed, He could Himself have punished them; but He has ordained it thus that He might test you, the one by the other.

As for those who are slain in the cause of God, He will not allow their works to perish. He will vouchsafe them guidance and ennoble their state; He will admit them to the Paradise He has made known to them.

(8:65) Prophet, rouse the faithful to arms. If there are twenty steadfast men among you, they shall vanquish two hundred; and if there are a hundred, they shall rout a thousand unbelievers, for they are devoid of understanding.

God has now lightened your burden, for He knows that you are weak. If there are a hundred steadfast men among you, they shall vanquish two hundred; and if there are a thousand, they shall, by God's will, defeat two thousand. God is with those that are steadfast.

A prophet may not take captives until he has fought and triumphed in his land. You [Muhammad's followers] seek the chance gain of this world, but God desires for you the world to come. He is mighty and wise. Had there not been a previous sanction from God, you would have been sternly punished for what you have taken. Enjoy therefore the good and lawful things which you have gained in war, and fear God. God is forgiving and merciful.

(3:169) Never think that those who were slain in the cause of God are dead. They are alive, and well provided for by their Lord; pleased with His gifts and rejoicing that those they left behind, who have not yet joined them, have nothing to fear or to regret; rejoicing in God's grace and bounty. God will not deny the faithful their reward.

Rules for Daily Living

Usury (2:275) Those that live on usury shall rise up before God like men whom Satan has demented by his touch; for they claim that trading is no different from usury. But God has permitted trading and made usury unlawful. He that has received an admonition from his Lord and mended his ways may keep his previous gains; God will be his judge. Those that turn back shall be the inmates of the Fire, wherein they shall abide for ever.

God has laid His curse on usury and blessed almsgiving with increase. God bears no love for the impious and the sinful.

Food (5:3) You are forbidden carrion, blood, and the flesh of swine; also any flesh dedicated to any other than God. You are forbidden the flesh of strangled animals and of those beaten or gored to death; of those killed by a fall or mangled by beasts of prey (unless you make it clean by giving the death-stroke yourselves); also of animals sacrificed to idols.

(5:96) Lawful to you is what you catch from the sea and the sustenance it provides; a wholesome food, for yourselves and for the seafarers. But you are forbidden the game of the land while you are on pilgrimage.

Drinking and Gambling (5:90) Believers, wine and games of chance, idols and divining arrows, are abominations devised by Satan. Avoid them, so that you may prosper. Satan seeks to stir up enmity and hatred among you by means of wine and gambling, and to keep you from the remembrance of God and from your prayers. Will you not abstain from them?

Hunting (5:95) Believers, kill no game while on pilgrimage. He that kills game by design, shall present, as an offering to the Ka‘bah, an animal equivalent to the one he killed, to be determined by two just men among you; or he shall, in expiation, either feed the destitute or fast, so that he may taste the evil consequences of his deed. God has forgiven what is past; but if anyone relapses into wrongdoing God will avenge Himself on him: God is mighty and capable of revenge.

Punishment for Murder (4:92) It is unlawful for a believer to kill another believer except by accident. He that accidentally kills a believer must free one Muslim slave and pay blood-money to the family of the victim, unless they choose to give it away in alms. If the victim be a Muslim from a hostile tribe, the penalty is the freeing of one Muslim slave. But if the victim be a member of an allied tribe, then blood-money must be paid to his family and a Muslim slave set free. He that lacks the means must fast two consecutive months. Such is the penance imposed by God: God is all-knowing and wise.

He that kills a believer by design shall burn in Hell for ever. He shall incur the wrath of God, who will lay His curse on him and prepare for him a woeful scourge.

Pilgrimage (2:196) Make the pilgrimage and visit the Sacred House for His sake. If you cannot, send such offerings as you can afford and do not shave your heads until the offerings have reached their destination. But if any of you is ill or suffers from an ailment of the head, he must pay a ransom either by fasting or by almsgiving or by offering a sacrifice.

(2:197) Make the pilgrimage in the appointed months. He that intends to perform it in those months must abstain from sexual intercourse, obscene language, and acrimonious disputes while on pilgrimage. God is aware of whatever good you do. Provide well for yourselves: the best provision is piety.

Fasting (2:182) He that suspects an error or an injustice on the part of a testator and brings about a settlement among the parties incurs no guilt. God is forgiving and merciful.

Believers, fasting is decreed for you as it was decreed for those before you; perchance you will guard yourselves against evil. Fast a certain number of days, but if any one among you is ill or on a journey, let him fast a similar number of days later; and for those that cannot endure it there is a ransom: the feeding of a poor man. He that does good of his own accord shall be well rewarded; but to fast is better for you, if you but knew it.

In the month of Ramadān the Koran was revealed, a book of guidance with proofs of guidance distinguishing right from wrong. Therefore whoever of you is present in that month let him fast. But he who is ill or on a journey shall fast a similar number of days later on.

Preparation for Prayers (5:6) Believers, when you rise to pray wash your faces and your hands as far as the elbow, and wipe your heads and your feet to the ankle. If you are polluted cleanse yourselves. But if you are sick or travelling the road; or if, when you have just relieved yourselves or had intercourse with women, you can find no water, take some clean sand and rub your hands and faces with it. God does not wish to burden you; He seeks only to purify you and to perfect His favour to you, so that you may give thanks.

Male/Female Relations (4:34) Men have authority over women because God has made the one superior to the other, and because they spend their wealth to maintain them. Good women are obedient. They guard their unseen parts because God has guarded them. As for those from whom you fear disobedience, admonish them and send them to beds apart and beat them. Then if they obey you, take no further action against them. God is high, supreme.

(24:30) Enjoin believing men to turn their eyes away from temptation and to restrain their carnal desires. This will make their lives purer. God has knowledge of all their actions.

Enjoin believing women to turn their eyes away from temptation and to preserve their chastity; to cover their adornments (except such as are normally displayed); to draw their veils over their bosoms and not to reveal their finery except to their husbands, their fathers, their husbands' fathers, their sons, their step-sons, their brothers, their brothers' sons, their sisters' sons, their women-servants, and their slave-girls; male attendants lacking in natural vigour, and children who have no carnal knowledge of women. And let them not stamp their feet when walking so as to reveal their hidden trinkets.

(2:221) You shall not wed pagan women, unless they embrace the Faith. A believing slave-girl is better than an idolatress, although she may please you. Nor shall you wed idolaters, unless they embrace the Faith. A believing slave is better than an idolater, although he may please you. These call you to Hell-fire; but God calls you, by His will, to Paradise and to forgiveness. He makes plain His revelations to mankind, so that they may take heed.

They ask you about menstruation. Say: 'It is an indisposition. Keep aloof from women during their menstrual periods and do not touch them until they are clean again. Then have intercourse with them in the way God enjoined you. God loves those that turn to Him in repentance and strive to keep themselves clean.'

Women are your fields: go, then, into your fields whence you please.

(24:2) The adulterer and the adulteress shall each be given a hundred lashes. Let no pity for them cause you to disobey God, if you truly believe in God and the Last Day; and let their punishment be witnessed by a number of believers.

The adulterer may marry only an adulteress or an idolatress; and the adulteress may marry only an adulterer or an idolater. True believers are forbidden such marriages.

Those that defame honourable women and cannot produce four witnesses shall be given eighty lashes. Do not accept their testimony ever after, for they are great transgressors—except those among them that afterwards repent and mend their ways. God is forgiving and merciful.

(2:228) Divorced women must wait, keeping themselves from men, three menstrual courses. It is unlawful for them, if they believe in God and the Last Day, to hide what God has created in their wombs: in which case their husbands would do well to take them back, should they desire reconciliation.

Women shall with justice have rights similar to those exercised against them, although men have a status above women. God is mighty and wise.

Divorce [revocable divorce, or the renunciation of one's wife on oath] may be pronounced twice, and then a woman must be retained in honour or allowed to go with kindness. It is unlawful for husbands to take from them anything they have given them, unless both fear that they may not be able to keep within the bounds set by God; in which case it shall be no offence for either of them if the wife ransoms herself.

These are the bounds set by God; do not transgress them. Those that transgress the bounds of God are wrongdoers.

If a man divorces [by pronouncing the formula 'I divorce you' for the third time] his wife, he shall not remarry her until she has wedded another man and been divorced by him; in which case it shall be no offence for either of them to return to the other, if they think that they can keep within the bounds set by God.

Personal Perspectives

Document 2: A Westerner's View of the Koran

In his essay "The Hero as Prophet," British historian and essayist Thomas Carlyle offers his opinion of the Koran as a book. He grants that translation alters the effectiveness of the original; nonetheless, he believes the Koran is haphazardly organized.

Nothing but a sense of duty could carry any European through the Koran. We read in it, as we might in the State-Paper Office, masses of lumber, that perhaps we may get some glimpses of a remarkable man. It is true we have it under disadvantages: the Arabs see more method in it than we. Mahomet's followers found the

Koran lying all in fractions, . . . and they published it, without any discoverable order as to time or otherwise; merely trying, . . . and this not very strictly, to put the longest chapters first. The real beginning of it, in that way, lies almost at the end: for the earliest portions were the shortest. Read in its historical sequence it perhaps would not be so bad. Much of it, too, they say is rhythmic; a kind of wild chanting song, in the original. This may be a great point; much perhaps has been lost in the Translation. Yet with every allowance, one feels it difficult to see how any mortal ever could consider this Koran as a Book written in Heaven, too good for the Earth; as a well-written book, or indeed as a *book* at all; and not a bewildered rhapsody.

John B. Christopher, *The Islamic Tradition*. New York: Harper & Row, 1972.

Document 3: A King Advises His Son

In 1082 the ruler of a small kingdom in Persia, Kay Kā'us ibn Iskandar, recorded his advice to his son in the Book of Qābus (a "Mirror for Princes") to instruct the future king on how to appear kingly.

You must realize, my son, that the day of my departure approaches and the day when you will succeed me is near. Know that this world is ploughland; as you sow, be it good or ill, you reap. . . .

Be of ready speech, my son; yet never tell lies and do not gain the reputation of being a liar. Rather become known for veracity, so that if ever in an emergency you utter a lie it will be believed. Never utter a truth which has the appearance of a lie; for a lie which has the air of truth is preferable to an accurate statement which seems to be false, and this kind of lie will be believed where that kind of true statement will not. . . .

If you become king some day, my son, be Godfearing, keep eye and hand away from other Muslims' women-folk and let your robe be unspotted. In every task you propose, first consult with wisdom. As long as you see any possibility of leisurely action avoid haste; and whenever you propose to enter upon an undertaking, first ascertain the way by which you will emerge from it.

Be ever one that speaks the truth, but speak rarely and laugh rarely, so that those subject to your kingship may not become emboldened against you. Expose yourself to the public gaze only rarely, and so prevent yourself from becoming a spectacle commonplace in the eyes of your troops and your people. Maintain stern discipline, more especially with your wazīr (and) never be completely dependent upon his counsel. Hearken to what he has to say, but make inquiry into the circumstances of the case to ascertain if it is your welfare he is seeking, or his own benefit. Thus he will be unable to regard you as being governed by his views.

John Alden Williams, ed., *Themes of Islamic Civilization.* Berkeley and Los Angeles: University of California Press, 1971.

Document 4: Misunderstanding Between Two Cultures

Anthropologist Carolyn Fluehr-Lobban, doing fieldwork among Muslim women in the Sudan in Africa, reports the following embarrassing experience when she misunderstood a local taboo.

I recall with some embarrassment even today an exchange that took place early in my fieldwork in the Sudan when I was still learning conversational Arabic. Several young Sudanese women were questioning me about American culture and religion, when one of them broke in with the question, "Do you eat pork?" "Oh, not very often," was my response, proud that I could express a degree of frequency between always and not at all, whereupon a hushed silence replaced the banter that had been under way. I realized that I had made a terrible error in revealing this unclean, unacceptable pork eating behavior to them. Red-faced, I tried to turn the conversation to another subject, but I was unsuccessful as they looked at me now not just as an oddity but as an unhygienic one. It is this sort of experience that makes an indelible impression about the deep feelings associated with a food taboo in society, feelings that are not replicable for a researcher working with a text or document.

Carolyn Fluehr-Lobban, *Islamic Society in Practice.* Gainesville: University Press of Florida, 1994.

Document 5: Education of Girls

Jean P. Sasson has written the biography of Princess Sultana of Saudi Arabia because the princess was not allowed to write her own story. In the excerpt, Sultana tells how she managed to attend school and, simultaneously, reveals attitudes toward women in her royal family.

My mother, encouraged by King Faisal's wife Iffat, managed to educate her daughters, despite my father's resistance. For many years, my father refused even to consider the possibility. My five older sisters received no schooling other than to memorize the Koran from a private tutor who came to our home. For two hours, six afternoons a week, they would repeat words after the Egyptian teacher, Fatima, a stern woman of about forty-five years of age. She once asked my parents' permission to expand my sisters' education to include science, history, and math. Father responded with a firm no and the recital of the Prophet's words, and his words alone continued to ring throughout our villa. . . .

All children need to be stimulated, but my sisters and I had little or nothing to do other than to play in our rooms or lounge in the women's gardens. There was nowhere to go and little to do, for when I was a child, there was not even a zoo or a park in the city.

Mother, weary of five energetic daughters, thought that school would relieve her while expanding our minds. Finally, Mother, with the assistance of Auntie Iffat, wore Father down to weak acceptance. And so it came to be that the five youngest daughters of our family, including Sara and myself, enjoyed the new age of reluctant acceptance of education for females.

Our first classroom was in the home of a royal relative. Seven families of the Al Sa'ud clan employed a young woman from Abu Dhabi, a neighboring Arab city in the Emirates. Our small group of pupils, sixteen in all, was known in those days as a Kutab, a group method then popular for teaching girls. We gathered daily in the home of our royal cousin from nine o'clock in the morning until two o'clock in the afternoon, Saturday through Thursday.

It was there that my favorite sister, Sara, first displayed her brilliance. She was much quicker than girls twice her age. The teacher even asked Sara if she was a primary graduate, and shook her head in wonder when she learned that Sara was not.

Our instructor had been fortunate to have a modern-thinking father who had sent her to England for an education. Because of her deformity, a club foot, she had found no one who would marry her, so she chose a path of freedom and independence for herself. She smiled as she told us that her deformed foot was a gift from God to ensure that her mind did not become deformed too. Even though she lived in the home of our royal cousin (it was and still is unthinkable for a single woman to live alone in Saudi Arabia), she earned a salary and made her decisions about life without outside influence. . . .

Miss Sakeena told Mother that Sara was the brightest student she had ever taught. After I jumped up and down and yelled, "What about me?" she thought for a long moment before answering. With a smile, she said, "And Sultana is certain to be famous."

That evening at dinner, Mother proudly passed on the remark about Sara to Father. Father, who was visibly pleased, smiled at Sara. Mother beamed with pleasure, but then Father cruelly asked how any daughter born of her belly could acquire learning. Nor did he credit Mother with any contribution to the brilliance of Ali, who was at the top of his class at a modern secondary school in the city. Presumably, the intellectual achievements of her children were inherited solely from their father.

Even today I shudder with dismay while watching my older sisters attempt to add or subtract. I say little prayers of gratitude to Auntie Iffat, for she changed the lives of so many Saudi women.

Jean P. Sasson, *Princess: A True Story of Life Behind the Veil in Saudi Arabia*. New York: Avon Books, 1992.

Document 6: Wives in a Harem

In the excerpt from her biography, Iranian-born Sattareh Farman Farmaian relates stories about her mother, the third wife who, at twelve, was married to Shazdeh, a man over fifty. Farmaian's mother Khanom, separated from the two older wives, was ignorant, frightened, and alone when Shazdeh was sent on government or military missions. Farmaian tells of the hope and joy Khanom felt when the fourth and fifth wives came into the harem.

And while he was away, Shazdeh had found her [Khanom] a present. He had taken another new wife, named Batul (as with the Kurdish bride, the marriage was to seal a political pact). Now he sent her to live at Ezzatdoleh's, too.

My mother was overjoyed. The new wife was a beautiful, statuesque girl only a couple of years older than herself. Batul-Khanom had already borne Shazdeh two enchantingly pretty little daughters, Maryam and Mehri, with whom my mother at once fell in love. Here at last was someone who was close to her own age, and in the same situation.

She quickly found that she had never known anyone even remotely like her new companion. Batul was from a modern, educated family in Kermanshah, a border city open to cosmopolitan influences. Not only could she read and write, but she even had a scrapbook with a collection of poems she liked. My mother, however, was disconcerted to find that there were things about the new wife that startled and shocked her. Khanom, as a proper Moslem, thought that above everything a woman had to be pious, serious, self-controlled, and reserved, whereas Batul-Khanom was by nature impulsive, openhearted, fun-loving, and volatile. . . .

For the first time in her serious, anxiety-ridden life, my mother had a companion her own age. She did not want to lose her. With Batul-Khanom there was someone with whom to sew, visit the baths, and enjoy the jokes, games, and clowning with which women entertained themselves. . . .

The Iranian government hoped that Shazdeh, whom the leading men of Shiraz remembered as a good and able governor from his first appointment, would be able to calm the resentful citizenry and somehow deal with the famine and the marauding tribes. . . .

To ensure his acceptance by the Shirazis, my father also took a wife from one of the leading families and raised an all-Iranian regiment to patrol the roads and oil pipelines on condition that the British, as was customary, reimburse and pay him for the protection. This, he knew, would take the teeth out of some of the opposition to the occupying forces, while his marriage would encourage the citizenry to trust their new governor. . . .

Before his departure for Shiraz my mother had given birth to my older sister Jaby, while Batul had borne her first son, Manucher. My father therefore did not send for them until the war's end. . . .

Luckily, they reached Shiraz safely and there began making the acquaintance of my father's new wife. Fatimeh-Khanom was neither as lively and amusing as Batul nor as perceptive as my mother; instead she was quiet, timid, and plain, a follower rather than a leader. However, my mother and stepmother discovered that she always jogged along amiably with anything the two of them wanted to do, and my mother was cheered to find that Fatimeh-Khanom was a daughter of one of the town's wealthy mullahs, and therefore just as old-fashioned and devout as she. Now she had an ally—even if not a very brave one—whenever she felt constrained to gently chide Batul for one of her irreligious jokes.

My mother wondered if life might finally be taking a turn for the better. She humbly thanked the Merciful and Compassionate for safely reuniting them with Shazdeh and sending her and Batul their new friend. . . . Maybe, now that the foreigners' war was over, the *englis-ha* and *russ-ha* would tell their soldiers to leave Iran, and some way could be found to pull our country together. Then, perhaps, Shazdeh would take his harem back to Tehran and build them a real home there, and she and Batul and Fatimeh could settle down and raise their children together in peace. If all this turmoil were over, the roads might even become safe enough for her and Fatimeh to make a pilgrimage to the holy shrines at Qom or Mashad, if Shazdeh let them. She longed for security at last, for herself and the country. She wanted to stop wondering what new troubles God was going to send her next.

Sattareh Farman Farmaian with Dona Munker, *Daughter of Persia: A Woman's Journey from Her Father's Harem Through the Islamic Revolution.* New York: Anchor Books Doubleday, 1992.

Poets and Writers

Document 7: Hafiz's Ode to Wine

Fourteenth-century Persian poet Hafiz, like many Islamic poets, wrote odes praising wine and earthly beauty, both metaphors for the passion of spirituality. The message to forbid the drinking of wine occurred when Muslim leaders reputedly drank it to excess; perhaps it became a metaphor because it was forbidden. The fifth ode from "The Divan" addresses the wine Saki in rhymed couplets.

Up, Sákí!—let the goblet flow;
Strew with dust the head of our earthly woe!

Give me thy cup; that, joy-possessed,
I may tear this azure cowl from my breast.

The wise may deem me lost to shame,
But no care have I for renown or name.

Bring wine!—how many a witless head
By the wind of pride has with dust been spread!

My bosom's fumes, my sighs so warm,
Have inflamed yon crude and unfeeling swarm.

This mad heart's secret, well I know,
Is beyond the thoughts of both high and low.

E'en by that sweetheart charmed am I,
Who once from my heart made sweetness fly.

Who that my Silvern Tree hath seen,
Would regard the cypress that decks the green?

> In grief be patient,
> Night and day,
> Till thy fortune, Hafiz,
> Thy wish obey.

Robert Warnock and George K. Anderson, *The World in Literature.* Vol 1. Chicago: Scott, Foresman, 1950.

Document 8: Ibn-al-Fārid's Ode to Wine

Mystical poet Ibn-al-Fārid uses wine to symbolize the source of holy rapture, the Love of God made manifest in an earthly creation. The poet says that not to drink the symbolic wine is to miss gladness and wisdom in life.

Good health to the folk of the monastery! How oft they were

drunken with it;
and yet they had never quaffed it, but only aspired thereto.
But I—I was set awhirl with it, before ever I grew to manhood,
and with me that rapture shall abide forever, though my bones
   may crumble.
I charge thee to take it pure; yet if thou desirest to mingle it,
to turn away from the Beloved's mouth's lustre were wrong
   indeed.
So look thou for it in the tavern, and seek its unveiling there
to the tuneful notes of melodies, wherewith 'tis a noble prize:
for ne'er did it dwell with sullen care in the selfsame place,
as sorrow has ne'er cohabited with sweet tunefulness,
and be thy intoxication therewith but the life of an hour, yet shalt
thou see Time's self become an obedient slave, and thine the
   command of it.
No joy is there in this world for him who lives sober;
and he that dies not of drunkenness misses true prudence—
then let him weep for himself, whose life is all wasted
and he not in all his days of the Wine taken part or portion.

Excerpts from *Aspects of Islamic Civilization*, by A.J. Arberry. Copyright ©1964 by George Allen
and Unwin Ltd. Reprinted with permission of HarperCollins Publishers Ltd.

Document 9: A Recipe Written in Rhymed Couplets

*Baghdad caliph al-Mustakfī assembled a party to converse about food
and the poetry composed on the subject. One of the assembled men quoted
a famous musician and author, Ishaq iln Abrahim of Mosul, who describes his favorite dish in rhyme.*

If thou wouldst know what food gives most delight,
Best let me tell, for none hath subtler sight.
Take first the finest meat, red, soft to touch,
And mince it with the fat, not overmuch;
Then add an onion, cut in circles clean,
A cabbage, very fresh, exceeding green,
And season well with cinnamon and rue;
Of coriander add a handful, too,
And after that of cloves the very least,
Of finest ginger, and of pepper best,
A pinch of cummin, murri just to taste,
Two handfuls of Palmyra salt; but haste,
Good master, haste to grind them small and strong.
Then lay and light a blazing fire along;
Put all into the pot, and water pour

Upon it from above, and cover o'er.
But when the water vanished is from sight
And when the burning flames have dried it quite,
Then, as thou wilt, in pastry wrap it round,
And fasten well the edges, firm and sound;
Or, if it please thee better, take some dough,
Conveniently soft, and rubbed just so,
Then with the rolling-pin let it be spread
And with the nails its edges docketed.
Pour in the frying-pan the choicest oil
And in that liquor let it finely broil.
Last, ladle out into a thin tureen
Where appetizing mustard smeared hath been
And eat with pleasure, mustarded about,
This tastiest food for hurried diner-out.

Excerpts from *Aspects of Islamic Civilization*, by A.J. Arberry. Copyright ©1964 by George Allen and Unwin Ltd. Reprinted with permission of HarperCollins Publishers Ltd.

Document 10: Ibn Hazm's Treatise on Love at First Sight

Ibn Hazm, who lived in Muslim Spain during the first years of the eleventh century, was invited to write an essay on love. An excerpt from his essay refutes the notion of love at first sight and defines authentic love.

I indeed marvel profoundly at all those who pretend to fall in love at first sight; I cannot easily prevail upon myself to believe their claim, and prefer to consider such love as merely a kind of lust. As for thinking that that sort of attachment can really possess the inmost heart, and penetrate the veil of the soul's recess, that I cannot under any circumstances credit. Love has never truly gripped my bowels, save after a long lapse of time, and constant companionship with the person concerned, sharing with him all that while my every occupation, be it earnest or frivolous.

So I am alike in consolation and in passion; I have never in my life forgotten any romance, and my nostalgia for every former attachment is such that I wellnigh choke when I drink and suffocate when I eat. The man who is not so constituted quickly finds complete relief and is at rest again; I have never wearied of anything once I have known it, and neither have I hastened to feel at home with it on first acquaintance. Similarly I have never longed for a change for change's sake, in any of the things that I have possessed; I am speaking here not only of friends and comrades, but also of all the other things a man uses—clothes, riding-beast, food, and so on. . . .

I have meditated upon this theme in verse as follows.

True love is not a flower
That springeth in an hour;
Its flint will not strike fire
At casual desire.

Love is an infant rare
Begotten, slow to bear;
Its lime must mingle long
Before its base is strong.

And then not soon will it
Be undermined, and split;
Firm will its structure stand,
Its fabric still expand.

This truth is readily
Confirmed, because we see
That things too quickly grown
Are swiftly overthrown.

Mine is a stubborn soil
To plough with arduous toil,
Intractable indeed
To tiller and to seed.

But once the roots begin
To strike and thrive therein,
Come bounteous rain, come drought,
The lusty stem will sprout.

Excerpts from *Aspects of Islamic Civilization*, by A.J. Arberry. Copyright ©1964 by George Allen and Unwin Ltd. Reprinted with permission of HarperCollins Publishers Ltd.

Document 11: Poetic Tributes to Lowly Insects

Islamic poets write profusely about spiritual life, but Arab poets in Spain also occasionally treated lowly subjects in rhyme and metaphor. Al-Ṭalaiṭilī paints a picture of an ant, and al-Sumaisir transforms mosquitoes into musicians.

Slender her flank,
Narrow her shank,
Carved to design
Exceedingly fine.

Ethiop-hued,
Lugging her food

Gripped between claws
Like a pincer's jaws.

Look at her rump:
A little lump
Of blackness, which
Is new-dripped pitch.

Or you may think
It's a blot of ink,
The hasty smudge
Of a learned judge.

•　•　•　•　•　•

Mosquitoes are sucking
My blood like sweet wine,
And hey noddy-noddy
They merrily sing.

How nimbly they're plucking,
These minstrels divine!
Their lute is my body,
Each vein is a string.

Twentieth-Century Resurgence of Islam

Document 12: Khomeini and the Iranian Revolution

In 1960 Islamic scholar and politician Ayat-Allah Khomeini mounted political protests against Iranian government policies, actions that resulted in his exile. In 1979, after the defeat and departure of the ruling shah, Khomeini returned to Iran and became Iran's spiritual and political sovereign. While in exile, Khomeini laid out his fundamentalist goals and strategies in speeches and interviews, excerpted here.

I have no coalition with any group. I am with the Iranian people. Whoever agrees with our points (independence from foreign influence, absolute freedom and the establishment of the Islamic Republic) is one of us and one of the Iranian people. If anyone disagrees [with these points] he has moved away from the interests of Islam and we will have nothing to do with him. Those who agree with us are in harmony with us. However, we have no special relation with anyone. . . .

I ask the nation to continue its revolution until the establishment of a just Islamic political order. . . . No Republic, no Democratic Republic, no Democratic Islamic Republic; only an Islamic Republic. I request that the nation be vigilant. Do not allow your sacrifices and efforts to be wasted. Do not be intimidated by the word "Democratic." These forms are western; do not accept them. . . .

I will vote for the Islamic Republic and I ask you to vote for the Islamic Republic, not one word less, not one word more. Those who talk about "Republic" alone mean no Islam. Those who talk about "Democratic Republic" mean not the Islamic Republic. . . .

If we had been truly revolutionary we would not have allowed them [the opposition parties] to be established. We should have established one party, the party of the oppressed. . . . I will warn these corrupt groups all over the country that if they do not stop we will deal with them differently. . . . It is the duty of the revolutionary tribunal to ban all these newspapers and magazines which do not reflect the path of the nation and to arrest their writers and put them on trial. . . .

It is reported that they [the Islamic Republic of Iran] kill people. People imagine that Iran executes human beings. To this day Iran has not killed even one human being. Iran only deals with those beasts who attack Islam, the nation, and humanity. It rectifies and edifies them by training or imprisonment. And if that is not possible it eliminates them. This is a method that prophets have followed from the beginning of existence to the present.

Farhang Rajaee, *Islamic Values and World View: Khomeyne on Man, the State and International Politics.* Vol. 13. New York: University Press of America, 1983.

Document 13: The Nation of Islam in America

In America the resurgence of Islam involved black participation in the religious-political movement Nation of Islam, led by Elijah Muhammad, Messenger of Allah. In 1961 Muhammad spoke in Atlanta, Georgia, urging blacks to follow him.

We, the Nation of Islam, who believe in freedom, justice and equality stand not only before you today, but before the entire world as we declare this truth about the American so-called Negroes. The nations of earth are faced today with a worse problem than has ever presented itself in the history of mankind, and the primary ingredient of this great "world problem" involves the condition and position of the so-called Negro here in America . . . 20 million ex-slaves who have become a nation within a nation and who are now crying out for something that they can call their own.

This is creating a problem not only for America, but for the entire world, and that problem is: how to give you a knowledge and understanding of yourself, teach you the knowledge of your own God and your own religion, and to teach you the knowledge of your own nation so that you can make a stand for yourselves as other nations are making for themselves.

This problem is so delicate and complicated that only God Himself can solve it. I am not a man who has grabbed a suitcase with a bible in it upon my own impulses. No! I stand before you as a man who has been chosen for you by God Himself. I did not choose myself. This must be made clear! The Divine Revelation which I have received and which I am preaching to you and to the entire world came to me from the Mouth of God. . . .

Let the infidels curse and swear at me. Let the infidels go on the warpath of propaganda against Elijah, but I warn you: "You better listen today to him who has received his instructions directly from the Mouth of Almighty God." I did not receive this gospel from a paper, nor a book, nor from a vision, nor from an angel, but directly from the Mouth of Almighty God Himself.

My beloved people: I know your problems and your burdens; I know your problems and your burdens; I know what you go through; you don't have to tell me . . . for I have the ABSOLUTE CURE for all your problems and ailments. All you have to do is listen to what I say, and then jump up on your feet and follow me.

Louis E. Lomax, *When the Word Is Given.* Westport, CT: Greenwood Press, 1963.

Document 14: Malcolm X Stirs the Nation

Though the Black Muslim movement began in America in the 1930s, it did not garner widespread attention until the rise of fiery speaker Malcolm X, leader of the New York Muslims. In a 1960 speech at the Harvard Law School Forum, Malcolm X outlined his defense of an all-Negro state in America.

Our people have been oppressed and exploited here in America for 400 years, and now with Mr. Muhammad we can leave this wicked land of bondage, but our former slave master is yet opposing his efforts and is unjustly persecuting his followers who have left the Christian church and accepted the religion of Islam. . . .

Pick up any daily paper or magazine and examine the anti-Muslim propaganda and the false charges leveled against our beloved religious leader by some of America's leading reporters. This only points up the fact that the Caucasian race is never willing to let any black man who is not their puppet or parrot speak for our people or lead our people out of their enslaving clutches without giving him great opposition. . . .

The Christian world has failed to give the black man justice. This Christian government has failed to give 20 million ex-slaves justice for our 310 years of free slave labor. Despite this, we have been better Christians even than those who taught us Christianity. We have been America's most faithful servants during peace time, and her bravest soldiers during war time. And still, white Christians have been unable to recognize us and accept us as fellow human beings. Today we can see that the Christian religion of the Caucasian race has failed us. Thus the black masses are turning away from the church back to the religion of Islam. . . .

Therefore, Mr. Muhammad has declared to you, and to your government, that if you don't want your 20 million ex-slaves to leave you and return to our own land and people . . . and since your actions have proved that the Caucasian race will not accept these 20 million ex-slaves here among them as complete equals . . . then let us separate ourselves from you right here, into a separate territory that we can call our own, and on which we can do something for ourselves and for our own kind.

Louis E. Lomax, *When the Word Is Given*. Westport, CT: Greenwood Press, 1963.

Glossary

Abbasids: Third and last caliphates, originating from the family of Muhammad's uncle; the Abbasid capital was Baghdad, 750–1258.

Abrahamic: Pertaining to the patriarch Abraham, to whom Jews, Christians, and Muslims trace their spiritual origins.

Allah: God.

Ashura: Tenth day of the month in the Islamic lunar calendar; among Shi'a Muslims the day commemorating the death of the Prophet's grandson Husayn.

caliph: Successor of the Prophet, elected, appointed, or designated to head the Muslim state.

darwish: Initiate in a Muslim mystic brotherhood of Sufis; in English, "dervish."

dhimmi: Jews and Christians living within lands under the caliphate and retaining their non-Muslim religious status in exchange for payment of a poll tax.

du'a: Prayers of supplication or petition to God.

ghazu: Raids on caravans, chiefly for camels.

hadith: Oral tradition of sayings attributed to the Prophet, but not his revelations in the Koran.

hajj: Pilgrimage to Mecca, the fifth Pillar of Islam; a pilgrim to Mecca is a hajji.

hanif: A pure monotheist, such as Abraham, who was not Jew, Christian, or Muslim.

hijab: "Cover, curtain, veil"; the Muslim practice of veiling women by covering the hair or the entire head and face.

hijra: "Emigration"; refers to Muhammad's move to Medina in 622.

ijtihad: Individual legal reasoning; freedom of interpretation of Islamic law.

imam: The leader of group prayer; in Shi'ite Islam, the divinely inspired successor to the Prophet.

iman: "Faith"; a religious virtue more highly regarded by the Koran than Islam; "surrender."

iqra: "Recite"; the suras of the Koran.

jihad: "Striving" (for physical, moral, spiritual, and intellectual perfection); often translated as "holy war."

jinn: "Genies"; the evil or mischievous spirit creatures that possess poets.

Kaaba: Cube-shaped stone building in the center of the courtyard of the Great Mosque in Mecca; the most important shrine in Islam, serving as a focal point of prayer (*salat*) and destination of the pilgrimage (hajj).

Kharijites: One of the major traditions of Islam, beginning in 657 when a group seceded from the army of the caliph.

madrasah: School or academy.

Mamluks: Originally Turkish slaves; leaders of the Islamic regime in Egypt and Syria, 1250–1517.

Mecca: City in Saudi Arabia, Muhammad's birthplace and site of the Kaaba.

Medina: City in Saudi Arabia to which Muhammad and his followers migrated in 622; burial site of Muhammad.

minaret: The tower of a mosque from which the call to prayer is issued five times daily.

Moors: Spanish Muslims.

muezzin: The person designated to call faithful Muslims to prayer.

mufti: Islamic legal officer; legal adviser to the ruler.

Mughal: Sunni rulers in Delhi.

Muslim: "One who has surrendered" to God through Islam.

nadhir: A warner.

qari: One who has memorized the Koran and may be employed to recite suras.

qibla: The direction one faces during prayers.

Quraish: Leading tribe in Mecca at the time of Muhammad, who was a member of the Quraishi clan of Banu Hashim.

Quran: The revelations Muslims believe the messenger of God spoke to Muhammad; the heart of the Islamic faith and the foundation of Islamic law; in English, Koran.

Ramadan: Ninth month of the Islamic lunar calendar; the month of fasting from before sunrise to after sunset.

rashidun: Rightly guided caliphs; the period of the first four caliphs, 632–661.

salat: Prayer, the second Pillar of Islam, performed five times a day facing Mecca.

Saracens: Sunni Ottoman Turks.

shahada: The profession of faith, a statement of the fundamental belief of Islam: "There is no deity but God, Muhammad is the messenger of God."

shahs: Safavid kings of a Shi'ite dynasty ruling Persia, 1500–1779.

Shari'a: Sacred Islamic law derived from the revelations in the Koran and from the words and examples of the Prophet as recorded in the *hadith*.

Shi'a, Shi'i, Shi'ite: The Muslim minority who trace their spiritual heritage to the Prophet through his cousin Ali; Muslims living primarily in Iran and Iraq today.

Sufi, Sufism: Dimension of Islam stressing the immanence or inner existence of God; the Islamic form of mysticism.

Sunni: The vast majority of orthodox Muslims who acknowledge the authority of the Koran but not the need for a messianic leader descended from the Prophet.

sura: One of the 118 chapters in the Koran.

tawhid: "Union" or "unity"; applied to the oneness of God and the single sovereignty of God in the universe; in modern Islamic thought, a term applied to the unity of religion and politics and religion and economics.

ulama: Collectively, the learned men in the Islamic tradition.

Umayyads: Second period of the caliphate ruled by the Meccan Umayyad family from the capital in Damascus, Syria, 661–750.

umma: "Community"; the total community of believing Muslims worldwide.

Yathrib: Oasis town to which Muhammad and his followers migrated in the *hijra* in 622; name changed to Medina.

zakat: Alms or pious tax to provide for the poor; the third Pillar of Islam, calculated according to personal income.

Chronology

570 Muhammad is born

595 Muhammad marries Khadija

610 Muhammad receives first revelations

613 Muhammad begins preaching of Islam in Mecca

619 Muhammad faces crisis following deaths of Khadija and his uncle-protector Abu Talib

622 Hegira of Muhammad and seventy followers from Mecca to Medina begins; year 1 of the Islamic calendar

624 Muslims defeat Meccans at Badr

630 Muslims occupy Mecca, making it the spiritual capital of Islam

632 Muhammad dies; Abu Bakr becomes first caliph

634 Abu Bakr dies; Umar becomes caliph

637–641 Muslims conquer Jerusalem, Syria, and Egypt

644 Umar is assassinated; Uthman becomes caliph

652 First authoritative text of the Koran

656 Uthman is assassinated; Ali becomes caliph and fights at Battle of the Camel

661 Ali is killed by a Kharijite; Mu'awiyah of the Meccan Umayyad family becomes caliph and moves capital to Damascus; beginning of the Umayyad dynasty

680 Ali's son Husayn is killed October 10; the date becomes a major Shi'a anniversary

691–694 Dome of the Rock is constructed in Jerusalem

711 Muslim forces cross Strait of Gibraltar and begin the conquest of Spain

717–718 Failure of Arab siege of Byzantium

732 Charles Martel's forces hold back Muslims at Tours, containing the Muslim threat to western Europe

750 Abbasids overthrow Umayyad rule; capital subsequently transferred to Baghdad

756 Umayyads establish an independent caliphate in Cordova, Spain

785 Construction begins on Great Mosque of Cordova

786–809 Height of scientific, literary, and philosophic achievements in Baghdad

813–833 House of Wisdom promotes Arabic translations of Greek scholarly works

836 Abbasid capital moved to Samarra for half a century

840 Death of expert mathematician al-Khuwarizmik

870 Death of al-Bukhari, expert on the *hadith*

910 Fatimid caliphate takes control of North Africa

923 Death of ar-Razi, physician, skeptic, and musician

969 Fatimid caliphate seizes Egypt; capital transferred from Tunisia to Cairo

1001 Ghaznawid Turks begin conquest of northwest India

1037 Death of Avicenna, renowned scientist and philosopher of medieval Islam

1055 Seljuk Turks capture Baghdad

1056 Berber conquest of Black Empire of Ghana, giving Muslims their first foothold in sub-Saharan Africa

1071 Byzantium defeated by Seljuk Turks

1085 Christians reconquer Toledo, the intellectual and scientific center of Moorish Spain

1099 First Crusade takes Jerusalem

1123 Death of Omar Khayyám, astronomer and poet

1147–1149 Europeans launch Second Crusade

1171 Saladin conquers Cairo: end of Fatimid caliphate

1187 Saladin recaptures Jerusalem for Muslims

1189–1192 Europeans launch Third Crusade

1202 Europeans launch Fourth Crusade

1221 Mongols destroy Persia

1258 Mongols take Baghdad, ending the Abbasid caliphate

1260 Mamluks defeat Mongols

1276 Death of Ahmad al-Badawi, founder of the rustic Ahmadiya dervishes in Egypt

1290 Muslim merchants from India secure first missionary base in Indonesia

1453 Ottoman Turks capture Byzantium

1492 Christians capture Granada, the last Moorish stronghold in Spain

1520–1566 Süleyman the Magnificent takes power and makes Istanbul the center of Ottoman power and culture

1527 Ottoman forces stopped at Vienna

1556–1658 Empire of the Turkish Mogul dynasty at its height in India; building of the Taj Mahal

1683 Ottomans defeated at Vienna

1792 Death of the founder of the puritanical Wahhabi movement, which sought to limit Sufi excesses

1798 French troops land in Egypt

1803 British occupy Delhi, India

1853 Crimean War begins

1869 Opening of the Suez Canal, a symbol of Western imperialist supremacy

1905-1906 Revolution in Persia, beginning a long struggle to modernize the monarchy and end European imperialist controls

1912-1913 Ottomans lose territories in Balkan Wars

1914-1918 World War I destroys the Ottoman Empire

1916 Arabs begin revolt against Ottomans

1918 Great Britain agrees to Zionist demands

1922 Shah Reza Pahlavi begins modernization reforms in Iran

1924 Turkish Republic abolishes the caliphate and abandons the Shari'a

1930-1950 Nationalism movement in Muslim lands

1934 Ibn Sa'ud founds modern Saudi Arabian kingdom; Elijah Muhammad becomes leader of the Nation of Islam in America

1947 Partition of Indian subcontinent into predominantly Muslim Pakistan and largely Hindu Republic of India

1948 Israel founded; Arab League formed in response

1949 Indonesia gains independence from Dutch colonial rule

1952 Black Saturday, January 26, in Cairo marked by anti-Western riots; Egyptian revolution of July 23-26 ends the monarchy and brings Gamal Abdel Nasser to power

1965 Malcolm X, leader of the Muslim Mosque, assassinated by members of the Nation of Islam

1967 Israel defeats Arabs in Six-Day War

1978-1979 Shi'ite revolution in Iran, led by Ayatollah Khomeini

1980-1988 Iran-Iraq War

1991 Persian Gulf War

For Further Research

Karen Armstrong, *Muhammad: A Biography of the Prophet*. San Francisco: Harper, 1992.

Steven Barboza, *American Jihad: Islam After Malcolm X*. New York: Doubleday, 1993.

George W. Beshore, *Science in Early Islamic Culture*. New York: Franklin Watts, 1988.

Joel Carmichael, *The Shaping of the Arabs*. New York: Macmillan, 1967.

David Carroll and the editors of the Newsweek Book Division, *The Taj Mahal*. New York: Newsweek Book Division, 1972.

Frederick Mathewson Denny, *An Introduction to Islam*. 2nd ed. New York: Macmillan, 1994.

Michael Eric Dyson, *Making Malcolm: The Myth and Meaning of Malcolm X*. New York: Oxford University Press, 1995.

John L. Esposito, *Islam: The Straight Path*. New York: Oxford University Press, 1991.

Sattareh Farman Farmaian with Dona Munker, *Daughter of Persia: A Woman's Journey from Her Father's Harem Through the Islamic Revolution*. New York: Anchor Books Doubleday, 1992.

Alfred Guillaume, *Islam*. London: Cassell, 1963.

Dilip Hiro, *Holy Wars: The Rise of Islamic Fundamentalism*. New York: Routledge, Chapman, and Hall, 1989.

Muhammad Zafrulla Khan, trans., *The Quran*. New York: Olive Branch Press, 1991.

Bernard Lewis, *Islam in History*. Chicago: Open Court, 1993.

Thomas W. Lippman, *Understanding Islam: An Introduction to the Muslim World*. Rev. ed. New York: Mentor, 1990.

Peter Mansfield, *The New Arabians*. Chicago: Ferguson, 1981.

Jean Mathe, *The Civilization of Islam*. Translated by David Macrae. New York: Crescent Books, 1980.

Sayyid Abul A'La Mauduli, *Towards Understanding Islam*. Translated and edited by Khurshid Ahmad. Lahore, Pakistan: Idara Tarjumanul-Qur'an, 1980.

Robert Payne, *The History of Islam*. New York: Dorset Press, 1990.

Don Peretz, *The Middle East Today*. 3rd ed. New York: Holt, Rinehart and Winston, 1978.

Malise Ruthven, *Islam in the World*. New York: Oxford University Press, 1984.

Edward W. Said, *Covering Islam: How the Media and the Experts Determine How We See the Rest of the World*. New York: Pantheon Books, 1981.

Khairat Al-Saleh, *Fabled Cities, Princes and Jinn from Arab Myths and Legends*. New York: Shocken Books, 1985.

Jean P. Sasson, *Princess: A True Story of Life Behind the Veil in Saudi Arabia*. New York: Avon Books, 1992.

Annemarie Schimmel, *Islam: An Introduction*. New York: State University of New York Press, 1992.

Desmond Stewart, *Mecca*. New York: Newsweek Book Division, 1980.

Sufism: The Alchemy of the Heart. San Francisco: Chronicle Books, 1993.

William Montgomery Watt, *A Short History of Islam*. Oxford: Oneworld, 1996.

John Alden Williams, ed., *Islam*. New York: Washington Square Press, 1961.

Richard Worth, *Israel and the Arab States*. New York: Franklin Watts, 1983.

Index